'Robyn has written a brilliant, no nonsense, straight-talking guide about how to navigate the daunting world of people and relationships – not just the obvious stuff, but the subtle things that women on the autistic spectrum are lik_____ with. This is a useful book for women t_____ out for them.'

– *Sarah Hendrickx,*
Trainer and Consultant
author of severai ∪∪∪ĸs on Asperger syndrome

'It does not matter how bright a young person on the spectrum is, you cannot send them out into the world without skills for living, loving and resilience. Robyn's book comes framed with experience and the personal knowledge that autism does not stop with childhood... Knowledge keeps us all safe... This is a book everyone who works with teenagers and young adults with autism should have as a reference and it forms an essential resource for women with autism, providing the kind of insight only a woman on the spectrum could provide.'

– *Lynne Moxon, Chartered Psychologist who teaches socio-*
sexual skills, Senior Lecturer, University of Northumbria

'This book provides a how-to guide for spotting unsafe situations while offering concrete tips for safer living for women on the autism spectrum. Spoken from the voice of a young woman with autism, readers will be given practical strategies for navigating socially vulnerable relationships and situations – a useful tool for helping independent women living on the spectrum stay safe.'

– *Dr Elizabeth Laugeson, author of* The Science of
Making Friends, *Assistant Clinical Professor, UCLA,*
Founder and Director, UCLA PEERS Clinic

The Independent Woman's Handbook for
Super Safe Living on the Autistic Spectrum

of related interest

The Aspie Girl's Guide to Being Safe with Men
The Unwritten Safety Rules No-one is Telling You
Debi Brown
Foreword by Sarah Attwood
ISBN 978 1 84905 354 9
eISBN 978 0 85700 703 2

Safety Skills for Asperger Women
How to Save a Perfectly Good Female Life
Liane Holliday Willey
Foreword by Tony Attwood
ISBN 978 1 84905 836 0
eISBN 978 0 85700 327 0

Aspergirls
Empowering Females with Asperger Syndrome
Rudy Simone
Foreword by Liane Holliday Willey
ISBN 978 1 84905 826 1
eISBN 978 0 85700 289 1

The Complete Guide to Getting a Job for
People with Asperger's Syndrome
Find the Right Career and Get Hired
Barbara Bissonnette
ISBN 978 1 84905 921 3
eISBN 978 0 85700 692 9

Love, Sex and Long-Term Relationships
What People with Asperger Syndrome Really Really Want
Sarah Hendrickx
Foreword by Stephen Shore
ISBN 978 1 84310 605 0
eISBN 978 1 84642 764 0

Making Sense of Sex
A Forthright Guide to Puberty, Sex and Relationships
for People with Asperger's Syndrome
Sarah Attwood
Illustrated by Jonathon Powell
ISBN 978 1 84310 374 5
eISBN 978 1 84642 797 8

THE INDEPENDENT WOMAN'S HANDBOOK FOR SUPER SAFE LIVING ON THE AUTISTIC SPECTRUM

Robyn Steward

Jessica Kingsley *Publishers*
London and Philadelphia

First published in 2014
by Jessica Kingsley Publishers
73 Collier Street
London N1 9BE, UK
and
400 Market Street, Suite 400
Philadelphia, PA 19106, USA

www.jkp.com

Library of Congress Cataloging in Publication Data
A CIP catalog record for this book is available from the Library of Congress

British Library Cataloguing in Publication Data
A CIP catalogue record for this book is available from the British Library

ISBN 978 1 84905 399 0
eISBN 978 0 85700 765 0

Printed and bound in Great Britain by Bell & Bain Ltd, Glasgow

This book is dedicated to three people.

Mum and Dad: You are two amazing people, and I am lucky to have you. Thank you for always loving and accepting me for who I am. For being so proactive throughout my life and never giving up on me. For letting me try, fail and try again.

And MF: For making me not feel alone, for sharing things we both like. Most importantly, for forgiving me when I get things wrong and for connecting with me. It means a lot!

Acknowledgements

This is my first book in a career that spans almost a decade so there are a lot of people to thank!

All the women who filled out my surveys, Jessica Kingsley, Micheline Ellison Steinberg, Robin, Sam and Theo Ellison, Niall and Isabel Spooner Harvey, Judith Gould, Wendy Lawson, Katy Ladbrook, Gad Roberts, Lynn Moxon, Sarah Hendrickx, Rudy Simone, the Autcast community, Gloria and David Steward, Dr Elizabeth Laugeson, Dr Alex Gantman, Carol Povey, Mark Lever, Anna Nicholson, Dr Tony Attwood, Temple Grandin, Lisa Clark, Lucy Buckroyd, Lisa (Zaffy) Simone, my purple hat, William Davenport, Pete Langdon, Ian Ensum, Glenys Jones, NAS (National Autistic Society), Danusia Latosinski, Rudy Simone, Matt Eaves, Hal MacLean, Creative Learning Systems, Mark Wallis, Julie Ballam, Isabelle Hesse, Hannah Barnett, Ben Connors, Sarah Niles, Mary Woozley, S.R., R.B.

Contents

Chapter sub-headings are listed at the beginning of each chapter

The Purpose of this Book

The purpose of this book is to provide other women and girls on the autistic spectrum (whether diagnosed or not) with information about some of the safety issues and concerns they may face, and strategies that can help to deal with them. We will look at the following areas: friends; sex; romantic relationships; drugs, alcohol and other substances; preparation for leaving your home (e.g. to go to a shop); the internet, mobile devices and information sharing; money; work; emotions and mental health. These issues are discussed on the premise that you will be engaging in relationships with peers as an adult. I have also written about why certain things happen and what non-autistic people might already know. This book is intended not to scare you but to give you the information that will help you to do the things you want to do in your life more safely.

You do not have to read every chapter consecutively (one after the other) and I have created or provided (from my research) strategies and activities that I hope will be useful. However, everyone is different, and if a strategy is not helpful to you, you should not feel this is because you have not done it correctly, or because you are somehow not autistic enough or too autistic. Everyone is different, and it is simply that what works for one person does not work for everyone. Everyone is different and has different needs.

I am worried that when you read this book, you will say, 'Well, this made no sense to me'; however, this book is written for many people, not just one person, and if I was there sitting next to you when you were confused or did not understand something, I would try to explain it in a different way.

Definition of safety

The Oxford Dictionary says that safety means:

> The condition of being protected from or unlikely to cause danger, risk, or injury.

My personal definition is:

> When you are safe, something unpleasant/harmful/hurtful is unlikely to happen to you, so safety is when you use a strategy to make sure you are safe (i.e. as unlikely as possible to come to harm) from things or people who might hurt you.

For example:

> The traffic policeman, when directing a group of children across the road, was careful to ensure the children's safety by not allowing any cars to knock the children down.
> There was still some risk that one of the children might have run into the road or that a car would run them down, but the traffic policeman did everything he could to minimize the risk and keep the children as safe as possible.

If you or other people keep telling you that a particular activity is 'too risky', you (or they) will limit your right to have the lifestyle you choose. A better way to deal with risk is to investigate what the risks are and what you or others around you can do to minimize these risks, while still giving you as much choice and freedom as possible. Risk is the probability that something will happen, so using a book such as this one to learn strategies will reduce risk.

Language

It has now become almost impossible to please everyone in terms of which words are used to describe autism and people who are diagnosed as being autistic.

Autism is part of a person; it can't be removed or separated from a person. To try to reflect this, I have described people as being *on the autistic spectrum*.

You may ask, why 'on the autistic spectrum' rather than 'autistic'? The reason is that there are many people who share some but not all of the difficulties of people who are diagnosed as autistic; however, these people do not have a diagnosis and wouldn't receive one. This could be for many reasons, but their difficulties in life are real. To my mind, using the word 'spectrum' suggests a broader scope of readers than those who identify with being autistic. It is my hope that this causes no offence and is as inclusive as possible.

I have described people who are not on the autistic spectrum as *non-autistic*.

At various points in the book I have defined the words that I've used, to try to make what I mean as explicit as possible. These definitions are indicated by the magnifying glass symbol 🔍.

There are many different learning styles. Because of the type of book this is, I have found it nearly impossible to decide on key points for each chapter. What is an important piece of new information to one reader may be something familiar to another. Instead, I have included at the end of each chapter my 'Top 10 things to remember', but you can write your own lists. You could add a sticky note or fold down the corner of the page or highlight what you feel are important points in each chapter and then collate them in one place to help you remember them.

Important Information

Some of the information contained in this book uses swear words, but they are used in context so that if you hear or see them you will know what they mean.

This book aims to make no judgement on you, the reader, and instead tries to help you make your own decisions. Some of the topics discussed in this book may seem controversial. But as a woman on the autistic spectrum, I can assure you that it is important that this information is made available to other women and girls on the autistic spectrum, so they can keep themselves safe. Without this information, people are at risk of getting abused, hurt and confused. For example, if you were abused but did not know it was OK to tell someone, you might suffer in silence for years, or you might not even be able to identify that you are being or have been abused. This book provides information on topics such as this. Even if you know what domestic abuse/violence is, if you are in a situation where it is happening to you or other people in your home, you may not know it is wrong. Sometimes relationships can start healthy and later become abusive, and sometimes it is hard to know when this change occurs. Non-autistic people also experience these difficulties, but they may have a wider peer group to check things out with.

Your views on whether something is right or wrong will depend on your family, culture, faith and where you are in the world. This book is intended for people around the world. If you are a parent or someone supporting someone on the autistic spectrum, I would ask you to remember that the topics discussed in this book are topics discussed by most young people and adults; they are almost unavoidable. It is better to have information on them than not. If you are concerned that your daughter or the person you support may be frightened by the book or have ideas put into her head by this book, work through it together. If your faith or culture forbids particular behaviour or activities, discuss this with your daughter or the person you support, even if it is painful for you to think that she might be in some of the situations discussed in this book, and even if, as an adult making decisions of her own, she makes decisions you do not agree with. It is better for her and you that she has appropriate information to make help her make those decisions. People on the autistic spectrum often do not read between the lines and often do not have a peer group to learn from. I work with and support other people on the autistic spectrum and have experienced abuse myself – that is why I wrote this book. I have been frank about topics such as prostitution and drugs, not because I want to encourage any particular behaviour or activity other than people thinking about the choices they face and making the right choices *for them*. As an author, I do not know most of my readers personally, and it would be wrong for me to exclude information that could be vital to keeping someone safe just because I was concerned that I would encourage a particular behaviour. When I was young, my parents had a frank discussion about drugs with me. Because of this conversation, when it came to making my own choices I knew which choices I wanted to make.

Some of the information in this book may seem basic to you or even just common sense. I have written this book with the awareness that readers will have different knowledge levels when they begin reading it. Because of this, I have started discussing topics at a basic level. I felt it was important to ensure all readers had at least some of the same knowledge to start with.

I want you to know that I did not write this book in the way described above to belittle anyone or insult anyone's intelligence. When writing the book, I was conscious to include important information that I felt every woman should have. If some readers did not already know this information, then at least it would be in the book.

The research for this book was carried out in several ways. (It wasn't designed as scientific research.)

- An online survey on safety issues was completed by 106 non-autistic women and 109 women on the autistic spectrum.

- The issues included in the survey were decided with my publisher and were based on my own personal and professional experiences.

- I also interviewed people on the autistic spectrum and professionals who work with people on the autistic spectrum.

- I also interviewed very social non-autistic people.

- All the quotations used in this book are used with the kind permission of the research participants who chose their own pseudonyms.

Finally, I wouldn't describe myself as a writer. Putting my words on a page is troublesome for me. I tried my best!

About Me (The Author)

I'm Robyn Steward. When I started this book in June 2012, I was 25, and I was 26 when I finished it in February 2013. I live in London on my own.

At the age of 11, I received a diagnosis of Asperger's syndrome. I also have nine disabilities.

I started teaching people about autism when I was 17, and now I train many different professionals, including teachers, support workers, psychologists and social workers. I also provide mentoring to others on the autistic spectrum and consultancy for individuals on the autistic spectrum, their families and professionals in the autism field.

Every year since 2008, I have organized a speaking tour around the USA. I also toured Australia in 2010 with Dr Wendy Lawson.

Below are some of the boards/panels/groups I am a member of:

- Steering group member for the PAsSA (People with Asperger's and Anxiety) trial at the University of East Anglia (UEA).

- Sub-select committee for psychology doctorate (UEA).

- Advisory board, National Autistic Society (NAS) E-learning project.

I am also an ambassador for the NAS. This is a varied voluntary role which includes activities such as responding to government consultations that will affect people with an ASD/C (autistic spectrum disorder/condition).

I spoke at the launch of the Autism Bill in 2008 (now the Autism Act 2009) at the House of Commons.

I co-chaired the NAS Professionals conference 2012 and the Women and Girls conference 2012.

The autism community in my local area is important to me. I try to champion the rights of others on the autistic spectrum and their families, particularly people who would otherwise not have a voice. I am a member of the Wandsworth Autism Action Plan steering group and the ASD education group. I meet regularly with the lead commissioner on autism in Wandsworth. I also helped to set up a parents and carers group.

I am also an artist. My art work is very important to me and I have won a few small awards for it. I also play the guitar and cornet. I love London and my favourite underground line is the Victoria Line because it is blue on the map and goes from north to south London fast.

I still have many challenges, partly because I am a human being but also because I am on the autistic spectrum.

This is my first book.

Here is my website address: www.robynsteward.com.

Introduction

HOW DOES BEING ON THE AUTISTIC SPECTRUM AFFECT SAFETY ISSUES?

Everyone on the autistic spectrum is different. Everyone has different needs and is affected by autism in different ways. Not everything in this chapter will apply to you, but I thought it important to explain how the theories used to describe autism can affect safety.

I realize that reading this section of the book could be depressing for some readers.

It's important to understand the difference between people on the autistic spectrum and non-autistic people. It is also important to understand that non-autistic people are not all the same, and some will share the same difficulties as people on the autistic spectrum, although possibly not as intensely. Autism is really just a cluster of human behaviours taken to their extremes. You are still a human being and therefore share things that are common to all human beings – for example, not always knowing what someone else is thinking. It's also important to remember that there are positives to being on the autistic spectrum, just as there are to being non-autistic.

🔍 **Positives** are good things about a situation, object, person, plant or animal.

Communication

There are many different types of communication that can be affected by autism. Below I have listed some.

> ⊘ **Communication** is 'The ability to use one's language skills to establish social relations and to seek assistance or information from others' (Krantz and McClannahan 1993).

From a safety perspective, this means that it can be hard to communicate with other people. Sometimes, for example, you may need to use the phone to convey or receive important information, and if something has happened to you that you need to tell someone else about, it may be hard for you to explain it or write it down.

Initiating communication and language retrieval (knowing which words you want to say) can be difficult for many people on the autistic spectrum; this difficulty is greater when a person is in a stressful situation, and this can be frustrating and upsetting.

Speech

Many people on the autistic spectrum have difficulty speaking when they become overloaded by emotions, sensory information or any other kind of information. There may be other triggers (situations) that make it difficult to speak.

> ⊘ **Triggers** are situations that cause a particular emotional reaction. For example, a noisy supermarket can trigger a headache or a panic attack.

> ⊘ **Overloaded** means to be unable to process or understand more information. For example, after a two-hour maths class you may feel overloaded and as if you can't take in any more information and need to have a rest.

When a person cannot speak, they are often described as being nonverbal. If you know that you sometimes become nonverbal, you should make a plan of what to do when this happens – for example, how you will communicate using an iPhone app.

Understanding others' speech and being able to respond

Difficulties with this area of language may vary. It could be that what others say to you makes no sense. For example, in young children on the autistic spectrum, it is common when asked a question for them simply to repeat the question. This can be because they do not understand the question, do not understand how to answer it or do not understand that, if they answer, they can obtain something they want (or refuse something they do not want).

Sometimes phrases can be misunderstood, often because they are non-literal – metaphors and idioms, for example. You may take what is said literally when it is not supposed to be taken literally. A lot of language that non-autistic people use is not literal. It is important to be able to understand what is said to you, because if someone is asking you to do something and you do not understand what they are asking, then you would be unable to say yes, you did want to do what was being asked, or no, you did not want to do what was being asked of you. For example, someone might say to you, 'Do you want to sleep with me?' If you were to misunderstand this and take it literally, you might think the person just wanted to sleep in the same bed as you; you might conclude that this was because it would be cheaper or warmer. However, this phrase almost always means 'Do you want to have sex with me?' It's important to develop the skills to be able to ask questions to make sure you have understood what the other person is asking you, rather than just assuming you understand. If you assumed you understood someone, you could find yourself in a very stressful situation and be unable to speak to get yourself out of the situation. A person on the autistic spectrum may be able to speak very clearly and convey complex ideas, but this does not mean that they do not have problems with processing information and understanding information. I have met many people on the autistic spectrum who use a script which they write for themselves before they have a conversation with someone else.

See the resources section at the end of this chapter for a dictionary by Ian Stuart-Hamilton that might be helpful.

Intonation and vocal tone

Voices can make all kind of sounds, and non-autistic people often use their voice to communicate things such as boredom or sarcasm. Many people on the autistic spectrum also do this. However, if this is something you find hard, it is important to understand that, without being told, a non-autistic person may not know that you do not understand voice inclination or tone.

Body language

Body language is a term used to describe a number of things including:

- eye movement and eye contact
- facial expression
- hand gestures
- body movements.

The difficulties some people have understanding and reading body language could be because:

- The majority of non-autistic people intuitively understand and learn about body language, and therefore it is assumed that people on the autistic spectrum will also be able to read and understand body language. But many people on the autistic spectrum do not learn about body language intuitively. You would think that listening was just an activity done using your ears, but to understand what someone is saying you also need to understand the person's body language.

Intuitively means to do something naturally or without tuition. Therefore, intuition is an automatic (i.e. without thinking) feeling about a situation. For example, when you go into a pub or bar, your intuition could make you think that this is not a safe place for you to be alone. Quite often, people get a feeling in their gut/stomach area which indicates to them that they are uncomfortable in a situation, even though, until they really think about it, they could not tell you why they felt uncomfortable.

- Some people on the autistic spectrum have learnt to read body language. Sometimes this can impact on how much time it takes to think/process information, because as well as processing what is being said and what is happening in the environment they are in, they also have to process and understand other people's body language. Non-autistic people mostly do this automatically; however, they are not all good at it.

- Many people on the autistic spectrum find it hard to filter out information. A person speaking to them may be expressing themselves with body language, words and voice intonation, but there is also sensory information such as their clothing and smell to process, as well as other stimuli within the environment. It can be hard to know what to pay attention to – what to think about and what to ignore. This can mean that people on the autistic spectrum misunderstand or do not process important information that is necessary for making decisions. For example, a friend might ask you if you would like a ride or lift – that is, if you would like them to let you sit in their car while they drive to a destination you both want to go to. If you are unable to process information, you may not notice that your friend smells of alcohol and you would not make the assumption that they had been drinking alcohol and that it would be unsafe for them to drive.

Difficulties in processing information could be for lots of different reasons. One reason is that many non-autistic people are born polytropic, but people on the autistic spectrum are often monotropic.

(?) **Polytropic** means to be able to concentrate on more than one topic at a time.

(?) **Monotropic** means to be able to concentrate only on one topic at a time.

Additionally, many people on the autistic spectrum find making eye contact painful, overstimulating or pointless.

Many people on the autistic spectrum misinterpret body language. You may feel, for example, that someone is staring at you – in fact, you might be very sure the person is staring at you. But often they are not, and, if they are, the best thing to do is move away from them and carry on living your life. If you worry about people staring at you, it will stop you from being able to do other things; your attention is being used to concentrate on whether you are being stared at, instead of something constructive.

Not being able to read and understand body language or missing information conveyed (transmitted) via body language can cause difficulties from a safety perspective because some of the danger signs about a person might be conveyed in body language. For example, some people would consider not making eye contact to be shifty.

    A person who is **shifty** is someone who is untrustworthy (i.e. not worth your trust) and may be trying to lie to you.

However, there are other reasons why someone may not make eye contact – for example, if they are upset. You need to consider the context of the situation (see Chapter 10 for more about contexts), the tone of a person's voice, the way they are sitting and what they have just said. Non-autistic people – and some people on the autistic spectrum – can decide (although they are not always correct) why the person is not making eye contact and what they are trying to communicate.

Body language is also used to understand when someone is joking and when they are not. This can be important when trying to avoid arguments and misunderstandings.

I think it is important to try not to be anxious or depressed about finding it difficult to understand body language. It's important to be aware that you find it difficult. You have many things to offer the world, and this book aims to enable you to access more of the world in a safe way, so that you can find your niche in life and achieve the things you want to achieve.

Social imagination

People on the autistic spectrum can be very imaginative. It is a myth that everyone on the autistic spectrum is unimaginative. But it is important to remember that autism is a spectrum of abilities and that there are people on the autistic spectrum who have great difficulty with social imagination.

Sometimes information about social imagination seems to be misunderstood. There is a difference between creative imagination and social imagination.

There have been many artists, musicians, scientists and other people, all on the autistic spectrum, who have used creativity to be successful.

Children on the autistic spectrum may not play imaginative games in the same way as non-autistic children. For example, a child on the autistic spectrum might play schools, but rather than make up (create) their own scenario (story) about what happens in their game, they recreate what has happened in real life (not necessarily on that day but at any point in their school career) or what they have seen on TV or in other forms of media. Non-autistic children naturally make up their own stories and act them out. This can be very difficult for children on the autistic spectrum. It is important to receive help early on to develop these skills.

Theory of mind

Social imagination can be used to describe many different things, but I see the biggest problem with regard to safety as being the difficulties that some people (but not all) on the autistic spectrum have in understanding what is called 'theory of mind'. Theory of mind is when you imagine what it would be like to be someone else, how they might feel, what their intentions are and their perspective of the world.

For example, if you were watching a film trailer and someone was having a fight with someone else, a non-autistic person might be able to imagine what it would be like to be the person who started the fight and why they might have started fighting. Some people on the autistic spectrum, however, may find it difficult to imagine this.

This is important for safety. Sometimes people will say things such as 'Would you like to come and see this amazing thing?' and their intention is to lead you away from your friends so they can hurt you. However, in another circumstance it could genuinely be that the person wants to show you something. Theory of mind is one skill people use to help work out whether the person wanting to show them something is genuine or not.

People on the autistic spectrum need to learn about their own emotional reactions more consciously than perhaps a non-autistic person does. Emotional reactions can help you work out whether someone is geniune or not. For example, if your heart starts to beat fast and your stomach feels as though it is 'dropping' when somebody asks you to get into their car, your body is giving you physiological signals that you are nervous. This information can be used to help you choose a safe action (i.e. not getting in the car). You can learn through practice how to notice the physiological signs that will help you recognize which emotion you are feeling, This will increase your confidence, because you will know how you are feeling and either you will know what to do or you can ask others to help you decide what to do.

> ⊘ **Genuine** means to be telling the truth and not trying to get you to do something just so the other person can benefit from it. For example, the benefit to them of hurting you might be that they were having fun.

Theory of mind is not a skill that you simply do or don't have – it varies in skill level from person to person. Some people are very skilled at it, whereas others are not – just like a driving licence shows that someone has the skills to drive a car, or a large lorry, or a bus or an ambulance. Some people have very good driving skills, while other people are not very skilled.

Many people on the autistic spectrum build up a sort of cognitive theory of mind – that is, rather than knowing it intuitively, they think about what someone might be thinking using knowledge they have of previous situations to understand why someone might behave in a particular way (i.e. what the other person intended them to think or feel).

Repetitive and routine behaviours

Repetitive and routine behaviours include flapping, rocking and twirling. Many people on the autistic spectrum use what is often referred to as stimming (self-stimulation) for many different reasons, including to communicate feelings such as anxiety and happiness, to calm down/relax or to calm their sensory system.

Some people might be scared of someone who is stimming because they do not understand it. However, stimming is often a very important coping mechanism for someone on the autistic spectrum. It is important while stimming not to hurt yourself or others, or to stop yourself or others from doing things such as concentrating. Although it is important that you have the effect that stimming gives you, it may mean you need to change your stim so as not to hurt or disturb others. You might change it to something providing similar stimulation in that area of your body or have specific times in the day when you can stim. It is important that people who know you learn to accept your stimming and understand that it has a purpose, but you also have to accept that you may have to change your stim if it hurts you or other people, or stops you or other people from doing something. The embarrassment of others, however, should not be a reason to change a stim, in my opinion.

It is important to understand that your behaviour can change other people's perception of you, particularly people who do not know you.

You may also find that you rely on a routine to make sense of the world or to make life less scary. Any change or deviation from your routine may cause you great anxiety. However, it is possible to learn coping mechanisms to overcome this anxiety.

Obsessions and special interests

It's important to understand that there is a difference between obsessions or special interests and having obsessive compulsive disorder (OCD).

OCD is characterized by having both an obsession such as contamination and a compulsion such as hand washing. People who have OCD feel that if they do not carry out their compulsion, something bad will happen. For example, someone with contamination OCD may experience a compulsion to wash their hands; if they do not do this, they become anxious about being contaminated.

OCD is not the same as an obsession or special interest. An obsession or special interest is something you think about a lot or engage in doing a lot which you enjoy. It normally involves achieving something such as learning new information, building something or providing for the needs of an animal. It also makes you happy.

There is another common difficulty relating to obsession, and although it's not strictly an obsession, I think it is an appropriate time to mention it here. Sometimes people on the autistic spectrum can get stuck on the topic of anxiety and find it hard to let go of it.

Getting stuck on a topic means not being able to think about anything apart from that topic.

Letting go of a topic means accepting the facts about it – for example, saying 'I can't do anything about it. Something has happened and I cannot change it' – and then being able to think about other things.

Difficulties in social situations

Many people on the autistic spectrum have difficulties talking to other people in social situations. This could be for many different reasons, including finding it hard to move from one topic to another.

People on the autistic spectrum often have difficulties with emotional competency and regulation – that is, being able to identify the emotion you are feeling and to recognize other emotions in other people, and being able to control emotions. For example, when something upsetting happens, it can be hard to carry on with your daily life and it can take a long time to process the emotions. See Chapter 9 for information on this and how to release and process emotions.

Many people on the autistic spectrum are teased or bullied. If you have had this experience, it may have damaged your confidence (i.e. you feel less confident) and this could make you less likely to stand up for yourself (say what you do and don't want).

> Confidence is when you feel happy about who you are and that you can and will achieve things. If someone damages your confidence, this means that you feel less confident because of what someone else has done to you. For example, if you felt confident about how you looked, but someone called you fat and then you started to worry that you were fat, this would be an example of having your confidence damaged due to bullying.

Being bullied can also cause difficulties with mental health. Sadly, bullying has caused some people to commit suicide. This is sometimes because they have felt overwhelmed or deeply hurt by the experiences they have had, or they may have felt that things would never get better.

Many people on the autistic spectrum have felt unable to cope because they haven't been able to find effective strategies for themselves. We know that autism means that the brain is wired differently. Imagine the brain as a road system. Non-autistic people and people on the autistic spectrum have identical road systems, but in non-autistic brains the traffic is allowed to go both ways, whereas some of the traffic in the autistic brain only goes one way. It's not bad and it can have advantages as well as disadvantages, but because the brain processes things differently to the non-autistic brain, it is logical to assume that a person on the autistic spectrum may need different strategies – particularly as emotions are so abstract.

> When someone or something that happens to you gives you a negative emotional response (e.g. if you were bullied, you might feel sad), this is known as **having your feelings hurt**. It is important to take others seriously when they say you have hurt their feelings, and it is equally important that they respect you when you say your feelings are hurt.

Sensory issues/perception differences

People on the autistic spectrum can have difficulties with sensory perception.

The **senses** are hearing, sight, touch, taste and smell, and also vestibular (sense of balance) and proprioception (sense of where our bodies are, sense of pressure and sense of hot and cold).

There are many different ways in which sensory perception can be different for people on the autistic spectrum.

- *Hypersensitivity* is when a sense or senses are very sensitive. This could change depending on how you feel emotionally – for example, some people have hypersensitive hearing when they are stressed. Also, for some people on the autistic spectrum, hugging, handshakes and touch used in sex can be painful due to hypersensitivity. Refusal to touch may be interpreted as rejection by friends or partners. Understanding whether this is your experience will help you to make choices about what you do and don't want to do. You may decide, for example, that you will shake hands but not hug people. You can then tell people you know well, such as friends and family, what your needs are. If you are able to tolerate it, practising a regular social touch such as a handshake with someone you trust (e.g. a therapist or family member) can be a helpful skill to learn.

- *Hyposensitivity* is underreaction in the senses. Again, this could change with your emotional state and affect one or all of your senses. It may mean that you seek out sensory stimulation. You may underreact to sexual stimulation, which can lead to difficulties having orgasms or to your requirement for sexual stimulation to be more extreme.

  If you seek specific things to touch, such as people's hair, avoid touching strangers or acquaintances, as people may find this threatening.

  If you are hyposensitive to sexual stimulation, avoid any sexual stimulation that causes injury or soreness. Be aware that if you are hyposensitive to sexual simulation, you will need to be gentler with a partner (as they may not be hyposensitive). Talk to your partner about ways you can both enjoy sexual stimulation. Ask them what they do not like and make sure you avoid doing those things.

- *Sensory overload* is when the sensory system becomes overloaded and cannot take in any more information. This is quite a common reaction in supermarkets and malls. This could make someone vulnerable to teasing and bullying by others and it may also mean that they are not aware of where personal belongings (e.g. purse, keys) are and how to get out of the situation safely.

Many people on the autistic spectrum also have other sensory perception difficulties. Visually, objects and faces can appear like a mosaic (very distorted), or sound could be scrambled. It may be hard to distinguish what you are hearing and what is written on a classroom wall, for example. Or you might find it hard to distinguish what someone is saying when lots of people are talking, and this could mean you mishear or misunderstand an important piece of information.

There are many other sorts of sensory perception difficulties. Look for Olga Bogdashina's books to find out more about this topic (see the resources section below for one example).

Top 10 things to remember from the Introduction

1. The autistic spectrum is very wide and everyone is different in the way difficulties affect them.

2. People on the autistic spectrum can have difficulties with communication. These may include:

    □ finding it difficult to put thoughts into audible words

    □ sometimes being nonverbal/mute

    □ finding it hard to make eye contact – some people find it painful, distracting, overwhelming, confusing, pointless

    □ finding body language and facial expressions difficult to interpret

    □ taking things literally – such as directions, instructions, idioms and metaphors.

3. People on the autistic spectrum can experience and process sensory information in a different way to the non-autistic population (Bogdashina 2003). This can make the world hard to interpret and may mean you miss important information. These experiences may include but are not limited to:

   □ hyper- or hypo- (over- or under-) sensitivity to particular senses, which can vary according to emotions

   □ distorted senses where the images look 'scrabbled'

   □ mono channel, which means only processing one sense at a time.

4. It can be difficult for people on the autistic spectrum to understand another person's intentions, which can be due to difficulties with social imagination. As a result, many people on the autistic spectrum have been taken advantage of.

5. Many people on the autistic spectrum stim. Stim is short for self-stimulation. Stimming can include hand flapping, rocking or leg shaking. Stimming can be a very important tool for some people on the autistic spectrum to regulate their sensory or emotional experiences.

6. Many people on the autistic spectrum find a change of routine very difficult to cope with. This could be for many reasons, including not being able to perceive what will happen after the change, fear of the unknown and a need to complete the task they are working on. Chapter 9 talks more about change.

7. Many people on the autistic spectrum have a special interest/ obsession. This could be on any topic; it just means that the person is intensely interested in that topic. It is different from OCD.

8. People on the autistic spectrum can have OCD (obsessive compulsive disorder) in addition to being on the autistic spectrum.

9. Some people on the autistic spectrum are monotropic. This means they concentrate on one task at a time. Non-autistic people are often polytropic, meaning they concentrate on multiple topics at a time.

10. There are many positives to being on the autistic spectrum. It is important to find what you are good at and work on your skills in that area as much as possible.

Resources

Books

Baron-Cohen, S. (2008) *Autism and Asperger Syndrome (The Facts)*. Oxford: Oxford University Press. ISBN: 0192623273

A book about autism for parents, originally written in 1993.

Bogdashina, O. (2003) *Sensory Perceptual Issues in Autism: Different Sensory Experiences – Different Perceptual Worlds*. London: Jessica Kingsley Publishers. ISBN: 1843101661

This book explains the many different types of sensory issues people on the spectrum experience. It also contains a sensory profile tool, which may be a useful starting point for assessing your sensory issues, particularly if you are unable to see an occupational therapist.

Stuart-Hamilton, I. (2006) *An Asperger Dictionary of Everyday Expressions*. London: Jessica Kingsley Publishers. ISBN: 1843105187

This is a dictionary of phases, each of which has a star rating of rudeness so you know whether or not you can use the phase in situations when you need to be polite. This is a great, easy-to-use resource if you tend to take things people say or write literally.

Vermeulen, P. (2012) *Autism as Context Blindness*. Overland Park, KS: Autism Asperger Publishing Co. ISBN: 1937473007

The world we live in consists of many contexts, and many people on the autistic spectrum find it hard to differentiate between contexts and adapt their behaviour accordingly. This book explores what context means, how it affects us and what this means in the world of autism.

1

PLATONIC FRIENDSHIPS

In this chapter

1.1 Introduction

Platonic means non-romantic or non-sexual.

1.1.1 Why I included this chapter

This chapter does not assume that everyone wants friends. There are many people on the autistic spectrum who do not want friends. However, there are also many people who do want friends. Friendship can be a way of keeping safe because:

- Going somewhere in a group makes you less vulnerable. If someone wanted to attack another person, they would most likely choose someone who was alone rather than someone in a group, because if they attacked someone in a group, other members of the group would seek help or fight back.

- Being part of a group also provides you with the opportunity for a second opinion when trying to make decisions or choices. For example, if someone asked you out on a date and you weren't sure how to say no politely, you could ask one of your friends if they had had a similar experience and what they did in that situation.

- Having friends may increase your self-esteem. This could be because spending time with them may make you happy and feel good about yourself if they encourage you to try new things.

- Having friends can also make you feel loved and have benefits for your mental health.

- Having friends can help you become more independent. Many people feel more willing to do something that scares them if they can do it with someone else. For example, when someone is first learning to go shopping by themselves and not with their parents, they might go with a friend, because they might feel safer and more confident when they are with someone else. Their friend will not care for them in the same way a parent would, so the person going shopping will learn to feel more confident with less support.

- Having friends can provide you with people to speak to when life is stressful, and this can be calming. Friendships should be equal, so if you want to share your problems/stresses with your friends, you also need to be willing to hear them talk about their problems and stresses. Some people also enjoy helping their friends. Sometimes the most helpful thing you can do for a friend is listen to them. You don't have to try to solve their problems for them.

- Having friends can make you feel wanted as a person. Many of my clients have felt rejected by many people. When they have a good friend, they don't feel so rejected by the world.

In the context of platonic friendships, **love** means to care for another person and want to support them; it is a stronger feeling than just liking a person.

1.1.2 Thinking about friendships

Having friends should work both ways. Not only do you benefit from a friendship but so do your friends, and it can feel good to do the things described above (e.g. share information and encourage your friends).

You also have to learn how to maintain a friendship, just as you would maintain a car. Relationships need maintenance. Most people become unhappy if they argue a lot.

However, there are some people who may pretend to be your friend when they are not really your friend. It is important have some skills to help you tell the difference between someone who genuinely wants to be your friend and someone who may want to hurt you. It is important to know that non-autistic people do not always know if someone is genuine or not. If you are unsure whether someone is genuine, here are three things to remember:

1. Check out what they are telling you – ask someone else who could verify whether what the person is saying is true.

2. Ask for advice from someone you trust.

3. How has this person behaved in the past? For example, are they dishonest?

1.1.3 It's OK not to want friends

It is OK not to want friends, but be sure you understand the reason you don't want friends. Is it because you have had bad experiences in the past? Because if it is, you can overcome your past difficulties, and knowing that this is the reason will help you to decide what to do next. However, it may be that you feel you don't need friends. Do you enjoy your own company or prefer the company of animals to the company of other people? Or you may have tried to make friends when you were younger but didn't succeed or didn't know how to maintain a friendship. As a result, you may have given up, feeling you cannot get things right. Many people on the autistic spectrum feel this way. However, you can overcome your difficulties. You may find Dr Elizabeth Laugeson's book *The Science of Making Friends* helpful (see the resources section at the end of this chapter).

If you have had bad experiences in the past, there may be ways of finding people who are more like-minded (i.e. have similar interests and opinions on life). A person probably won't agree with you all the time, but perhaps some of your bad experiences with friends were because people did not understand you or because social activities were not structured enough. At school, it may have been because people in your age group at the time did not understand disability – some of their views might have developed because their parents told them what to think. In the last 10–15 years, attitudes to disability have been changing, and now people are more positive. Also, as adults we form our own opinions on issues such as disability.

So perhaps friendship might be worth another try.

This chapter is now split into two parts. Part 1 is about people who are not friends but may pretend to be. Part 2 is about how to find friends and maintain friendships.

Part 1: People who are not true friends – what this means and what you can do about it

1.2 Introduction to Part 1

It is important to understand and be aware if someone is not a true friend – for example, if they are exploiting you.

> A **true friend** is someone who is not pretending to be your friend or pretending to like you because they want something. A true friend is someone who likes you and enjoys being friends with you.

> Later on in this chapter I talk about **acquaintances**. An acquaintance is a person you know but do not have a close relationship with. Acquaintances are not true friends but they aren't necessarily going to exploit you.

> If you have been **exploited** in the context of friendship, it means that someone has pretended to be your friend. They only wanted to be your friend because you had something they wanted (e.g. money). They thought that by pretending to be your friend they could get that money.

Some people also like to control and manipulate people. As with exploitation, a person might pretend to be your friend so that they could manipulate and control you.

It is important to know that non-autistic people can also find friendships confusing and find it difficult to understand other people's behaviour.

In this chapter I aim to try to explain some of the common safety considerations around friendships. I have also written about what you can do to keep yourself safe. To begin with, perhaps it would be helpful to consider what some warning signs/red flags might be in friendships. If someone was trying to hurt you, how might you know it was happening?

1.3 Warning signs/red flags

A **warning sign** is something (such as a way of behaving) that could alert you to danger. For example, a warning sign that someone is angry is that they are shouting. Sometimes people call warning signs 'red flags'.

'I think even those of us on the [autistic] spectrum are aware of "red flags" or that intuitive feeling that comes up when a situation is wrong or dangerous. Many of us are taught to ignore them, we're made fun of when our instincts tell us to get out of a situation, and over time that causes damage by way of us then getting involved in abusive situations where we might otherwise listen to ourselves and avoid them. It's so important to listen to what's inside us, whatever gut feeling, inner voice, some unspoken sense, whatever it is that is signalling us, no matter how small, to pay attention to something that doesn't seem right.'

Pavitra, research participant

Not everyone on the autistic spectrum knows when they are in a bad or risky situation (i.e. a situation that has risks such as someone exploiting you). If you do not feel that you notice warning signs that would alert other people to the fact that they were in a bad situation, that is OK. It is possible to learn skills to help you know when a situation might be bad or dangerous. Having to learn these skills does not make you any less of a valuable person.

Being able to read body language can help you decide if a situation is dangerous or not. For example, if someone has their fists clenched and they can't stand up without swaying, then you could conclude that they were drunk and angry. However, a lot of body language is more subtle than this.

There are some non-autistic people who find reading body language difficult. You can learn to read body language. This book is focused on safety. There are other resources that contain more detailed information about body language. Please see the resources section at the end of the chapter for details of a book by Barbara and Allan Pease that will give you further information about body language.

A **bad situation** is one where the outcomes are likely to be negative. For example, you would be in a bad situation if you were walking home late at night through a neighbourhood that did not have many street lights, and where people were dealing (selling) drugs and often carried weapons. The situation is bad because your life is at risk. Drugs can make people volatile. If you see someone dealing drugs they may worry that you will tell someone, and this may mean they want to hurt you to make sure you don't tell anyone.

Below are some examples of warning signs/red flags:

- *Gossiping.* This is when people are talking about you behind your back. You may hear about this from other people or suspect it. Ask someone you trust if this is what is happening. If it is, ask the person who is gossiping to stop. They may deny that they were gossiping (because they might feel embarrassed or ashamed) but they should stop. If they do not, then consider not being friends with this person.

   Sometimes this happens. There is a phrase 'to rise above something', which means to think, 'Well, the people who know me know what kind of person I am, so if this gossip is spreading lies about me, then only people who do not know me well will believe it.'

Behind your back means that someone talks negatively about you without you knowing.

- *Making you feel guilty* for not doing something. For example, if you said you did not want to go to an event or you had planned to go but were then unwell, someone could make you feel guilty, as if you had done something wrong intentionally. They might say something like 'You're not a good friend because you do not support me enough.'

   See the boundaries section later in this chapter. You may want to add to the list of boundaries the amount of time you are prepared to spend with a particular person.

   If you feel that your friendship is equal (also discussed later in this chapter) – that is, you are both making equal amounts of effort – then say so. For example, you might say, 'I'm sorry, I do my best, but if you feel I'm not doing enough, then maybe we shouldn't be friends?'

If this happens a few times, perhaps the person is enjoying the reaction you are giving them, so it may be best not to continue with this friendship.

- You leave a situation and feel that *you have been used* in some way. For example, someone might make fun of you or tease you. You ask them to stop, but they ignore you. If they were your friend, they would not want to make you feel unhappy. In this case, they are simply using you as entertainment.

  In these scenarios it is usually not helpful to tell the person that you don't want to be used as entertainment. Just leave the situation and don't speak to that person any more than you have to.

- *If someone keeps touching you*, ask them to stop. If they do not stop immediately, leave wherever you are and go home. If you are in your home, ask them to leave. If they will not leave, call the police. If you are abroad or a long way from home, go to your hotel room, or if you do not feel safe there, go to the front desk/reception desk and ask for help. If you are staying with the person you want to get away from, rather than in a hotel, consider whether there is somewhere else you could stay.

- *Being open about life on first meeting.* If, when you first meet a person, they start telling you about all their problems, this could mean they are emotionally needy – they need to be listened to all the time or they are someone who shares too much information. However, be aware that this person could just want you to give them money or feel sorry for them.

1.3.1 How can I tell if someone is emotionally needy or sharing too much information or that they want something?

It can be difficult to know someone's intentions. You may only really know the answer by getting to know more about the person. For example, do they give as much information about their life to you as they do to other people? If they ask you for something when you have first met them (except if it is to borrow your cigarette lighter, as this is quite normal), then it is possible that they want to take advantage of you.

Use the ladder of trust (see section 1.14) as a guide for how much information you should share, but if you feel someone is sharing too much information, you may not want to share as much information as they are sharing. Think about the potential consequences of information you might share with a person.

1.4 Who is my friend and who is not?

In my research and in the work I have done with people on the autistic spectrum, I have met individuals who have found it hard to tell who is their friend and who is not. This could be because, for many people on the autistic spectrum, the way people behave and their intentions may seem contradictory or confusing, and therefore it is hard to understand the other person. For example, someone may be nice to you one day and rude the next day.

Many people I have met on the autistic spectrum have made a new friend and the friendship has become very intense (i.e. being in contact with that person daily, wanting to spend time only with that person).

It's very important not to get too intensely involved with a new friend straight away, as this can lead to arguments, misunderstandings and difficulties if the friendship ends. This is often because the person doesn't know what to do when they no longer spend time with their former friend.

At the start of a friendship, you might ask the person to do a particular activity with you (perhaps something that relates to a shared interest). When you get home from the activity, if you want to, you can send them a message to say you had a nice time and you'd like to spend more time with them.

Then wait a few weeks for them to ask you to do an activity. They may contact you sooner, but if you haven't heard from them after a couple of weeks, you could send them a message. Say that you would like to spend time with them, and if they respond positively ask what they would like to do.

You might also introduce your new friend to your existing friends (if you want to/can) and they may invite you to meet their friends. You might spend time at each other's homes, and you might also meet their family or choose to introduce them to your family.

1.5 Teasing

Sometimes people say things to joke with you. This might be called gentle teasing or bantering – for example, if you had blonde hair, a photographer taking your photo might call you Blondie. But if the person says these things deliberately to hurt you, or you ask them to stop and they don't, then this is bullying.

1.5.1 Why would anyone enjoy being teased?

Non-autistic people often tease each other in the initial stages of friendship (e.g. inventing nicknames) but they can usually judge how far to go. If you are becoming upset by teasing, then your friend's behaviour has become inappropriate. You should tell them you do not like them calling you that name or teasing you. If they do not stop, then they are probably not a good person to be friends with, as they don't respect your feelings.

It may sound strange, but sometimes people like being teased and find it funny, because they learn to 'laugh at themselves'. This means that they learn to understand the comic value of a situation or something about themselves.

1.5.2 What should I do if I am being teased by a friend?

If a friend is teasing you and it makes you unhappy, your friend may not know how hurt you are. Before assuming that they are not a true friend, try to find a quiet moment with them (a time when nobody else is around, perhaps at the end of the day if you work with them). Say:

'You know I'm a bit sensitive and I don't really like it when you...'

If the person cares about you, then they will say something that acknowledges your feelings, such as:

'Sure, OK' or 'I'm sorry'.

And they either won't do it again or if they start to do it they will apologize and the amount of times it happens will reduce.

Teasing can be a way that people bond with one another, but it may not work for you, and that is OK.

1.5.3 Tease the Tease

Tease the Tease is great, particularly if the teasing is from someone you don't know or are not friends with, or someone you have asked to stop and they haven't.

Tease the Tease is part of PEERS® (Program for the Education and Enrichment of Relational Skills), which was designed at UCLA (University of California Los Angeles). It's a programme to teach social skills to teens and adults on the autistic spectrum. Tease the Tease teaches participants to use a selection of phrases such as 'whatever' or 'yeah, and?' or 'anyway' with the appropriate tone of voice, as a suitable response to being teased. This strategy is versatile and can be used in lots of situations, decreasing the likelihood of future teasing because it makes the teasing less fun for the teaser. Asking a family member or a non-autistic friend to help you practise this strategy can be helpful. If you have a counsellor, advocate or psychologist, they may also be able to help.

PEERS is run in different parts of the world, including North America, South America, Europe and Asia. Professionals can access the programme by purchasing *Social Skills for Teenagers with Developmental and Autism Spectrum Disorders: The PEERS Treatment Manual*, written by Dr Elizabeth Laugeson and Dr Fred Frankel (see the resources section at the end of this chapter). Parents and young people who do not have access to a PEERS group in the community can learn more from *The Science of Making Friends* by Dr Laugeson (again, see the resources section at the end of this chapter for details). This book also includes a DVD companion to demonstrate what the skills look like and a mobile application for smartphones called *FriendMaker* to provide social coaching in the real world.

1.6 Intentions

'If I was ever unsure of the intentions of a person, I would back away from the situation, call or text another friend who I trusted deeply and ask them for advice on the situation. They were usually right and I escaped a lot of near misses with this practice.'

Stella, research participant

It is important to be aware of your own limitations. For example, you may find it hard to understand other people's intentions if they are very different from your own. This is because many people on the autistic spectrum have difficulties with theory of mind (Baron-Cohen, Leslie and Frith 1985). If this is the case, then if you are unsure of someone's intentions, you could discuss this with someone you trust.

In this context, **case** means circumstances or the way you are experiencing something. For example, you could say 'in case of getting lost, phone a friend'; this means 'if you get lost, call a friend'.

It is possible to improve your understanding of other people's intentions. One book that may be helpful is *Comic Strip Conversations* written by Carol Gray (see the resources section at the end of this chapter for more information). You may find this helpful to aid your learning about other people's intentions.

The activity below aims to help you think about other people's intentions.

Write down situations you have experienced in life (there are some examples listed below if you need suggestions). Write down two or three potential intentions that the people in the situations may have had. You could talk about this activity with a counsellor or psychologist. Some suggested answers are given at the end of this chapter.

Situation 1

Raj and Kat are living in a shared house. Raj went to bed on Monday evening after Kat, but he did not do the washing-up (washing the dishes – plates, knives, forks, etc.). Raj and Kat's house rules state that they will do the washing-up before they go to bed.

Why might Raj not have done the washing-up?

Situation 2

Sarah and Fatima agreed to go shopping on Saturday morning. They agreed to meet at the bus stop near Sarah's house. But Fatima did not come. Fatima is often late, but when Sarah tried to call her, she did not answer her phone.

What were Fatima's intentions? How could Sarah find out?

Situation 3

Luke, Shane and Faye are friends. They go to town one night and Luke puts vodka in Faye's drink. Faye then vomits and Luke and Shane leave the club, but they are waiting for Faye when she gets home.

What were Luke and Shane's intentions? How could Faye find out?

Situation 4

Dave has been friends with Louisa for ten years. One day Dave tells Louisa that he can no longer pay the bill for his car, and he asks her to sign a form as a witness to say he can't pay the bill. Louisa agrees; she trusts Dave and so does not read the form he asks her to sign. Later that month Louisa gets a letter from a car company claiming that she owes them money for Dave's car.

What were Dave's intentions ? How could Louisa find out?

1.6.1 Other ways of learning about intentions

You may feel that some of the suggestions below are not appropriate for your age or ability. That is OK. However, this book is going to be read by a multitude of ages so I have tried to include things that I think may be helpful for people aged 14 and over.

- If you have family or friends who are supportive (or you may be able to do this on your own), there are some games that can help to develop flexible thought. For example, *Bubble Talk* is a game where you have to match captions with photo cards. Several captions could go with each photo, and it helps you to think of different reasons why people may think or say different things. (I appreciate older readers may not want to do this.) See the resources section at the end of this chapter for a link to the *Bubble Talk* website.

- Other people on the autistic spectrum have said they have found drama useful for learning about people and their intentions. However, many people on the autistic spectrum find it hard to generalize skills and to know what information should and should not be used in different situations. For some people on the autistic spectrum, it is natural to look at situations at face value, which means to consider what they can see in front of them. For example, if a policeman was rude to them, some might generalize that all policeman are rude. There may have been other reasons why the policeman behaved like this; some of these reasons may have nothing to do with the person he was rude to – for example, the policeman was having a bad day, or it might be that it was almost time for him to finish work and he was tired. It is essential but difficult (online forums may be helpful) to try to understand what you can't see – you can't see that the policeman is having a bad day but you can see his facial expression. When there are situations in your life that are new or do not happen often, or if something negative happens a lot, it is helpful to analyse them in a notebook. What went well? What didn't go well? Have I been in similar situations in the past and behaved differently? What was the outcome? What might have happened if I had behaved differently?

Stay positive when you analyse the past. Do not think, 'Oh, it's because of my autism' or 'I cannot do anything right' or 'I am stupid' or other similar thoughts. Think about the things you have learnt.

If you have access to a counsellor, psychologist or therapist, this work could be done with them.

1.7 Thinking time

For many people on the autistic spectrum, it's important to have a greater amount of time to consider different choices than non-autistic people often need. Techniques such as Tease the Tease can be useful because they are pre-scripted and so may need less processing time. Also consider the advice below.

'I have learned to say "let me think about that for a short while".'

Anouschka, research participant

What Anouschka is explaining is a bit like a script; she has learnt a standard response to being asked to do something. This is an example of a generalized skill, rather than being specific to a particular context. It is helpful to think about and write down a few possible responses that you could give if you needed some thinking time. Thinking time may make it easier to say no or to get yourself out of a bad situation.

'Don't do things in a hurry, think about it, give yourself the processing time. [Non-autistic people] want you to think straight away. Tell them to wait – this saves making a big mistake.'

Jacinta, research participant

1.8 Lending money/things to friends

Several people in my research commented that they no longer lend people money. I think you should also be cautious about lending money or other objects to friends. I thought the following advice would be particularly helpful to readers.

'If someone makes you feel uncomfortable you must tell him/her, and if he/she doesn't respect that, then that person isn't a friend at all. Be honest with yourself and others. Life is much easier that way and people get to know the real you. If someone asks for money, don't feel obliged to give it – it is yours after all and so it is up to you what you do with your money. Anyone who goes out of their way to insult you isn't worth knowing or even listening to. Have no regrets, the past is not worth worrying about, what matters is the present. Make a positive present for a more positive future.'

Angharad, research participant

1.8.1 Buying people things will not make them your friends

The professionals I interviewed for this book almost all commented that many people on the autistic spectrum would spend money on people because they thought this was a way to make friends.

> Friendship should be **reciprocal** – for example, if you go to the pub with a friend and you buy them a drink, then they should buy you your next drink. When you buy a drink for yourself and a friend(s), this is normally called a round. Sometimes you may find that by the end of the visit to the pub you have bought one more round than your friend, but this means they should buy the first round next time you go to the pub. Occasionally, someone might buy a person they don't know well a drink to be nice – for example, if you are enjoying the person's conversation with you – but this is not a way to make friends.

If you are desperate to have friends, it will not help you to buy people things. People may just pretend to be your friend so that you continue to buy things for them, but if, for whatever reason, you become unable to buy them things, they will not want to be your friend. Friendship is something that is built up over time, not just in one evening, and it works both ways.

> **Give and take** in the context of friendship means that both people take and receive things in equal amounts – for example, you give (buy) someone a drink at the pub/bar and then you take (receive) the next drink.

It is your choice. If you just want to buy someone a drink or something else because you like the person or perhaps it's a special occasion such as their birthday, and you understand that it may not be reciprocated, then that is fine – just as long as you understand that buying something for someone does not make them your friend.

1.9 Obligation

Feeling obliged to spend time with a friend was a common occurrence among the people I interviewed, with more than 50 per cent of women on the autistic spectrum reporting this.

Of course, part of being friends with someone is spending time with them. With some friendships, this may be only online (if you have only met online and live a long way away from each other), but friendships where you see each other in real life and not just on the internet do involve spending time with each other. When people make friends, they often have expectations.

Friendship should be something that is fun. If it is not fun, then either change the way your friendship works by telling the person that you are unhappy and want things to change, or leave the friendship. There are many people in the world to be friends with, and there are online forums for people on the autistic spectrum. There are also self-advocacy organizations such as ASAN (Autistic Self-Advocacy Network – see the resources section), which may provide an opportunity to meet others on the autistic spectrum.

> 'When I feel I want to help someone out, but I am uncomfortable with what is required of me to do so, I try to imagine the "someone" isn't there (and isn't asking anything of me) – then I ask myself if I would still want to take part. That way I can work out if the wish to be involved is truly my own, or I am feeling pressurized by the other person.'
>
> *Leigh, research participant*

1.10 How do I know what I should do to keep the friendship going?

It may make life easier to have friends you see at a group event. If you want to spend more time with that one person, you could ask them to do another activity with you – for example, going for a drink at a pub.

1.11 Other ways to prevent manipulation

- If you have a friend who is constantly trying to manipulate you, and you find it hard to say no to them, write a script of how you will say no. Memorize the script and practise reciting it in front of a mirror. Practise the script until you feel comfortable enough to speak to the person.

- If you are finding it hard to speak to the person, is there someone else who could speak to them – either with you (some people gain confidence just by knowing someone else is standing next to them and understands what they are trying to communicate) or on your behalf? Alternatively, you could write the person a letter or an email.

- If you are desperate for friends, it can be hard to know when you should stay away from people, because you so badly want it to be all right. If you find scales are a useful way of making decisions, you could ask yourself, 'On a scale of 1 to 10, how much emotional stress is this person causing me (10 being a great deal so that I am unable to cope with daily life and 1 being none at all)?' If your answer is 5 or higher, do you really want this person to be your friend?

- List the positive and negative things about being friends with this person. The more negatives there are, the more emotional damage they are doing to you, and therefore logically you would be happier without them.

- Sometimes it can be very hard to imagine what life would be like without a particular person in your life. In this situation, think about what it is your friend enables you to do and then think of ways of doing those things without them. You could try asking other friends or professionals in your life how you might be able to do those things without that friend.

- It can be very hard to leave a friendship – it takes great inner strength. It's important to understand and try to accept that not all situations can be resolved; sometimes you have to walk away and stop being friends with the person.

Loneliness may be scary, but it is better than being hurt. Loneliness is an emotion that can go away, whereas some emotional pain stays with people for the rest of their lives.

I appreciate that the above advice may make it sound easy, when in reality it is hard to (a) know you are being manipulated and (b) leave a friendship. This is especially true when you don't have many friends or many opportunities to make friends.

'When in doubt, talk with a trusted person about your doubts. This may be hard when you do not have real trusted persons in your life. Then I'd suggest you may join an Asperger or autism forum. There are people who are reasonably anonymous but much like yourself and they may offer really wise advice.'

R. Wolf, research participant

1.12 Leaving a friendship

There are different reasons why someone might not want to be friends with someone else any more and want to leave the friendship. Some of these reasons may be resolvable and others may not be.

For example, if your friend made you feel anxious, you could consider telling them how you feel and the circumstances in which you feel this way – for example, when they are late. You could then agree on what to do if these circumstances happen. For example, you could agree that they text you or use another method of communication to inform you that they are going to be late. It is important to agree on something you are both happy with. You also have to accept that people are not perfect and do make mistakes. Sometimes it's not possible to do what you both agreed – for example, if your friend's mobile/cell phone battery ran out, then they would be unable to text or call you. A true friend, however, would make an effort to make you feel less anxious. The people to stay away from are those who intend to hurt you.

If a friend is abusive or doesn't care about you, then do not be friends with this person. Abusers tend not to change their behaviour – that is, they usually continue to be abusive once they have started. There may be periods of time when they are nice to you. However, they are only being nice to you so that your friendship continues and they will be able to abuse you again. In this scenario, their intention is to manipulate you into thinking that they are a true friend and to continue abusing you.

You may have friends with whom you find it hard to spend time because they do things you do not like, such as going to bars, and so they may not be a close friend but someone you see occasionally. You could describe this kind of friendship as a 'casual' friendship. Your friendships are unlikely to all be the same; you will spend more time with some people than with others. Also, people's views and opinions change over time, and sometimes people may decide that they don't want to be friends because they no longer enjoy the other person's company.

It is perfectly acceptable not to want to be friends with someone, and you do not have to give them a reason.

Below are a few ways to stop being friends with someone:

- Don't spend time with them. Ignore their messages and phone calls and hope they go away. This is OK, but they may not go away and they may keep calling or messaging you.

- Send short replies to their messages and don't ask questions. Over time, they are likely to stop messaging you.

- Tell the person you no longer want to be friends with them. You do not have to do this face to face, although some people would consider it cowardly not to do so. If they continue to contact you, ask them not to. You do not have to give them a reason for no longer wanting to be friends with them.

Sometimes people drift apart. This is when social contact with that person reduces over a period of time. Friends come and friends go; most friends will not be your friends for your entire life.

Part 2: Positive friendships (friendships that are not exploitative or manipulative)

1.13 Defining friendships

Everyone's definition of what a friend is will be different, as there are many different types of friendships.

On social networking websites, such as Facebook, we request and accept people as our friends. We may not have met these people in real life, and it is likely your friendship with people on Facebook will be different from friendships with people you know in real life.

Below I have described different kinds of friendships. There are different levels of friendship. A level of friendship is the closeness of the friendship.

Emotionally close, often referred to simply as close, is a term used to describe people who tell each other about their emotions, thoughts and feelings. You could also be close to someone who is not your friend, such as a teacher. This means that you tell them how you are feeling. It is important to understand that friendship is a two-way relationship. This means that both people should be sharing equal amounts of information about thoughts and feelings. If you are both sharing equal amounts of information about thoughts and feelings, then you are close to each other. However, sometimes people share thoughts and feelings in support groups. This is a therapeutic context – that is, the reason you are sharing thoughts and feelings is to receive therapy or support from a professional or from the members of the support group. You are not necessarily friends with the other members of the support group, because the aim of meeting at the support group is different to when you share information informally (not in a support group) and as a way of getting support and building trust with a person. If you share thoughts and feelings with another person outside of a support setting, then they are most likely your friend, but only if you are spending time with them and if you are both sharing equal amounts of information.

Sharing information means to communicate information – for example, if I tell you that I am 25 years old, I am sharing the information that I am 25 years old with you. Sharing information is a phrase used with any type of information, including emotions.

(?) **Building trust** means to increase the level of trust, for example between two people in a friendship (see the ladder of trust in section 1.14).

1.13.1 Types of friendships (from least close to most close)

ACQUAINTANCE

This is a person who you cannot rely on always to be loyal to you. For example, you might go to an event you don't want to go to, but you go to be supportive to an acquaintance. You cannot expect your acquaintance will always do the same for you. You are unlikely to discuss feelings and emotions with an acquaintance. However, some acquaintances can become your friends over a period of time.

VIRTUAL FRIEND/ONLINE FRIEND

This is a friend with whom you only spend time online – for example, chatting via a website, Xbox LIVE or Skype. You enjoy their company, but you haven't met face to face. Sometimes you can tell them your secrets and other times it is unwise to do so. Share as much information as they are willing to share with you. There are some people who lie, so it is always important to question how likely it is that what this person is telling you is true and why might they be telling you this information.

REAL-LIFE FRIEND, WITH WHOM YOU SPEND TIME IN A GROUP BUT NOT ON THEIR OWN

This is someone who is similar to an acquaintance but more likely to come to events you invite them to, particularly if other members of the group in which you normally spend time with them are also invited. They are people who know your name and ask you about your life and your interests, not just 'How are you?' You would also ask them similar questions.

REGULAR FRIEND

A regular friend is someone you spend time with. You enjoy each other's company and you are mutually supportive of each other. But you do not share your thoughts and feelings about certain topics because you worry about the other person's judgement of you.

CLOSE FRIEND

This does not mean physically close; it does not have to involve living near each other, hugging or kissing. A close friend is a friend with whom you share your thoughts, feelings and opinions, and who also shares their thoughts, feelings and opinions with you. You trust each other, and the trust you have in each other is demonstrated in the way you both behave. For example, if they tell you something scares them, such as spiders, and you think that is silly, you respect the fact that they feel scared and try to be supportive. You respect each other's opinions even if they are different; everyone is entitled to their own opinions.

> Teachers and other professionals are not your friends. You might have similar interests or similar political or religious views to them, but they are professionals who are paid to provide you with a service. They have a duty of care towards you; this means they have a responsibility to keep you safe. It would not be appropriate for them to be your friend, because this would mean they might treat you more favourably than someone else for whom they also have a duty of care.

1.14 Ladder of trust

When you **trust** someone, it means you believe that they will do what they have said they will do, or that they will not hurt you, or they will protect you from danger. For example, we trust airplane pilots to fly us safely to our destination.

The above definitions of types of friendships talk a lot about trust. It is important to build up trust with a person, so you know that they will not hurt you.

Trust may seem like an abstract topic to you. One activity I use with my clients is called the 'ladder of trust'. You can either draw this or use post-it notes (sticky notes), as described on the following page.

1. Place two post-it notes side by side. On the first one write, 'Information that is OK to share and types of touch that are OK.' On the other post-it note write, 'Information and types of touch that are not OK.' These two post-it notes are the bottom rung of your ladder.

2. Write on the first post-it note what it would be OK to share/talk about when you first meet someone and what kind of touch would be OK (e.g. a handshake). On the other post-it note write down what information is not OK to share/what kind of touch is not OK. Table 1.1 shows an example of the bottom rung. However, the answers are very dependent on how old you are, where you live in the world and how you met the person, so you need to discuss this ladder with someone else who can help you. Think about the issues and be as specific as possible.

3. Next, place one post-it note above the first two post-it notes. On this one write, 'What I would expect to happen before I can move up the ladder.'

4. Write down what kind of reaction you would be expecting – for example, the other person sharing as much information as you had shared, or the person not touching you in an inappropriate place (e.g. your breasts). In other words, what would make you feel comfortable/happy to share more information with this person?

Repeat steps 1–4 for the next level of friendship – see Table 1.1 for a worked example. Note that the categories are repeated on each rung of the ladder (your ladder is likely to go much higher than this example as it is only designed to illustrate the idea), but each rung means more trust is given by both people.

As you are making your ladder, try to think about why it might not be OK to share certain information.

This is just an example to get you started. I would expect you to add more items to both rungs on the ladder and for the ladder to have many more rungs than the two below. This strategy is really useful just for thinking about trust and it may be that a particular situation means you miss a rung on the ladder or share particular pieces of information on the ladder that are personal to you, before sharing all the other information. That means that the information you share with a person may not be in the same order as on the ladder, but the aim of this activity is for you to think and begin to understand that friendships have different levels of trust. The rungs of the ladder represent the different levels – the higher up the ladder you and your friend are, then the closer you are as friends.

Table 1.1 Ladder of trust: What would you expect to happen before sharing more information?

Information that is OK to share/touch that is OK		Information that is not OK to share/touch that is not OK
At this point some people might share their surname/ family name so that they could be found on Facebook or other social networking websites, but other people would not feel comfortable doing this. If you don't feel comfortable doing so, then don't share your surname.		You would probably not share your middle name or if you had ever changed your name. (This might allow people to find information about you on the internet or wonder why you changed your name.)
It would be safer for you to use a pseudonym (see Chapter 6 for more about this).		
Area of town you live in.		Still not sharing your street address or house number.
Before I can move up the ladder I would expect the other person to share information about themselves on the topics we have discussed.		
I would not expect the person to bear-hug me.		
Information that is OK to share/touch that is OK		**Information that is not OK to share/touch that is not OK**
First name.		Not surname. (Why? Because you can search for someone's first name and surname in a telephone directory, which means they would have your telephone number and address so they could start to harass you, e.g. keep calling you.)
Age.		

Town you live in.	Not OK to share street name or house number (for the reasons described above).
	Also not OK to say you live on your own as this may make you vulnerable. (As described earlier in this chapter, people are safer in groups.)
What job you do or if you study.	Not where you work, how much you earn or if you are on benefits.
Gender.	Not that you have had gender reassignment, unless you are in a support group or with other members of the lesbian, gay, bisexual and transgender (LGBT) community. Gender reassignment is seen as being something that you keep private as other people may judge you negatively.
Hobbies/interests.	Unless you are in a religious setting such as a church or the other person mentions their faith/belief as being the same as yours, avoid discussion about religion as it can cause people to judge you.
	You probably wouldn't share your marital status, although it is usually OK to say you are married if you are. Some people may judge you negatively if you are divorced as some people feel divorce is immoral, or people may talk about painful memories if you say you are widowed.
Shaking hands. High five.	Bear-hug.

START HERE

Some people do not want to be emotionally close to their friends. Other people enjoy helping their friends. It is important that you know what is important to you in your friendships. What is it that makes a friend a friend to you? Is a friend just someone you spend time with, or is it someone you share your problems with? Do you have different types of friendships with different people? In this chapter I have already written about trust and different types of friendship. It's important, however, that you make this information meaningful for yourself; otherwise, you can't use the information on a day-to-day basis because it doesn't relate to how your friendships work. Below is my own personal definition of what a friend is to me. Also consider if emotional closeness is important to you.

1.15 Robyn Steward's definition of a friend (and add your own)

A **friend** is a person who does not have authority over me (e.g. a teacher). They are someone who I enjoy spending time with face to face, on the phone or on the internet. I enjoy some, but not all, of the same activities as my friends. I feel I can say no to activities that I do not want to take part in, and I trust my friends to respect my decisions. Friends won't bully me. If they tease me and I don't like it and express this, they are likely to apologize and they won't do it again. My friends are people who do not want to be my friend just because of any wealth or other material possessions I may have. Friendship should be give and take; you may do things for your friends and they should do things for you, such as listening to each other or supporting each other at events. My friends will learn to understand me, just as I will learn to understand them, and we will not try to change each other's personalities.

Within a school, work or care environment, there is a **social hierarchy**. Everyone is a part of the hierarchy. Teachers, doctors and managers are at the top; pupils, patients and employees are at the bottom. Normally, to reach the top of the hierarchy you have to have particular qualifications and experience, and do particular tasks, such as job interviews or take on the responsibility of patients. The people lower down the hierarchy are unlikely to have had as much experience as those higher up and this is why people who are lower down the hierarchy have to listen to what those at the top tell them. This could be described as the people lower down the hierarchy being under the authority of those at the top. If you are at the top of the hierarchy, you get to make the rules. However, it does not allow you to break the law or abuse/hurt people. Social hierarchies are one of the reasons teachers get to make and enforce rules in a school. They have earned their position. Rules they make should benefit everyone under the teacher in the hierarchy.

Below is a space for you to write your own definition of what a friend is.

My definition of a friend

1.16 What is a boundary?

Boundaries can be physical – for example, between two countries.

Friendships can have their own boundaries, which are a bit like rules. As an adult, some boundaries change.

An example of a boundary could be not going to pubs or bars with friends because it makes you feel scared. Many people on the autistic spectrum do not like what might be viewed as stereotypical social environments such as night clubs and bars.

Sometimes a person might change their boundary temporarily. It can be helpful to think about your boundaries and write them down, because that way you have decided what you will and won't do, and you have had time to process this. You should find this means it is easier to make decisions that involve boundaries.

Many people on the autistic spectrum will be desperate to have friends and will therefore do things that they are uncomfortable with, but this will not always help you make friends and may compromise your safety.

⊘ To be **uncomfortable with** something means to not like doing it because it makes you feel that you are doing something wrong, scary or anxiety-provoking. For example, I feel uncomfortable going to a night club because people stand too close to me.

Below are some examples of boundaries that a person might apply to friendships. Different friendships may have different boundaries because you may trust some friends more than others.

Physical boundaries

I do not like being hugged.
I do not like being touched.
I do not mind people touching my shoulder briefly.
I do not want my friends to visit me at home.
I do not want to be kissed.

Emotional boundaries

I cannot cope with a friend who rings me up to just moan about their problems.
I do not like friendships which involve a lot of contact – for me this is twice a week.
I do not enjoy people who want me to share personal details about my life.
It makes me incredibly anxious when people are late without telling me first.

'Learn to think about where your own boundaries lie. Think for yourself per situation whether you want to extend a boundary (for instance, because you want to meet new people, you are willing to risk feeling a bit scared when going to social events), or whether you are perfectly happy with where your boundary is (for instance, that people should not touch you constantly, even if they do that to everyone). These things are easier to think about when you're alone.'

Carol, research participant

Write down your boundaries in a list like the one on the previous page.

My boundaries

1.16.1 How do I use boundaries and the ladder of trust together?

Good question. The ladder of trust has different levels or rungs of the ladder, with different responses you are waiting for between them, so your emotional boundary could be that you wait for a suitable response before moving up the ladder (e.g. sharing more information). You might find it helpful to name the rungs on the ladder 'level 1', 'level 2' and so on, and the bits in the middle 'responses to level 1', 'responses to level 2' and so on, and these can be your boundaries. For example, 'I will share information on level 3 of my ladder of trust if...'

1.16.2 Why do people have boundaries and a ladder of trust?

I've advocated using both because sometimes a boundary is too rigid – for example, although you may not usually share personal details with people, you may choose to share more personal details with someone after they have shared personal details with you and you feel you can trust them. However, boundaries are important because there may be things you would never share or never do.

1.17 What is your comfort zone?

A comfort zone is not actually a physical zone (or space). A comfort zone is the things you feel confident and happy doing. You may find that thinking about your comfort zone as well as your boundaries gives you greater self-awareness and confidence to say what you do and don't want to do, because you have thought about it ahead of needing to make a choice. I have provided a visual way of representing comfort zones in Figure 1.1.

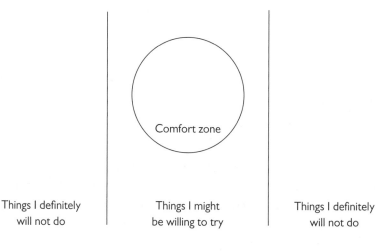

Figure 1.1 Comfort zone

You could either draw your own or use Figure 1.1. Things you are confident and happy doing can be written in the circle. You can write things in the spaces between the lines in the centre of the page that you would find hard, but possible, if you were with friends who would support you or if you had pre-planned a way to get out. By doing the things you write down in the 'Things I might be willing to try' section a few times, you are likely to become more confident about doing them, in which case you could consider writing them in your comfort zone circle at a later date.

In the space between the lines and the edge of the page are things you would definitely not want to do.

You could also specify the frequency. For example, it might be out of your comfort zone to visit a friend in hospital, but you would make an exception once. You could also include information you won't share, such as your bank details.

Think of some activities that you would like to do with your current friends or future friends. As you do this, think of things you wouldn't want to do and why, and add them to your comfort zone diagram. For example, you may not enjoy talking. This could be because you feel that this puts a lot of pressure on you. Deciding upon activities might also give you ideas about places where you could meet new friends.

⑦ **Pressure**, in this context, means to make it hard for you to think or to make decisions.

⑦ **Context** is the place, situation or circumstances in which a word is used. For example, pressure in the context of science means something different to the social context in which the word pressure was used in the above paragraph. Words have different meanings in different contexts.

1.17.1 Why is establishing my comfort zone important?

If you know what your comfort zone is, then this helps you to keep yourself emotionally safe.

⑦ To be **emotionally safe** means to be able to think rationally about your wellbeing without being overwhelmed by emotions. Knowing what you do not want to do should also help you to avoid being manipulated, since it creates a framework to refer back to when trying to make decisions.

⑦ **Manipulation** is when someone plans to make you do something that is not in your best interests. For example, someone might manipulate you into giving them money, telling you they will give it back, when they do not intend to do so.

It isn't just us!
By the way, the difficulties with people attempting to manipulate their friends are shared by non-autistic women and women on the autistic spectrum.

In my survey, 53 per cent of non-autistic women had experienced attempts by others to manipulate them, compared with 79 per cent of women on the autistic spectrum.

1.18 Needs and wants from friendship

An important question to consider is what you *need* and what you *want* from friendships. Needs are essential; wants are things that would be nice but are not essential. You should also consider other ways of meeting your needs and wants.

Your initial answer to the question 'What are my needs from friendship?' may be 'I want to spend time with someone.' After further thought, a more complete way of describing this need may be that you feel a need to spend time with another person doing structured activities (i.e. something with a clear start and end) – for example, watching a film or going to a restaurant. Or you might feel you need to spend time with someone else doing something constructive such as writing a play or playing music. You might also feel that being emotionally supportive, as you would be in a close friendship, is too intense or overwhelming.

On the other hand, you may feel that emotionally supporting someone else and them supporting you is exactly what you do want, as well as spending time with someone else doing particular activities.

On the other hand is a phrase used to suggest that there is an alternative view. For example, some people may think that cats are better than dogs. On the other hand, some people think dogs are better than cats.

It is OK not to feel a need to have close friends. Some people feel that they just need to spend time with other people to meet their social needs. If unstructured, noisy social gatherings are difficult to cope with, a solution might be to attend a structured social gathering such as a poetry gig. You could talk to other people at the gig about the poems, and this would provide the opportunity to meet new people. Over time, if you kept going to the same venue, people will start to recognize you. Although brief conversations may not always result in friendship, they would be a chance to chat to people about something factual. There is the possibility that you might meet someone who then becomes your friend. Or you may find these brief conversations meet your social needs.

It is also important to list what you *do not* need. Many people on the autistic spectrum benefit from thinking about these issues because it gives them time to process information, instead of having to make an immediate decision, and it may help you to find new ways of meeting your social needs. Without thinking about them, you may not have considered what you need and do not need. You may have tried to have a social life that involved things you do not need and which could actually hinder your attempts at social interaction. For example, you might have tried to be like other young people and go to night clubs, but you were overwhelmed by the sound, which would mean you would find social interaction even harder than usual.

> 'I know what it's like to desperately want friends and to do anything to make them happy and accept you. In the end it's not worth it because it just makes you more miserable. It's taken me nearly 30 years to understand that not everybody who is friendly towards me has nice intentions and that a real friend would not make you feel bad about yourself. Better to have no friends than friends who treat you like dirt.'
>
> *Kel, research participant*

1.18.1 I do not like meeting in busy places to socialize. What alternatives are there?

One of your boundaries might be that you do not want to go to noisy, busy places; however, you do still want to make friends. How can this be resolved?

Many people on the autistic spectrum do not like noisy and busy places. It is a misconception that all non-autistic people like places such as malls, supermarkets, clubs and bars. Many do not.

From a safety perspective, if you experience information or sensory overload or other difficulties with processing information, quieter activities may be better. It is still possible to socialize and make friends without going to noisy places.

There are online communities for people on the autistic spectrum. There are also communities that are not specifically for people on the autistic spectrum but are centred around an interest such as needlework or computers.

If, however, you want to meet people in real life, then here are nine ways that might help you do this:

1. Use websites such as www.meetup.com to search for groups of people with similar interests (e.g. creative writing).

2. If you have an interest that involves vocational skills, such as caring for animals, then you could apply to volunteer at an animal shelter or other places that feature your interest.

3. If you have an interest in in computer gaming (playing computer games), there are often groups of gamers who meet up to play together. Xbox LIVE involves wearing a headset, so this may be beneficial if you are sensitive to noise.

4. If you like to read, the local library (and some bookstores) may have a reading group, or there may be events such as poetry readings.

5. There are some very small venues for things such as poetry, comedy and some music. If you like these activities, researching small (or 'intimate', as they are sometimes described) venues would be a way of finding places you could go for semi-structured activities. For example, in London there is a place called the Poetry Café. It has a room downstairs where they have poetry readings. This is where everyone sits down on chairs facing the front and listens

to people reading poetry. At the interval, most people go upstairs to buy a drink or have a smoke, so downstairs is usually quiet during the interval.

6. Some people on the autistic spectrum say that they find busy environments much easier to cope with if they have a specific role to focus on because this helps to filter out the other information. If this is the case for you, you could consider the following:

    ▫ If you like to perform, you could sign up at an open mic night. These nights allow anyone to volunteer to put their name on a list of performers for that evening.

(?) In this context, **night** means the duration of an event – for example, a gig might be from 9 to 11pm. People would consider the night to be over at 11pm, because that is when the music will stop. It has nothing to do with the concept of day and night. It is still night-time; it's just that the music or other event you went to see has finished.

(?) **Mic** is short for microphone.

(?) **Open**, in this context, means that you do not need to audition.

(?) **Put on**, in this context, means to arrange and advertise a particular event – for example, the Poetry Café puts on open mic poetry nights.

You will normally be told what time you will be performing. But be prepared for other people not getting off stage on time, meaning your time slot changes, and sometimes there may not be time to hear everyone. It is important to learn not to outwardly show that you are annoyed that your time slot has changed, as everyone else playing after you will have had their time slots changed too. It would be disrespectful to other people to get annoyed as they might perceive that you think you are more important than they are.

    ▫ If you are at college or university, there may be what are called societies (socs). These are clubs based around specific interests. For example, ents (entertainment) is a society that organizes entertainment such as music.

There are many different roles that members can take, such as sound technician, lighting technician or DJ, and these are roles you could learn to do even if you have no experience but were interested in learning.

- AmDram is an amateur dramatics society/club; these are often non-profit/charity organizations and not just in colleges and universities. AmDrams organize plays. There are many things you could do there, such as costume design (if you were interested in needlework) as well as acting. You could Google amateur dramatics and your city – for example, amateur dramatics + Los Angeles – and contact the group to ask if you can come and what you could do.

- If you play an instrument, you may like to join an orchestra or other musical group. If you sing, you could join a choir.

7. If you are religious, churches can sometimes be a good source of social relationships. Your local church may run study groups, for example.

8. There may a local group that goes on walks in the countryside, or perhaps there is countryside accessible to you via public transportation or car, and the walking group may be based there or at a nature reserve. You could research the websites of nature reserves to see if these groups exist in your area.

9. The local newspaper may contain advertisements for local groups. There may also be specialist newspapers – for example, music newspapers.

It is important to understand that it is unlikely that you will make close friends with people immediately. Friendship takes time to build and it's important to maintain the friendship.

1.19 Ways to work on a friendship and why this is important for safety

Once you have made friends, you have to work on your friendship. This is because you're only going to benefit from a friendship (including the added safety benefits that friendship can provide) if you continue to be friends with that person. Therefore, you need to use some friendship maintenance skills to keep the friendship going.

An analogy that may be helpful for this is learning to play a musical instrument such as the guitar or piano. Once you have mastered a skill, such as playing a particular piece of music, you have to practise regularly to keep being able to play that piece of music so that you maintain the skill in your memory.

People often told me that you had to work on friendships and I did not understand what they meant until I observed what other people did.

Working on a friendship does not mean always doing things that make you uncomfortable or unhappy. Below are some suggestions for ways you could work on a friendship.

> 'Be true to yourself and you'll gain the respect of others.'
>
> *Jenn, research participant*

I have found it helpful to be in touch with my friends regularly. How frequent this communication should be is hard to work out if you do not have a lot of experience or find it hard to read the social cues.

> *Social cues* are things that provide information on social situations, such as a person's behaviour or tone of voice. For example, if you called someone on the phone and they said, 'I am just writing an email,' this is a social cue that tells you to tell the person you are calling that you will call them back later. Or you can ask, 'Is now a good time to talk?'

If you are unsure about how often to contact your friend, one rule that is helpful to apply to this situation is this: when you have contacted them, wait for them to respond before contacting them again, unless it is an emergency. Friendship is two-way; you may want to talk to your friend once a week, but they may feel this is too much contact. You have to respect each other's needs. Ask your friend how often they want to be in touch with you.

🔍 **In touch** means to be in contact with someone. For example, I might say I am in touch with my parents daily, but it does not refer to physical touch (e.g. I touched my mum's shoulder).

If you feel yourself becoming isolated, or you want more frequent contact with other people, consider finding out if there is a weekly music night, Scrabble night or similar event you could attend that you would enjoy. This would enable you to see people regularly, but there is less to worry about in terms of frequency of contact as you see one another at the shared activity. Here are some more ideas:

- Choose an event you want to go to, preferably around an interest you share with a friend, such as a particular type of music, and invite your friend to go with you. You might try to invite them a week in an advance. However, some people live very spontaneous lives, so, depending on your friend's personality, it may be better to invite them on the day.

  Inviting them to something increases the likelihood of them inviting you somewhere. If your friend continually says no to your invitations, then perhaps they do not want to spend time with you. Do not take this personally; maybe there are other commitments in their life (e.g. children). Is there someone else you can invite instead?

  If it has been difficult to arrange going to a social event with them, perhaps you could do an activity together that is not time- or date-specific. For example, if you both like to paint or draw, you could do this any day that you are both available.

  If you are unsure if your friend wants to spend time you, you could ask them when would be a good time for you to do something together. If they are a bit vague, then find other people to spend time with and perhaps your friend will want to spend time with you in the future.

🔍 To **take something personally** means to feel something was said or done deliberately to make you upset.

- Be assertive and make choices about your friendship that suit you as well as your friend. If someone really cares about you, they will want to spend time with you, regardless of whether or not you want to attend the mainstream pub/bar and social events. If this is not the case, then perhaps there are other people who may be better friends for you.

- If a friend does something that upsets you and which is aimed at you – for example, calling you a negative name such as 'freak' – it is perfectly acceptable to tell them that you do not like them doing this.

  However, be aware that you cannot control the whole world and that sometimes people may do things to others that you do not like (e.g. swearing). If you feel strongly about it, then you have to make a choice as to whether you want to be friends with this person or not. Most people will become angry if you tell them what to do, although you could try asking politely. However, people are entitled to their own choices, and if you decide you cannot tolerate the person doing something that you do not like, or they if are hurting you in some way, then don't be friends with them. The energy you are using putting up with things that make you unhappy could be used having fun with someone you do enjoy being with.

- Ask your friends to be straightforward and literal when they talk to you. For example, if they are bored with a conversation, ask them to tell you instead of just sounding uninterested, as you may not be able to pick up on their tone of voice.

  Many people struggle to pick up on subtle social cues such as someone not sounding interested. For people on the autistic spectrum, this could be because you are monotropic (able to concentrate on only one thing at a time). Also, your sensory system may be mono-channel (concentrating on one sense at a time). In some situations, this can be advantageous – for example, hearing things in music that others do not hear. However, in this situation, it is not so helpful.

(?) To **pick up on** something means to notice and process the information.

1.20 Strategies for conversations

Talking, whether this is online or face to face or using sign language, is important because it allows for the friendship to continue. Using skills that make sure that neither of you is bored or annoyed with the conversation is helpful, because this means there is less risk of misunderstanding and a greater likelihood that the friendship will continue.

When speaking to your friends:

- Make sure your friend wants to talk to you at that point in time – for example, ask, 'Is this a good time to talk?'

- It's important that conversations are conversations, as opposed to monologues, and that you and your friend are both interested in the topic that you are discussing, unless you both like talking in monologues to each other.

(?) A **monologue** is like a mini-speech – essentially a list of statements, facts, opinions or thoughts or a mix of different types of information, given by one speaker, which does not include contributions from the listener.

- If you are not interested or feel that you have spoken about a topic or your friend has spoken about a topic for long enough, you can change the topic. If your friend changes the topic, this could be a sign that they have had enough of talking about the previous topic. It is best not to discuss that topic for the remainder of the conversation. Even if you find your friend's topic of conversation boring, if they let you talk about a topic for a certain length of time, then try to allow them the same amount of time to talk about their topic.

- To help you know if someone is interested in a topic or not, you could learn what people's voices sound like when they are interested and when they are not interested. To do this, ask people you know to demonstrate what their 'bored' and 'interested' voices sound like.

A person who is interested in a topic is likely to ask questions; a person who is not interested is unlikely to ask questions. If you are talking about a topic and the person you are talking to does not ask questions, change the topic. Sometimes people do not like to say how they are feeling because they worry about offending other people. If you are unsure whether or not you are boring your friend, you could ask, 'Shall I continue or should we change topic?' This gives the person an opportunity to say how they feel, in a non-direct way. Rather than saying, 'I am bored,' which would be a direct way of explaining how they feel, they can just say, 'Let's change the topic.'

'When you hear the phone ring and the caller ID tells you a friend is calling, you shouldn't be feeling dread. If you do, it's not a healthy friendship.'

Beth, research participant

It might be useful to have a visual, auditory or physical representation of what you are good at and your qualities. Below is a suggestion of how you can do this. Refer back to these suggestions when you feel low and bad about yourself, in order to remind yourself that you are a unique and important person. These suggestions are somewhat similar to the ones I discussed with Dr Tony Attwood as part of my research for this book. However, I wrote this section before I spoke to him.

1.21 Non-autistic (NA) council

One strategy I have found very useful is to have a non-autistic (NA) informal council. This is a group of non-autistic people whom I ask for advice. I may ask each person about the same scenario to get different perspectives. If I am unsure about something, I find this works very well.

I am unable to explain in this book every single situation in which someone's intentions may not be good – that is, the other person wants to hurt you – because these situations are so person- and situation-specific. I feel frustrated not to be able to offer you more information on manipulation, as it is so obvious that this happens a lot to people on the autistic spectrum. But I feel that if you have greater confidence in yourself and if you develop ways of seeking information, then you can use these to help you to understand what is happening around you and to stand up for yourself to get out of bad situations.

I think it is important to remember that non-autistic people also experience negative situations, and that perhaps some readers may feel that their life has been somewhat over-clinicalized. In other words, the difficulties of just being a human being have been highlighted as being part of being on the autistic spectrum. Because autism is such an integral part of each individual person, it is not possible always to attribute a particular circumstance to the fact that the person is on the autistic spectrum. I think therefore that a person is most likely to gain success if they can find people – both people who are friends and people who are there to support the person – who can give them information.

Mentoring, for example, can be a very useful tool. I have a mentor who is a woman and we discuss women's issues. She is not much older than me, and I find hearing about her experiences incredibly useful, helping me to think about what I might do. In life it is important to take risks, but it is equally important to make sure those risks are 'acceptable' – that is, we have worked out how likely or unlikely it is that a very negative consequence, which we will be unable to cope with, will happen because of the risk we take.

For example, there is always a risk of having a car crash every time you drive a car, but when you think of how many car journeys are made a year and how many result in crashes, the number resulting in crashes is quite low. Therefore, it is an acceptable risk to drive a car as long as you have a driver's licence, but it would be an unacceptable risk to drive a car while drunk, because many car crashes happen as a result of the driver being drunk. Being drunk slows down reaction times and therefore increases the likelihood that you will have a car crash. Driving when drunk is therefore an unacceptable risk.

It is true that people take unacceptable risks, and that is their choice. And it is your choice to decide which risks you do and do not want to take. Using a tool such as the NA council can help you work out how much risk is involved in an activity or in a decision you are trying to make.

1.22 Equal friendships

One way to know you are being exploited is if your friendship is not equal. The seesaw/scale strategy in Chapter 3 can also be used for friendships. This may be a helpful tool in evaluating your friendship.

Being friends with someone does not mean that one of you always gets to choose what activity you do or what film/movie you see. Who makes the choices should be divided equally between you both. If it is not equal – if your friend is always telling you what to do – this means that they are dominating you. It is important not to be dominated but also not to dominate other people, as this can make them and you unhappy.

1.23 Emotional support in friendships

It is important to understand that what is important or hurtful to one person may not be important or hurtful to another person. If your friend wants to talk to you about something that has upset them, but you think it is trivial or silly, respect that your friend feels differently and listen to what they have to say.

Many people feel happier just because they told someone what they were worried or upset about; this is sometimes described as 'getting it off your chest'.

I wasn't always popular (and other personal thoughts on friends)

I am lucky now to have lots of friends, but when I was at school and in my late teens, I did not have many friends at all. If you are someone who does not have friends, please don't feel that there is something wrong with you, because it is likely to be an environmental issue – you have not met like-minded people because of your circumstances. If you feel your social skills limit your ability to make and maintain friendships, you could ask people who know you for feedback on this and suggestions about what you could do to improve. However, do not take what they tell you to mean that you must do as they say; they are merely suggestions.

> **Feedback** is information on what is good and bad about something.

Below are descriptions of some of my close friends. I have met most of my close friends in the last five years.

Alex is a woman who is on the autistic spectrum. She experiences many of the same autism-related difficulties as I do. We have similar interests. I go through periods of time when I see her twice a week and then not at all for several months. Sometimes we chat and sometimes we listen to music.

Tom is a man who is probably on the autistic spectrum and works in the creative industries. I go to see his work and we meet fortnightly for a drink at a pub. I am also friends with his wife, although I do not know her as well as I know Tom.

Leah and *Chris* are older than me and they have children. They live about 6000 miles from me, but I see them once a year, and we keep in touch over Facebook and speak on the phone once a week.

I have been friends with *Mark* and *Dessaray* for several years and see them roughly once a month, but we talk on the phone perhaps once a week or maybe once a fortnight. Sometimes we go to gigs together and I have also been involved in creative projects with them.

I used to live with *Sam* at college and we have stayed in touch. We talk on the phone occasionally. We meet up three times a year and talk via Facebook.

I don't see *Florence* often, perhaps once a year, but we talk on Facebook once or twice a month. She is a good listener and I do the same for her.

I have many other friends who are not as close but with whom I keep in touch on Facebook, by phone and by email, and there are those whom I see face to face.

1.24 Unresolved arguments

Sometimes arguments cannot be resolved. If this is the case, it is important to walk away; sometimes people are just incompatible with each other. This is not your fault or your former friend's fault.

To **walk away** means to stop arguing with a person; you can physically walk away or change the subject. You have to accept that people are entitled to their own opinions.

To be **incompatible with another person** means that you cannot spend time with a particular person without having an argument, or that you (or they) often feel upset or angry about something they (or you) have said. It means that your view is opposed to the other's view and you are unable to agree. Incompatibility is something non-autistic people also experience.

Sometimes when situations have happened that have upset you (e.g. arguments), it is hard to concentrate on anything else. If you find this difficult, make a timetable of activities and a list of alternative thoughts, instead of thinking about the argument you have had. The timetable of activities might help you to stay focused (concentrate) on something else. Alternative thoughts could include questions on your special interest, if you have one. It may be useful to write these things down beforehand.

Write a short list of alternative thoughts below.

Alternative thoughts

Alternative thoughts could be used as follows. It may be that you start to think about the argument you have had and then you think of the alternative thought and concentrate on that. Many people on the autistic spectrum think in association, and this might or might not be helpful. For example, if you had an argument about missing a bus, it may be helpful to think about something else to do with buses – for example, reciting a list of bus companies – but don't focus on the exact cause of the argument.

It is important to process arguments so that you can think about what happened, what could have been done differently and whether you would change your behaviour if the situation that caused the argument happens again. However, you need to be calm to do this, and you also need not to be thinking about something else. For example, it would not be a good idea to try to process an argument while you are trying to work, because it might mean you make a mistake. You might also be upset about the argument and need to wait until you don't feel as upset before you can think about the cause of the argument in a rational way. In both of these scenarios, using alternative thoughts would allow you to carry on your daily life until you could find a time in which to process what happened.

If you are at work and it is really bothering you, then you may need to take a break specifically to think about the argument, or to use your alternative thought to help you refocus on your work.

1.25 Friends who spend time with others

Do not think that if a friend enjoys having more than one friend it means they do not like you. Some people like to spend time with lots of different people; others just like to have one close friend. Do not take this personally; everyone is different. If you are concerned, you could ask your friend, 'Are we still friends?'

Top 10 things to remember from Chapter 1

1. It's OK not to want friends. However, if this is because you have given up trying to make friends, some of the skills you

learn from this book might help you, so trying to make friends again may be worthwhile.

2. Not everyone has good intentions, and it is important to use activities such as the ladder of trust and the intentions scenarios to help learn about possible intentions people might have and for you to decide what information to share.

3. Many people on the autistic spectrum need extra time to process information. There are phrases you can say such as 'Give me some time to think about that' to allow you more time to make a decision.

4. Friendships should be equal in terms of the amount of effort each person is putting into the friendship.

5. When you have a friend, especially if you do not have many friends, you may be very enthusiastic and want to spend all your time with them. But they may not want this and may feel overwhelmed if you keep texting/calling/messaging them. Wait for a reply to your message (unless urgent) before sending another or making another call.

6. There are different types of friendships and different levels of emotional closeness. There may be some things you would happily share with one friend but not another.

7. It is important to maintain a friendship.

8. Everyone has a comfort zone and boundaries. Make sure you have decided what yours are and that you adhere to them. (If you choose to change them, only do so when you are calm and able to think rationally about the change.)

9. A group of non-autistic people who you can go to for advice can be a helpful resource. Each person is likely to have a different opinion, so if you are uncertain about how to manage a social situation, your group of non-autistic people can be helpful.

10. Do not let people disrespect you. You cannot control how someone behaves towards people you do not know, but you can tell them not do a particular thing to you, such as teasing you. If they do not stop when you ask, they are not your friend.

Resources

Books

Gray, C. (1994) *Comic Strip Conversations: Illustrated Interactions that Teach Conversation Skills to Students with Autism and Related Disorders.* Arlington, TX: Future Horizons. ISBN: 1885477228

Comic Strip Conversations is a technique first developed by Carol Gray. The technique teaches you to process social information, by encouraging you to illustrate your conversation as you speak with figures and speech bubbles and thought bubbles, as well as using different colours to signify feelings.

Laugeson, E. (2013) *The Science of Making Friends: Helping Socially Challenged Teens and Young Adults.* Hoboken, NJ: Jossey Bass. ISBN: 1118127218

Dr Laugeson has been running a social skills programme called PEERS at UCLA for a number of years. This book is written for professionals and parents to help coach people on the spectrum to make and keep friends, but it may also be helpful for people on the spectrum to read themselves. It includes a DVD to demonstrate the information from the book. There is an accompanying app to the book called *FriendMaker*, which is available on iTunes (you can find details in the 'App' section below).

Laugeson, E. and Frankel, F. (2000) *Social Skills for Teenagers with Developmental and Autism Spectrum Disorders: The PEERS Treatment Manual.* New York, NY: Routledge. ISBN: 0415872030

This book is about PEERS, a social skills programme for children and adults on the autistic spectrum. This manual explains how each session of the PEERS treatment programme is intended to be run by therapists.

Pease, B. and Pease, A. (2005) *The Definitive Book of Body Language.* London: Orion Books.

Body language doesn't just confuse people on the autistic spectrum – non-autistic people can be confused by it too. Whilst this book is not written with people on the spectrum in mind, it may be very helpful in explaining how body language works.

App

FriendMaker. Available through the iTunes app store.

This app accompanies the book by Dr Laugeson, mentioned above. It can be used on all Apple mobile devices (iPad, iPod touch, iPhone, etc.) and contains videos that 'model' (i.e. demonstrate) particular skills, so it is like having someone to coach you socially in your pocket.

Board game

Bubble Talk. Available from www.nationalautismresources.com/bubble-talk.html.

This is a good game for developing your understanding of body language. In the game each player has a series of picture cards and some pre-written speech bubbles (and also some blank speech bubbles for you to write your own). The aim is to assess the pictures and match the speech bubbles with the right pictures.

Organization

ASAN (Autistic Self-Advocacy Network)
http://autisticadvocacy.org
This US organization is run by and for people on the autistic spectrum.

Answers to the intentions activity

These are just example answers to the intentions activity from pages 43–44. You may come up with additional answers/solutions and that is OK.

Situation I

Why might Raj not have done the washing-up?

- Raj might have forgotten.
- Raj might have been too tired.
- Raj might have been mad/angry at Kat and wanted to demonstrate that he was angry.
- Raj might have been feeling lazy and planned to do it the next morning.
- Raj might have had some upsetting news (e.g. one of his family had died) and felt too sad to do anything.
- Raj might have tried to do the dishes but realized they had run out of washing-up liquid.
- If there was a large pile of dishes, Raj might have worried about waking Kat up by moving them.
- Raj might have decided that some plates needed to soak overnight to get the food stains off.
- Raj might have come across an item he did not know how to wash and wasn't able to continue with the task.
- Raj might have been too anxious to concentrate on the task.
- Raj might not have been able to find the plug.
- The kitchen light might have broken.
- Raj might not have felt well.

How to resolve

- Doing the washing-up is a common problem for people living together. If this is the first time it has happened, then Kat should consider avoiding confrontation, doing the washing-up and talking to Raj about it in the evening, to say that she did the washing-up and make a decision about whether what Raj says is believable or not.

- In the morning Kat should consider how Raj looks/behaves. If he looks ill/sick and if this is his reason for not doing the washing-up, that is OK – as long as if Kat was ill/sick, Raj would be prepared to do the washing-up.
- You won't know 100 per cent what will happen in a situation until it happens. If Kat and Raj have never lived together when Kat has been ill, then it would be hard to know for sure if Raj would or would not help. However, it is important to focus on the current situation and try to divert thoughts/attention from anxiety about events that haven't happened and may not happen.
- Kat should ask Raj why he didn't wash up. She needs to consider how truthful Raj is usually and how probable it is that what he says happened is the truth.
- Raj may be quite happy to go and do the washing-up of his own accord, but if Kat immediately yells at him or gets mad/angry at him, he is less likely to want to do so.
- When Raj has been awake for some time (e.g. after he has washed, got dressed and eaten, if this is what he normally does in the morning), Kat should say calmly (or write Raj a note) to ask why he didn't do the washing-up.
- Then they both need to agree on a resolution and, if necessary, a plan for how to make sure this does not happen again.
- If this is the first time in a month that Raj has forgotten, then he probably did genuinely forget, but if he starts to forget frequently, then Kat should raise this issue with him (speak to him).
- Sometimes people don't behave (including apologizing) the way you want them to. It's important to accept that you cannot control other people, decide where your boundaries are and, if you have to, move out.

Situation 2

What were Fatima's intentions? How could Sarah find out?
- Fatima might have forgotten.
- Fatima might have been running late.
- Fatima might have left her mobile/cell phone at home.
- Fatima might not have heard her mobile/cell phone ring.
- Fatima might be somewhere noisy and not be able to answer her mobile/cell phone because she would not be able to hear Sarah.
- Fatima might have got lost, even if she knows the area well. For example, if the bus she had to take was diverted to a part of town she didn't know, she might have become disorientated.

- A member of Fatima's family might have become ill and she might have had to take her family member to the hospital. In this scenario she would need to focus her attention on her family member and be supportive. For example, if her family member was in pain, some people find it helpful to be spoken to. Also, in some hospitals you cannot use a mobile phone. It may seem simple to send a text message, but this can be very hard if you are anxious or trying to help someone.
- Fatima might have wanted to upset Sarah.
- Fatima might have been ill.
- Fatima might have had an accident on her way to meet Sarah.

How to resolve
- Sarah would need to ask Fatima in a calm way why she did not turn up/meet at the bus stop, and consider Fatima's answer before accusing her of deliberately trying to upset her.
- As you can see, there are many reasons why Fatima didn't turn up, so if you were in the position of Sarah waiting for a friend at the bus stop, it would be unhelpful to focus on the most negative possible reason why your friend has not arrived. It would be better to try to think about other things, such as your special interest.
- When your friend arrives or you next speak to them, ask them what happened, considering, as in situation 1, if this is the first time this has happened, if the other person is usually honest and so on.

Situation 3
What were Shane and Luke's intentions? How could Faye find out?
- Luke and Shane might have just wanted Faye to relax.
- Luke and Shane might have wanted to hurt Faye either physically or sexually (this would be easier if Faye was drunk).
- Luke or Shane might have wanted to have sex with Faye (sometimes people are more easily persuaded to do something when they are drunk).
- Luke and Shane might have thought it would be funny to see Faye drunk.
- It might have happened accidentally.
- They might have left Faye because they thought she had gone home already.
- They didn't care.
- They forgot where Faye was (because they were drunk).
- One of them passed out so the other carried him home and might have thought it better to go straight home.

How to resolve
- If Faye feels uncomfortable or unsafe when she gets home, she should go to a place of safety. Faye needs to question whether she

feels safe around Luke and Shane and identify somewhere else she could go if she doesn't feel safe.
- Because of the amount of alcohol she has drunk, she is unlikely to be able to have a sensible discussion with Luke and Shane, who are also drunk, so she should get a glass of water (only if it is safe to do so) and go straight to bed.
- If Luke or Shane tried to harm Faye in any way, she should leave the house and call the police.
- Presuming Luke and Shane do not want to harm Faye, in the morning she needs to wait for Luke or Shane to complete their morning routine and ask why they did it, taking into account whether they are usually truthful and whether this sort of thing has happened before.
- Spiking someone's drink is never OK, so it's unlikely this was an accident (unless Faye ordered a coke, and Luke or Shane ordered a vodka and coke and gave her the wrong drink, in which case Faye should say, 'I've got the wrong drink' and swap with Luke or Shane).
- Unless there are exceptional circumstances, it's rude and potentially dangerous to leave a drunk friend at a club. If their reason for doing so is that they thought Faye had gone home, she should ask what they did to check that was the case.
- Faye needs to be assertive to explain how she felt.
- If I were in this situation, I would talk to Luke and Shane as little as possible and move out!

Situation 4
What were Dave's intentions? How could Louisa find out?
- Dave might have given Louisa the wrong papers.
- Dave might have wanted to con Louisa into paying for his car.

How to resolve
- Louisa could ask Dave to check the papers.
- If Dave does not say that she signed the wrong papers, Louisa should tell him clearly what has happened and that she wants him to change it immediately.
- If he won't do so, Louisa should seek legal advice. In the UK, the Citizens' Advice Bureau (CAB) may be helpful to start with.
- Make sure you read carefully anything you sign, and if you don't feel you fully understand the consequences of signing a document, then ask for help from a neutral person. A neutral person is someone who will not gain from the decision you make. In this situation, Dave was not a neutral person because if he intended for Louisa to be tricked into paying for his car, then this is what he would have gained.

2

SEX

In this chapter

2.1 Introduction

In this chapter, the word **partner**, unless otherwise specified, is used to mean someone you are having sex with.

2.1.1 Why is there a chapter on sex? How does it relate to safety?

Most schools now provide some sex education, but it is mostly about how to have 'safe' sex, meaning using condoms or other means of protecting yourself from STIs and STDs (sexually transmitted infections/diseases). School sex education also often covers the risks of pregnancy, but the curriculum often doesn't make mention of the emotions involved in sex and the fact that many people are homosexual, just as many people are asexual and heterosexual. Sexual assault is also often not discussed in as much detail as people on the autistic spectrum may need.

The emotions experienced during or after having sex can make a person very unhappy or very happy, and for some people this could cause them to behave in a way they would not do in other circumstances. If you know this might happen, you can prepare yourself for it, or at least rationalize your change in emotional state.

An **emotional state** is how you feel emotionally. For example, I could say my emotional state when eating ice cream is happy.

You cannot consent to a sexual relationship unless you have some understanding of the emotional consequences.

Understanding your own sexuality is very important, as it can cause a lot of anxiety and sometimes depression, particularly if you are trying to be heterosexual when you are homosexual or asexual. Some people who are heterosexual may try to be homosexual or asexual to please others or fit in.

Some people are uncomfortable talking to people on the autistic spectrum about sex, and this could mean that you do not understand what the emotional and health risks (STIs and STDs) are. You may not even know what sex is if the TV channel has always been changed when a couple do more than kiss.

There are also different reasons why people have sex, and if you confuse a casual sexual relationship with a romantic one, this could cause you great confusion and upset, and you may feel rejected.

Sex can sometimes cause physical pain, but this can often be overcome. You may need additional help if you have sensory sensitivities.

Sex is not compulsory and you can choose to be abstinent (not have sex) at any time, even if you have had a sexual relationship in the past.

Asexuality is OK too! Many people on the autistic spectrum are asexual. This means they are not interested in having sex or having a romantic partner. Many people live happy lives being asexual. It is common for people who are asexual to feel that they are expected to have sex or a romantic partner, and that there is something wrong with them. As an adult, you are entitled to make your own choices in life. Many people are born asexual, just as people are born homosexual, bisexual or heterosexual.

Vocabulary of difference

- **Gender identity** means a person's internal sense or feeling of being male or female, which may or may not be the same as their biological sex.

- **Gay** is a word used to refer to a person who is physically and emotionally attracted to someone of the same sex. The word 'gay' can refer to both males and females, but it is more commonly used to identify males.

- A **lesbian** is a female who is attracted physically and emotionally to other females.

- **Bisexual** is a term used to refer to a person who is attracted physically and emotionally to both males and females.

- **Cross-dressing** refers to the act of wearing clothing and other accoutrements usually associated with the opposite gender within a particular society.

- **Sexual orientation** means a person's emotional and sexual attraction to other people.

- **Transsexual** refers to a person who experiences intense personal and emotional discomfort with their assigned birth gender and may undergo treatment (e.g. hormones and/or surgery) to change gender.

Transgender refers to a person who was assigned a sex, usually at birth and based on their genitals, but who feels that this is a false or incomplete description of themselves.

Q: How can you be assigned a sex?
A: Most people are born with either male or female genitals. This is how it is decided whether a baby is male or female, and this is then written down on their birth certificate. However, there are some people who are born with both male and female genitals. The parents then have to make a decision as to whether they will treat the baby as a boy or girl. Later in life the person themselves can choose whether they identify as male or female.

Sex reassignment surgery, sometimes referred to as either 'sex change' or 'gender reassignment surgery', is a surgical procedure to change the genitals and secondary sex characteristics from one gender to another.

Changing your gender is a big decision and needs medical help.

Heterosexism is the assumption that everyone is heterosexual and that this sexual orientation is superior. Heterosexism is often expressed in more subtle forms than homophobia.

Homophobia means fear and/or hatred of homosexuality in others, often exhibited by prejudice, discrimination, intimidation or acts of violence. Similarly, **transphobia** refers to the fear and/or hatred of transgender individuals and is exhibited by prejudice, discrimination, intimidation or acts of violence. **Biphobia** refers to the fear and/or hatred of bisexual individuals and is exhibited by prejudice, discrimination, intimidation or acts of violence.

Don't be embarrassed or ashamed or feel that you are necessarily missing out on something if you are asexual. Many people on the autistic spectrum form good relationships as they get older and more confident, so do not dismiss the possibility of a relationship for ever. Many people on the autistic spectrum do not mature emotionally as quickly as their non-autistic peers, so if you are at an age where everyone else has a boyfriend or girlfriend and you don't, do not feel this will be the case for the rest of your life. People change in their responses to things and what they want in life as they grow older. Focus your attention on things you enjoy in your life, rather than things you do not have.

There are also many women who do not have sex with other people but masturbate. This is OK too. There are many sex toys to help with this, which are used by many non-autistic women as well as women on the autistic spectrum.

2.1.1 Media and sex

> 'Don't feel like you have to have sex. It becomes like playing a role, but this is not TV and you need to work out if you like this person enough to really want to have sex with them, not just do it to feel normal.'
>
> *Hannah, research participant*

You may have seen, on TV or in films, where people were having sex or the lead-up to it.

The **lead-up** to having sex refers to the events that happen before sex to the two people who are going to have sex – for example, dates might be part of the lead-up to sex.

The people on TV and films are actors; they have been given scripts and the characters they are portraying (pretending to be) are not real people or real situations. Therefore, you need to understand that life does not happen as it does on TV or in film. Often TV and film overemphasize parts of life. Sometimes this is because it will get more viewers and other times it is done because it is considered humorous or more interesting. Therefore, what you see on TV is not necessarily an example of normal behaviour.

TV and film only show things in small amounts of time. For example, in a two-hour film you might be watching the fictional story of two people who fall in love taking place over two years. The person who wrote the film will only have included certain parts of the story. In reality, two people may go on ten dates, but a film script may only include information on two dates. This means that film and TV do not give you a full understanding of how relationships work or the diversity of people's attitudes, unless what you are watching is a documentary on these topics which gives all the relevant information.

There is not a normal age at which people lose their virginity or a normal number of sexual partners they have. There are averages, but this does not mean the same as normal. It is important to understand that, regardless of what your friends may be doing or have done in the past, choices about when you lose your virginity and how many people you have sex with need to be *your* choices. You should feel this is the right choice for you, not because you think that is what everyone else does. If you try to do the same as everyone else and not what makes you happy, then you are likely to become unhappy and get frustrated. Everyone is different, and people often tell lies or boast or fabricate stories about how many people they have had sex with and how often, because they think it makes them look cool or clever. People are less likely to do this when they are in a stable relationship.

2.1.2 Positives to having sex

There are many positives to having sex. It can be an amazing experience and can be used to create children, if and when you want them. For some people, sex is an important part of their relationship with their romantic partner. Some people feel it is the best way for them to express their feelings for their partner.

(?) To be **sexually attracted** to someone is when you are sexually aroused by or interested in having sex with that person.

(?) **Sexual arousal** is when the body starts to prepare to have sex. You may notice, for example, that your vagina tingles or your underwear becomes wet (not because of urine but because of fluid from your vagina). The fluid is released to lubricate your vagina so that when you have sex it is easier for a penis or sex toy to fit into your vagina.

This book is about safety and keeping safe. Therefore, it is not within the book's scope to talk about how wonderful and pleasurable sex can be. There are many people on the autistic spectrum who have great sex. Remember, if you are not enjoying sex it's important to think about why you are doing it. Is it because you feel you should? Is it because your partner wants it? These are not good enough reasons.

2.2 Definitions of sex

Here are two core definitions of sex.

2.2.1 Sex with self, sometimes called masturbation

This means to cause yourself sexual pleasure by stimulating (creating sensation) usually your genitals and/or other sexual areas of your body.

> ⑦ **A sexual area of your body** means an area of your body that can be touched to create sexual arousal, often referred to as the erogenous zones (see Appendix B).

Some people like to use sex toys when they masturbate.

> ⑦ **Sex toys** are devices used to stimulate and cause sexual pleasure.

Some people do not masturbate. This is OK.

It is important to know that masturbation should be done alone or with someone you are having a sexual relationship with. Normally, masturbation results in orgasm.

> ⑦ An **orgasm** is a physical reaction, and often also an emotional reaction, which is the climax of sex or masturbation. In a man, this is when his semen – the fluid that contains sperm – is released from his penis and enters the woman's body. In women, it is when their vagina muscles spasm. Emotions you may experience during an orgasm could be, but are not limited to, feelings of pleasure, relief or fulfilment. Everyone experiences orgasms emotionally in different ways. You may find it difficult to have an orgasm through sex or masturbation if you are not relaxed enough.

2.2.2 Sex with others

You can have sex with other people. This may involve touching, licking, stroking and caressing someone else's body and the person you are having sex with doing similar things to your body (during foreplay) and then being penetrated. You must have the consent of the other person before engaging in any kind of sexual activity with them.

Sex with others is a process that can be described in two parts: foreplay and sexual intercourse.

Foreplay is used to describe sexual activity that allows the woman's muscles in her vagina to relax and fluid to be released from her vagina (more so than just when she is just sexually aroused). This makes it easier for a penis or sex toy to enter her vagina. Foreplay helps the man get an erection in his penis. It also can help the two people to bond emotionally and feel safe with each other.

> **Bonding emotionally** means to understand another person's emotions and to feel emotionally close to them, and for them to feel close to you.

Foreplay is often used so that both people feel confident being naked in front of each other (some people find being naked in front of another person embarrassing, because they feel more vulnerable). It is also fun. During foreplay the man's penis will become covered in what is commonly known as 'pre-cum', which is semen but not as much as when the man has an orgasm. This acts as a lubricant so that the penis will fit in the woman's vagina or anus more easily.

Many men learn about sex by watching porn. At the time of writing, there appears to be a trend in porn films where the actors have anal sex. This can mean that some men expect a woman to have anal sex with them. Anal sex for women can result in fissures (tearing) of the anus. If you are going to have sex with someone, it is important to only have sex with a person if you feel confident you can tell the person what you do or do not want to do. Do not let someone pressurize you into doing something you do not want to do or that you are not completely comfortable doing. Someone putting pressure on you to have sex in any way is being disrespectful to you. Anal sex can be uncomfortable for some women, and many women do not like to have anal sex. It is absolutely OK not to want to have anal sex.

Alternative names for erections

Stiffy
Hard on
Getting it up
Boner

Sexual intercourse is normally when the woman's vagina is penetrated by a penis.

⑦ **Penetration** is when part of your body, or a sexual partner's body, is entered. For example, the penis penetrates the vagina. Penetration is not exclusive to the vagina. You can also be penetrated in your mouth or anus (bottom). You can be penetrated by a sex toy or dildo (a piece of plastic or other material in the shape of a penis).

⑦ **Sexual partner** is the person you are having sex with, but this does not necessarily mean you are having a romantic relationship with them. It also does not necessarily mean that they are your friend just because you had sex with them.

Regardless of the way people have sex, this part of the activity normally ends when each sexual partner has an orgasm. Sometimes people have orgasms at the same time as each other and sometimes they do not happen at the same time. Sometimes sex ends before either person has an orgasm, because one or both partners decide they do not want to continue the activity. Some women find it difficult to have an orgasm and may need to seek advice, but these difficulties can be overcome. You may be able to get advice from your family doctor or family planning clinic.

2.3 Erogenous zones

The erogenous zones (see Appendix B for a diagram) are areas of a man's and woman's body (they are different for men and women) that can be touched to arouse a person sexually. The zones can be a good guide for areas in which you might want to touch your sexual partner (with their permission).

If someone is suggesting sex with you, they might stroke, for example, the inside of your thigh, which is an erogenous zone for a woman. In this way, erogenous zones can also act as indicators of someone's sexual interest in you. Stroking the inside of your thigh is a nonverbal way of saying 'I would like to have sex with you'. If you do not want the person to touch you, or if they suddenly force themselves on you, this is sexual assault. If you are in a sexual relationship with that person, you and your sexual partner may come up with your own individual rules about where and when it is OK to touch each other and the kind of pressure you/they like on that area of your/their body. You may want to discuss this. Don't do anything you are not comfortable with – if you think, 'I am not sure I want to do this' (or a similar thought), then this is an example of feeling uncomfortable, so stop and don't do it.

2.4 Making a choice

When having any type of sex, it is important that both partners consent and have capacity (understanding) to be able to consent.

Consent means to agree that you want to do something. You can consent to one type of sex and not to another. For example, you may consent to having your vagina penetrated but not your anus. Most people do not discuss consent using the actual word 'consent', as it is regarded as a formal word; instead, most people just talk to their sexual partner about what they do or do not want to do.

It is important to understand that everybody has the right to decide what happens and does not happen to their body. There may be things your sexual partner would like you to do, but you do not enjoy it or want to do it, and the same applies to what your partner does or doesn't enjoy or want to do.

2.4.1 Asserting yourself

It is OK to assert yourself. It is also OK to change your mind. For example, you may like being kissed on your neck the first time your sexual partner does it. But you might not like it the second time your partner does it, in which case you can ask them not to kiss you on the neck. This is an example of asserting your choices.

You should never worry about telling someone that you do not like them doing something. It won't mean they will not want to have sex with you. If someone does not respect your choices and feelings, then they are not respecting you. If someone does not respect you, it is not a good idea to have sex with them because they are likely to hurt you emotionally.

The easiest way to assert your choices about sex is often to verbally tell (speak to) your sexual partner and say what you do and do not want to do. If you are unsure if you want to do what your sexual partner is suggesting, then you could try it but say that you are unsure. Agree with your sexual partner that if you do not like it, you will tell them to stop and they will stop. If your sexual partner does not stop when you have asked them to, this means you have been sexually assaulted.

2.4.2 Nonverbal communication

Be aware that some people do not naturally assert choices by speaking. Instead, they try to communicate nonverbally – for example, they might move your hand to a part of their body they would like you to touch. Or they might move your hand away from a part of their body they do not want you to touch. If you are trying to initiate sex, they may turn away from you if they do not want to have sex.

Many people on the autistic spectrum find nonverbal communication difficult to understand or use. If this is the case for you, you need to tell your partner that you want them to communicate verbally. Explain that you find nonverbal communication difficult.

You may like different things to your partner – for example, your partner may like you to kiss their arms but you do not like them kissing your arms.

2.4.3 Emotional responses to sex

Sex with another person can cause different emotional responses when compared with masturbation. Masturbation is a bodily function that serves a purpose, which is to relieve sexual frustration and to gain pleasure. Just as urinating empties the bladder, so you may feel pleasure and relief. Masturbation also allows you to learn about what you find pleasurable.

But when you have sex with another person, this often means (not for everyone) that you feel different emotions to when you masturbate. Sometimes sex makes people feel vulnerable, violated or scared. These are examples of negative emotions. If you feel these emotions during or after sex, you need to consider if you should be having sex with this person. Sex can make you feel valued, wanted, loved and beautiful. See Chapter 9 for more information on emotions.

The way you feel during or after sex will depend on whether you and your sexual partner wanted to have sex with each other, on whether your sexual partner is supportive of you, and on you as an individual. Some people experience no emotions after sex. It is impossible to tell before you have sex whether you will experience emotions or not. It is advisable, however, that you have sex with someone who cares about you and will support you if you feel negative emotions either during or after sex. It's important to try to think about why you are feeling these emotions. For example, if this is your first time having sex or the first time you are having sex with a particular sexual partner, then it is natural that you may feel a little anxious or nervous. You may even feel confused or overwhelmed. But if the other person is being disrespectful towards you and not listening to you when you say you do not want to do something, and this is making you feel scared, then this is a situation you need to get out of.

2.4.4 What to do if you feel threatened

If you feel physically threatened or if you suspect that person would not want you to leave and might physically try to stop you leaving, then take your clothes and get dressed in the bathroom. If the person you are trying to get away from is in the same room as you, then leave the room and get dressed in the hallway if you have to, and leave the building as soon as you can. If you are in your own home, you need to ask the person to leave. If they do not leave, then call the police, explain to the police officer that you are on the autistic spectrum, that a man or woman will not leave your home and that you feel your life is in danger, and ask the police to come and help.

The above steps might seem very obvious, but they can seem harder if you are in a situation in which you are scared. Sometimes people find it reassuring to read what they might already have thought in a situation, because it makes them feel less silly. For example, the comment about getting dressed may seem obvious, but if you were frightened, you might forget your clothes. Seeing it written down might help you to remember. In situations where you need to get away from someone, I can only provide general advice, because I do not know what the room or building you are in is like, so take the above statements about leaving a situation as guidance rather than a rule. When you enter into a situation in which you are going to have sex with someone, or if you suddenly find a man or woman wants to have sex with you, think first if this is what you want to do and then think about how you could leave the situation either immediately or if you were to feel uncomfortable. Do not invite strangers to your home, because you do not know if they will try to hurt you.

2.5 Sexual assault (including rape)

In the UK, sexual assault is defined as follows:

> A person commits sexual assault if they intentionally touch another person, the touching is sexual and the person does not consent. (Metropolitan Police 2013)

Sexual touching is when someone touches your body in an erogenous zone, with the intention of giving themselves sexual arousal or pleasure.

Serious sexual assault is defined as 'assault by penetration', as follows:

> A person commits assault by penetration if they intentionally penetrate the vagina or anus of another person with a part of the body or anything else, without their consent. (Metropolitan Police 2013)

In the USA, sexual assault is defined as follows:

Sexual assault is any type of sexual contact or behavior that occurs without the explicit consent of the recipient. Falling under the definition of sexual assault are sexual activities as forced sexual intercourse, forcible sodomy, child molestation, incest, fondling, and attempted rape. (US Department of Justice 2013)

Your body belongs to you and therefore you should choose what happens to it.

'I truly believed the only way to keep a friend/relative/etc. was to do everything they wanted and I thought everyone else did the same.'

luckymum0f6, research participant

It is common for people on the autistic spectrum to feel that they have to do something because 'that is what everyone else does'. But the truth is that when it comes to anything sexual you do not have to do anything you do not want to do! When you make a choice, there is a consequence. In terms of sex, making a choice not to have sex with someone should mean that you don't have sex with that person. It should not result in not being friends with that person (unless you no longer want to be friends with them) or the other person treating you differently to how they treated you before you said no. (Except, of course, that they should stop trying to have sex with you. If they try again, tell them clearly that you never want to have sex with them.) If someone is horrible to you in any way just because you said no to having sex or any sex-related act such as kissing, then that person is not worth spending time with and is not a true friend. They only wanted to have sex with you and did not care about how you felt.

You always have a choice. It is never wrong to say no or 'I don't want to do that' or 'No, I do not like you doing that' or 'I want you to STOP now!'

This applies to any situation. If your choice is taken away from you with regard to sex, then this is sexual assault. Being made to have sex, or saying you don't want to have sex but then the man puts his penis in you anyway, is rape.

'Even if a sexual assault seems trivial, or if you are not sure whether it is technically an assault (for instance, you feel like it may have been your fault), you MUST talk this through with someone you trust or a GP [family doctor]. I was brutally assaulted when I was 17 and thought that it was my fault. Only now I am older and more self-aware I realize that this person could have done the same to others and it was not my fault. If I had talked it through with someone at the time, it would have been reported to the police.'

Oceana, research participant

Oceana describes very well what to do even if you are unsure whether you have been assaulted sexually. Sexual assault means to be touched or hurt sexually; this can include rape and attempted rape.

Rape is when you express to a person that you do not want to have sex but your sexual partner or someone else forces you to have sex with them.

Often abusers will make you think, and feel, that the attack was your fault. You can be raped or sexually assaulted when you are in a relationship. Sexual assaults of any kind do not have to cause physical pain to be emotionally painful. If you think it was your fault, make sure you check with a trusted friend (not the person who assaulted you) or a doctor.

This book is not written to frighten you. It is important to do the things you want to do in your life, so, instead, this book gives you information to help you understand what risks there may be when choosing an activity, to help you plan your life so that you minimize risks, and to let you know how you can get help if you need it.

If you tell your family doctor about a sexual assault or about an incident that you think may have been assault, you may then be able to access services such as counselling or other types of therapy. The person who assaulted you is likely to deny that it happened, but this does not mean that people will believe them or that it did not happen. Just because someone says something does not make it true.

2.5.1 Saying no

> 'Lots of therapy has taught me that I can assert what I want sexually (which could simply be "no" or "stop") and that doesn't mean the other person will be offended. If I don't stand up for myself and make my personal boundaries clear, then I will always end up hurt (emotionally or physically). People who are offended by you saying that something hurts you, or who try to do so anyway after you've said no, aren't the kind of person who should be in your life.'
>
> *Aspergirrl, research participant*

As previously stated, if at any time during sex you say 'No, stop' or that you do not like something someone is doing to you, if they are worth keeping in your life, they won't be offended. Because they respect you and care about your feelings, they would want to stop doing something you do not like or do not want them to do, because they would not want to hurt you or make you unhappy. It is also important that you stop doing something your sexual partner asks you not to do during sex. If you are refusing to do something or saying no, do not smile; if you do, you may be misunderstood. People may think you do not really mean no (e.g. they might think you are playing a game with them).

2.6 Sexual harassment

Sexual harassment is when someone does something of a sexual nature, such as staring at parts of your body that are related to sex (e.g. your breasts), or says sex-related things to you such as 'I really want to suck your tits' when you are not in bed with them or in a relationship with them.

2.6.1 What should I do if I experience or think I am experiencing sexual harassment?

If this happens when someone passes you on a street, keep walking and go into the nearest shop, then look back down the road in the direction the person was walking to see if they have gone. Do not make eye contact with the person or talk to them. If they physically hurt you, then report this to the police.

2.6.2 What should I do if I know the person?

If the person who you feel is sexually harassing you is someone you know or see on a regular basis – for example, if a friend keeps slapping your bottom or talking about your breasts – ask them not to talk to you in that way or not to touch you in that way. If they don't stop when you have asked them to, stay away from the person. If you cannot avoid meeting them – for example, because you work with them – then talk to your manager, group leader or supervisor. Or speak to a friend or someone else who knows both you and the other person. Ask their advice or ask them to speak to the person on your behalf or with you (for moral support). If you live with the person, think about whether it is possible to move out.

If the person doesn't stop, then contact the police and explain what has happened with regard to the person touching you. This kind of behaviour is known as sexual harassment. If a man or woman is rude to you after you have asked them to stop touching you or saying inappropriate things to you, remember what they say is not true. They are simply trying to manipulate you by making you feel guilty for saying no. They do this because they believe it will make it more likely that they will be allowed to carry on behaving the way they want to behave or because they enjoy upsetting you or because they are angry. However, do not do what someone else wants because they are angry; they have to control their emotions just as you have to control yours.

After you have asked them to stop being rude to you, walk away from the situation (literally) and go somewhere else. Do not respond to them. Ignore them. It is not your fault.

It is important, however, to make a distinction between sexual harassment and flirting.

2.7 What is flirting?

Most of the time flirting happens when a person likes another person, either romantically or sexually (although it could be both), and wants to test out whether the person they like also feels the same, without asking them in a straightforward way. You can tell that someone is flirting with you if they keep complimenting you, regardless of what they are complimenting you on.

The reason people don't ask other people straightforwardly (e.g. 'Do you fancy me?') is partly because they may be scared of rejection – that is, they would feel embarrassed or even stupid if the person said no. By flirting, people can explore whether they are interested in each other romantically or sexually, and for some people it makes them feel less stupid or silly if the person doesn't flirt back.

If a man were to make a comment about your appearance in a jokey manner (e.g. if a builder on a building site were to call out 'Nice baps (breasts) love!' as you walked past), this is flirting but without the intent to have a romantic or sexual relationship. The man is just enjoying looking at you. Some people might describe this behaviour as teasing. If he does it again and it makes you feel uncomfortable or unhappy you should ask him to stop or walk away.

If a man makes a comment about your breasts, for example, during a conversation and it makes you uncomfortable or unhappy, you should change the subject. If he does it again, ask him to please not talk about your breasts (you could do the same if it was a woman too). If he still persists after you have explicitly asked him not to, this is sexual harassment (see section 2.6). Flattering comments are acceptable, but not if they feature sex-related topics. The exception to this is if it is a work situation and the person flirting with you is your manager who is appraising your work. This is not appropriate and is also considered to be sexual harassment.

2.7.1 In what other ways do people flirt?

Flirting can be very subtle, but below are a few signs that someone could be flirting with you. Without being in the situation, I cannot tell you for sure a person is flirting with you, but these signs will help you to know what to look for.

- In a social context, the person talks about sex a lot – that is, 50 per cent of what they say is about sex – but this would be odd as the rules of social etiquette generally disapprove of a direct expression of sexual interest.

- They keep touching your arm, hands, hair or other parts of your body, but not sexual parts. (If they were touching your sexual parts – e.g. breasts – ask them not to and move away from this person and talk to someone else.)

- They are obviously looking at your breasts briefly, but not staring.

- They keep complimenting you. One compliment (e.g. 'You look nice today') might not be a sign of flirting, but if the person keeps saying things such as 'Wow, that dress looks nice on you!' and later on in the conversation 'Haven't you got pretty eyes?' then this could be flirting.

- If you don't know them well and they put their arm around your shoulder when you are not talking about something sad.

- If you don't know them well and they try to cuddle you. You only cuddle people you are close to. It's important to learn the appropriate way of doing this, and this is something that needs to be demonstrated. YouTube and some help from a friend, therapist or someone you trust to pick out suitable examples could be a way of learning about this.

- Body language can include flicking hair, eye contact when not having a conversation, or if the person looks into your eyes for longer than most people do without looking away (it takes time to know this, and most people use their intuition to tell them).

- Verbal communication of interest can include the vocal tone, which includes pace, volume, intonation. Many people on the autistic spectrum find this difficult to pick up, but you could look at some YouTube videos to help.

- If, over the course of the conversation, they move closer to you and there is no logical reason for them to do this (e.g. if you were somewhere noisy, you might have to move closer so you could hear each other).

- If they kiss you on the cheek (kissing someone on the lips is usually only done when two people have a closer relationship).

- Pinching your bottom, depending on where you are in the world, might be considered sexual assault rather than flirting. This kind of behaviour could be described as 'groping'.

- Flirting is also possible in instant messaging and other types of social media (e.g. Facebook).

Sometimes people use phrases such as 'Would you like to come back to mine for coffee?' This quite often means 'Would you like to come to where I live to have sex?' I can't list all the situations in which 'come back to mine for coffee' does and does not mean 'sex', because they are context- and culture-specific. If you suddenly find you have misread a situation – for example, you get to where the person lives and then they start kissing you – this might be the point at which you realize they didn't actually mean coffee. You need to say, 'Stop! I'm really sorry but I misunderstood what you meant,' and then leave. Do this as soon as you possibly can. Do not go to someone's home unless you trust them.

2.7.2 What could I do if I think someone is flirting with me and I don't want them to / I am not interested in them romantically?

If someone is flirting with you and you are not interested in them sexually or romantically, it is important that you don't make them think you are interested in them. You might also simply feel uncomfortable when someone flirts with you. Below are some steps that might help in stopping the person from flirting with you:

- Don't smile back; turn away.

- Change the topic of conversation every time they talk about sex. After you have done this twice, they should stop talking about sex.

- Be direct and say, 'I don't really feel comfortable talking about sex with you.'

- If their hand reaches towards you and you don't want them to touch you, move your body out of their reach.

- If they keep touching you, move your chair. If you are standing, move a bit further away from them.

- Ask them not to touch you.

2.8 Suggestiveness

This is a common source of confusion for women on the autistic spectrum, and it can result in people flirting with you because they think you like it or want the attention when you don't. There are some things which women and men can do that are sometimes called suggestive. This means that the person's behaviour is making other people think that this person wants to have sex with them.

Some examples of suggestive behaviour are:

- Wearing clothes that show your cleavage (breasts) or legs (anything that is shorter than an inch above your knee) may be considered suggestive; it depends where you live in the world. If you need advice, ask a friend or parent or a helpful shop assistant.

- Lots of makeup might be considered suggestive. The amount of makeup that might be considered 'too much' will depend on the culture in your locality; ask a friend, parent or shop assistant for advice.

- If you make sexual references in your conversation when talking to a possible partner, this could also be seen as suggestive.

- Sitting with your legs wide apart could be considered suggestive. If you are wearing a dress or skirt, sit with your legs crossed or touching; you can sit with your legs slightly apart if you are wearing trousers.

Some people might think badly of women who behave in the ways described above.

Unwanted attention is when a man or woman keeps talking about sex, looking at sexual areas of your body (e.g. your breasts) or touching you when you do not want them to.

If someone is looking at you or making suggestions – for example, 'Hey, you wanna get a room?' (which means 'Do you want to go to a hotel or my home and have sex with me?') – you have every right to ignore them or, if they persist, ask them to leave you alone. If they are not directly in front of you or to the side of you – for example, they are calling out of a car window, at a bus stop or across the street, or you are walking in opposite directions from each other – ignore them and continue walking, Even if you were planning on stopping where they are, continue walking. You can go back to where you planned to stop in a few minutes, when they have gone.

The acting strategy in Chapter 10 could be useful for getting away from people in a non-direct way if you felt uncomfortable asking them.

2.9 Stalkers

As described in the last section, potential partners will want to get to know you. However, if you do not like that person or feel they act strangely, you can ask them to leave you alone. If this is hard to do verbally, write them a note and hand it to them, email them or ask someone else to speak to them for you (e.g. a teacher or friend). If they do not leave you alone, or they keep asking other people about you, following you, sending you friend requests on Facebook, emails or other communication, or do anything else that you are not happy with, tell the police. This is harassment or stalking. Stalking is following someone; harassment is when people keep talking to you or contacting you when you do not want to be contacted.

2.10 Contraception (birth control) and STI and STD prevention

There are many different types of contraceptive, but only condoms, femidoms and dental dams protect against sexually transmitted infections/diseases (STIs/STDs).

⊘ A **dental dam** (oral dam) is a piece of latex that can be placed over the vagina or anus during oral sex to protect the person giving oral sex from STIs/STDs.

There are many types available and there are also many sources of information on contraception, so below is just a brief list of the different types (please see the resources section at the end of this chapter for sources of information on this topic):

- oral contraceptive, sometimes called the pill

- intrauterine system (IUS)

- intrauterine device (IUD)

- implant

- injection

- contraceptive patch

- diaphragms and caps

- vaginal ring

- female sterilization

- emergency contraception.

In whatever circumstances you are having sex, make sure you wear a femidom or the man wears a condom. This protects against STIs and STDs and pregnancy. Sometimes people will say they don't have any STIs or STDs, but don't just believe them (particularly if you do not know them well). Make sure you and your sexual partner get tested for STIs/STDs before you start having sex without condoms or femidoms. You need to be sure that your partner is not having sex with anyone else. And, of course, if you are having sex with anyone else, you could still be at risk. When you stop using condoms or femidoms, if you are having sex with a man, make sure you are using some type of birth control/contraception, unless you want to get pregnant.

Also remember that no contraceptive is 100 per cent effective and there is always a small chance of pregnancy even with contraception.

It is also important to know that getting pregnant will not make someone love or like you any more than they did before you were pregnant, even if it is their baby.

> **Birth control** (sometimes called contraception) is a way of controlling whether you get pregnant or not. There are many different types of birth control – for example, condoms and the oral contraceptive pill (the oral contraceptive pill is often referred to as 'the pill'). The pill often needs to be taken for several weeks before it is effective. There is also an emergency contraception pill, often called 'the morning after pill', which is used to stop pregnancy. There are two types: one can be used up to 72 hours after unprotected sex and the other up to 120 hours (five days) after unprotected sex. See your doctor or family planning/planned parenthood clinic for advice on how to get emergency contraception

2.10.1 When and how to get tested for STIs and STDs

To get tested, go to a sexual health clinic. Use Google to find one in your local area.

Get tested if you have had unprotected sex (i.e. without use of a condom, femidom or dental dam), or if you suspect you might have an STI/STD. If you start to get warts, sores or any other unusual changes in your genital area, these may be signs that you have an STI or STD.

2.10.2 When and how to get tested for pregnancy

Most women's periods stop when they get pregnant, but this is not true for all women. If you think you might be pregnant, you can get a low-cost pregnancy test from a pharmacy or go to a planned parenthood/family planning clinic and ask for a pregnancy test.

Signs of pregnancy

Not everyone will experience all the symptoms listed below. This list is only meant as a guide.

- Period being late.

- Tiredness (more than usual).

- Morning sickness (although this can last all day) – feeling nauseous and vomiting.

- Urinating (peeing) more frequently.

- Sore, tender breasts which may become swollen.

- More sensitive to smell than usual.

- A metallic taste in the mouth.

- Craving particular foods.

- Disliking previously liked foods.

- In the first 12 weeks, some women can feel very upset.

- Constipation.

- Increased vaginal discharge.

(NHS Choices 2013)

2.11 Beginning of a romantic relationship

'Don't feel you have to do stuff that you don't want to just to be accepted. People who really care about you won't make you do stuff you don't want to.'

Jacinta, research participant

At the beginning of a romantic relationship, sometimes people will have sex to see if they are compatible. But this is not compulsory.

⊘ To be **compatible** with someone sexually means that you and your partner become sexually aroused by each other when having sex and enjoy each other's company while having sex together.

Some people have what are known as fetishes.

⊘ A **fetish** is something a person finds sexually arousing. Fetishes range from things such as feet to tying a partner up.

Having sex at the beginning of a romantic relationship allows both people to explore each other's fetishes to see if they too find them arousing.

⊘ **Exploring a fetish** means to try a fetish – for example, try licking someone's feet – to see if you find it enjoyable.

At the beginning of a relationship, men may find it difficult to get an erection because they are nervous. This does not mean they are not compatible with you; they are just nervous. If you are unsure, you can ask them if they are nervous. Some men find it hard to talk about their emotions. This may be because they worry that others may judge them.

⊘ To find something **hard to talk about** could mean that a person finds it hard to decide how best to explain something. Or it may be that they get upset or feel other emotions intensely when they think about a particular topic. This makes it hard to talk about, because just thinking about the topic is emotionally intense, and this could be overwhelming and unpleasant – just as walking into a room with a bad smell can be hard because it is so overwhelming and unpleasant. For example, it might be hard for a person to talk about a friend who has died because they find it upsetting to think about their friend being dead. The concept of finding something hard to talk about because of emotions may seem confusing to you, but respect the fact that other people find some things hard to talk about. In a sex context, it may be hard for a man to admit that he is feeling nervous, because this might make him feel that he is a failure or somehow inferior to other men.

If your sexual partner doesn't want to talk about his feelings, you could ask him if he would like to try having sex again in a bit. It may help to cuddle for a while. If he says yes and the next time it is easier (i.e. he gets an erection), then it is likely he was just nervous.

2.12 Relating and sex

You may have read in books, or heard from other sources of information, that people relate to each other sexually. Some people say that it might be difficult for people on the autistic spectrum to relate sexually to other people.

I think this concept can be confusing. I want to try to explain what is meant by the term 'sexually relating'.

Relating to someone is to understand them and to have an appreciation of why they think or feel particular things, or to think and feel similar things (but not in every subject necessarily) as each other. For example, if you met someone who had been bullied and they explained they had become scared of other people, and you had also been bullied and felt scared of other people (either now or in the past), this would be an example of relating to that person. You understand how they are feeling because you have had similar experiences.

Relating to someone sexually is a very individual experience. But there is a difference between relating to someone who you are in a romantic relationship with and someone you are in a casual relationship with:

- In a casual relationship (i.e. when you are not in a romantic relationship), it can mean that you understand that the relationship is only casual (see Chapter 3 for more information on this) and the other person also understands this. It means that you enjoy each other's bodies (looking and/or touching), that you enjoy having sex and that you have an understanding of how your sexual partner feels about the sexual activities (touching, licking, etc.) that you are doing to each other. It also means that you respect each other's choices.

- In a romantic relationship, it could mean that you understand the other person not just in terms of what feels good for them but also in terms of their beliefs in life and how they think. You should not try to change yourself to relate to someone sexually, because to do this means you are just pretending or acting.

It may not be important to you to relate to someone else, and if this is true for you, then that is OK. If relating is important to you, then it may be helpful to know that non-autistic people also have difficulties relating to one another and that it can be a solvable problem. Often people solve these problems by seeing a relationship counsellor. See the resources section at the end of this chapter for some book recommendations.

2.12.1 What if my views/beliefs are different to my sexual partner's? Can we still relate to each other?

Yes, you can still relate to someone, even if you think different things about particular topics, as long as you both respect each other's opinions. It can be a learning process to understand why someone feels a particular way, but you can find out by asking them. Think about whether there are any choices that you have made in your life for similar reasons. It is also important that you do not try to change the other person. Learning to understand them and not trying to change them is a way of demonstrating respect for them. But do not put up with people hurting you. You may not be able to change someone, but you don't have to have sex with someone who hurts you, emotionally or physically.

2.13 Expressing feelings through sex

When people use a sign language, such as Makaton, BSL (British Sign Language) or ASL (American Sign Language), they use signs to represent (express) feelings and thoughts. Rather than using words, they use their hands in shapes to represent their thoughts and feelings. Some people find this easier to understand than words.

When we have relationships with people, we use our bodies to express feelings. For example, you might give someone a thumbs-up when they do something well. People also might touch another person to communicate – for example, people 'high five' each other.

> (?) A **high five** is when one person puts their hand up with their palm facing you, and you slap (gently so as not to hurt them) their palm with your hand. Normally, this is done when you work as part of a team with someone in a non-formal setting; it express feelings of pleasure and gratitude to each other.

People also rub another person's back when that person is sad. This means 'I really care about you' or 'I'm sorry you're upset' or 'it will be OK'. Some people find this touch calming and reassuring, which is why people do it instead of using words.

If you love someone romantically or find someone very beautiful, you may feel you want to express these feelings by having sex. Sex (i.e. foreplay and intercourse) can involve touching, licking, caressing and stroking. Some people even bite and scratch each other (you need to find out if your partner likes this before you do anything that might hurt them). These actions can feel mutually good for you and your partner.

It is OK if this is not the way you express your feelings. However, in a romantic relationship you need to talk to your partner about their needs. For some people, sex is an essential part of their romantic relationship for many reasons, including needing intimacy.

> (?) **Intimacy** means the physical closeness and/or the exposure of parts of your body that are private. For example, if you have had sex with someone or touched their genitals (with their consent), you could say that you have been intimate with that person. You can also be emotionally intimate with people. This means you tell/share with them your emotions about things that are important to you.

Sometimes, though, when people have sex, they are not expressing any feelings apart from wanting sex. Sometimes a sexual partner might not care about you or your feelings.

2.14 Love and lust

It is very important to understand the difference between love and lust. Understanding the difference will help you to be able to understand how you might feel about another person.

Lust is an intense emotion of attraction to someone. Lust is an emotion that is normally experienced with physical sexual desire. It's basically when you really want someone. You might just want to have sex with them or enjoy looking at their body. If you feel lust for someone, this is sometimes described as 'lusting after a person'. If you find someone sexually attractive (i.e. you think you would like to have sex with them), sometimes this is described as being 'turned on'. This phrase is also used when a man or woman starts to becomes sexually aroused. This can be due to fantasizing (imagining having sex) or through physical touch either during masturbation or during sex with another person.

It is important to know that the terms 'lust' or 'lusting' can be used in other contexts, which are non-sexual, but when referring to people the term 'lust' generally has a sexual meaning.

Love is an emotion normally felt when you know someone really well and have learnt their bad points (bad points are things that are not so good about them – e.g. they are grumpy in the morning) and their good points (things that are good about them – e.g. they are a good listener). You feel love when you have accepted their good and bad points, when you relate to the other person and want to spend lots of time with them. Love can evoke feelings of wanting to be affectionate, but this is not always shown physically by cuddling and kissing and sex. When you have sex with someone you love, you are expressing feelings of love, pleasure and attraction.

People may also express this emotion through words, through the effort they put in to make the other person happy or by buying them gifts. (It is important to know, however, you cannot make a person love you by buying them gifts.)

When you first start dating a new romantic partner, you may just feel lust and then, at a later point in time (there is no definitive time at which this will happen), you may 'fall in love'. This does not involve physically falling; it means that you feel love for the other person. If you do not feel these emotions, this is OK.

It is also important to understand that the person who you feel lust or love for may not feel the same way about you.

⊘ **Dating** is the process people go through to get to know each other when starting a romantic relationship. Dating can include many different sorts of activities such as eating meals together or going to the cinema and for walks in the country. Dating is normally an activity done by two people on their own. It is different to spending time with a friend, because one of the main purposes of dating is to find out if you would be able to have a romantic relationship with a person. This will depend on both people's personalities, life choices and wants and needs from romantic relationships being similar. If you start dating someone and find that you are different to them and that a romantic relationship would not work because you would both argue or not enjoy it, then that is OK. Do not feel that this is a personal failing. Most people go on many dates before they find their lifelong partner. It is also important to know that not everyone wants a lifelong partner. Some people date just for fun and do not think about whether they want to spend their life with that person.

2.15 Why do people have sex, and why is it important?

'Neither curiosity nor a desire to fit in are good reasons for having sex. The only good reason for having sex is that a particular person really turns you on. Even then it is a good idea to establish if possible that that person is not betraying another before getting it on with them.'

Hanid, research participant

It is important to understand why you want to have sex, because without this understanding you may get hurt. For example, if you are having sex with someone because you love them, but they do not love you, this could make you feel rejected, which would lower your self-esteem and confidence. This could result in other difficulties such as depression.

So understanding why you want to have sex and why your sexual partner wants to have sex with you is very important. You can find out why your partner wants to have sex with you by asking them. If you don't know them well, they may not want to be honest about their feelings, but their behaviour may give you clues about the way they feel. It can take time to learn what behaviour to look for. Discuss this with someone you trust.

2.15.1 One-night stands

If you have a one-night stand, it means that you have sex with someone whom you may only have met that day or evening, and you only intend to have sex with them on that one night. This is not usually how romantic relationships start.

(?) Sometimes having sex with someone is referred to as **sleeping with them**.

Sometimes people may start a casual relationship (see section 2.15.2 below) but do not assume it will become a romantic relationship.

If you choose to have a one-night stand, it's important to be aware of the safety aspects of this choice. As I have previously mentioned, it could be dangerous to invite a stranger into your home, because you do not know how they will behave. It could also be dangerous to go to their home. Some people have one-night stands by booking a room in a hotel.

One-night stands are not advisable for people who are emotionally sensitive, unless you feel you can turn off your emotions.

(?) Being **emotionally sensitive** means being affected by emotions triggered by small events. Emotionally, sex is a big event for many people, and if they are sensitive, a one-night stand can cause them emotional hurt because they feel sad they will never see the person again or they may feel that they have just been used for sex.

(?) The man or woman you have a one-night stand with is unlikely to be supportive of you emotionally. To **emotionally support** someone means to listen to them when they tell you how they are feeling and to try to make them feel better if they want you to do this.

I don't advise inviting strangers back to your home, but it is your choice. If you do decide to invite a stranger to your home, here are some things to consider:

- Would it upset anyone you live with?

- How you would you get out of a bad situation (for example, if the man or woman became forceful and did not listen to you when you said no)?

- How would you feel about having sex with someone whom you may never see again?

2.15.2 Casual sexual relationships / 'fuck buddies'

This is when two people who are friends have sex. How often this happens will depend on the relationship – for some people it may be once a month or once a year and for others it might be more regular. The friends may care about each other, but they do not love each other and they are not committed to having sex just with one another; they may have other sexual partners.

Sometimes having sex with a friend is described as being 'fuck buddies'. Sometimes these friendships involve other activities that you would do with friend who you do not have sex with – for example, going to the cinema – and sometimes you would only meet up with them to have sex. Again, it is important to be aware that this kind of sexual activity will most likely not lead to having a romantic relationship. However, because you are friends with the person you are having sex with, they might be more supportive and caring towards you than someone you have a one-night stand with.

2.15.3 Romantic / committed relationships

This is generally when people decide they like each other more than just as friends – that is, the intensity of the feeling of liking the person is greater than with other friends. But they are not just an obsession or special interest. You may well both also have feelings of sexual desire towards each other.

Each person in the romantic relationship is supportive of the other emotionally. Romantic relationships are usually mutually exclusive, although sometimes people have open relationships, which means a romantic relationship where both people care deeply for one another but they also have sex with other people who are not in the relationship. When you both love each other, having sex is sometimes called making love, because you are expressing feelings of love to each other. Sometimes people use the term 'making love' to talk about sex even when they do not love their partner, because they think it sounds nicer to say 'I would like to make love to you' than 'I would like to fuck you.'

The word 'fuck' is a swear word and may offend some people. However, I have used it in the context of this book because you may hear it being used. If nobody has explained to you what this word means or how it is used, then that might put you at risk of misunderstanding a situation.

2.15.4 Threesomes and orgies/group sex

You or your partner may want to have sex with each other and another person at the same time. This is called having a threesome. You should only do this if you want to. It does not mean the other person (who you have sex with but who you are not in a relationship with) loves you, but perhaps you or your sexual partner just want to experience having sex with someone else as well as you/them (this is quite often a male fantasy). 'Orgy' is a term that means group sex. An orgy is when people have sex with different partners in the same room. This could involve more than three people.

2.16 Prostitution

I am giving prostitution its own section because it is an issue that is often not talked about and I felt it would be easier for people to find it in its own section.

Some people on the autistic spectrum find it very hard to find a sexual partner. Some people choose to use prostitutes. A prostitute is someone you pay to have sex with. It is important to know that the laws concerning prostitution vary in different parts of the world and in different states, cities and countries. For example, in some places in the world it is legal for a woman working on her own to offer sex for money, but it is illegal for her to work for someone else doing this. If you decide that you want to use a prostitute, check the laws to do with prostitution in the area where you want to use a prostitute – even if you know the relevant laws in your own city, the laws may be different if you travel to another city, state, county or country.

It is also important to choose carefully. Some prostitutes have become prostitutes to enable them to pay for a drug addiction. Having a drug addiction may mean that they are using drugs intravenously (injecting drugs into their veins). This causes health risks of contracting and then passing on to other people diseases such as hepatitis. Because of the drugs, the prostitute may also behave erratically.

Some prostitutes are managed by a pimp. This is someone who loans prostitutes to other people to have sex with them. This could also be a safety risk, because the prostitute may be being forced to work for the pimp or is being controlled by the pimp.

Some women and men are sex-trafficked. Often they are from foreign countries and have paid someone to come to the country they are now working in. The person they paid acts like a pimp, telling them that there will be work. When they arrive in the country they are trafficked to, they have their passport taken from them and are forced to work for the pimp. If they do not, then they may get hurt by the pimp.

However, there are prostitutes who are not drug addicts and are not controlled by pimps or trafficked. Ways to find them may include the websites listed in the resources section at the end of the chapter. If you decide to use a prostitute, discuss this option with someone who knows you well before making the decision, in order to avoid negative consequences or dangerous situations.

2.17 How can I tell what he or she wants?

Some people see other people as objects to give them pleasure, rather than people with thoughts and feelings.

People may try to use you for sex. This means that they just want to have sex with you because they need sexual satisfaction. For some people, it is better for them to have sex with another person because it gives them greater satisfaction than masturbation.

Some people also like having power or control over another person.

However, this does not apply to all men or all women. It is very hard to know the difference between someone who genuinely cares about you and someone who just wants to have sex with you.

Here are some signs that someone just wants to have sex with you:

- Whenever you meet, you just have sex and do not do anything else together.

- When you say no to sex, the person is less willing to see you again.

- The person does not listen to what you want or do not want to do.

- The person does not give any consideration to how you might be feeling, particularly during or after sex.

- The person does not take time to learn what you enjoy or don't enjoy, both sexually and in general.

- You don't have any similar interests.

- You do not know the person well.

2.18 How to decide whether you should have sex or not

Uncertainty can cause people on the autistic spectrum a lot of anxiety. For some people, what happens after sex is just as important as what happens during sex. For example, seeing the person again and being friends with them could be just as important as enjoying having sex with a person. So if you are someone who is made anxious by uncertainty, it may be helpful to use the system described in this section. You will not be able to guarantee that your assumptions will be right, but this system allows you to think about what is and is not important. However, you need to remember that people do not work like machines – every man or woman is different. Systems can be very helpful for people on the autistic spectrum (trains, filing and music are examples of systems). But people do not always fit neatly into systems – that is, people do not always behave in the way you expect – and sometimes it can be hard to know the consequences of a decision. Sometimes you won't know what the consequences will be until you make the decision.

One way to overcome this problem is to work out first what is important to you and how likely the things are to happen.

Below are some questions you could ask yourself. You could also mark the questions out of 10 (10 being most important, 1 being least). For example, if someone randomly asks you for sex, even though you may want to have sex, is it important that you will see the person again or that they will be your friend? If that is important to you, it might be unwise to have sex with them until you know them better and are friends, thus making it more likely you will see them again.

Below are some example questions:

How important to me is it that…
- I will see this man/woman again?
- They feel love for me?
- They like me as a person?
- They just want to have sex with me?

You can continue this list.

If it helps you, you can place these questions into a table like the one on the following page (Table 2.1). You can add an additional column for 'How likely is it that what I need to happen will actually happen?' For example, someone who has only just met you and asked for sex is unlikely to like you as a person since they do not know you. If it is important that someone you have sex with likes you as a person, then having sex with them is not a wise choice until you and the other person know each other (e.g. you know what each other's interests are) and have participated in social activities together. If you are unsure what to put in the 'likely' column, ask a trusted friend for advice.

It may be helpful for you to think about the question column and then think what has this person done to demonstrate the answer that you want.

Table 2.1 Deciding whether to have sex or not

Question	How important it is to me	How likely it is (10 very likely, 1 not likely) and why
How important is it to me that I will see this man/woman again?	10	1 (not likely) because I have just met them

This does not solve understanding if this person just wants sex or wants a relationship, but it makes sure you understand how important the answers to the questions are to you.

It also does not solve the problem of what to do if you have to make a decision very quickly and do not have time to ask a friend's advice. Some of the choices you make might go wrong – and this is true for non-autistic women too. Of course, it is much harder for people on the autistic spectrum, because people on the autistic spectrum have additional difficulties, such as finding body language hard to understand and having reduced access to the support of peers (i.e. people your own age). Non-autistic people learn about other people from each other. I would recommended not having sex with someone until you are able to decide what the consequences might be; if you find this difficult, discuss it with a trusted friend or professional.

Generally, romantic relationships build up over a period of time. Jay Blue's advice could be very useful here:

'Never rush into sex. Always wait for at least 2–3 months (or longer) to make sure you trust the person and you are in a committed relationship.'

Jay Blue, research participant

It is important to remember that everyone does things at different times; other research participants advised shorter lengths of time before having sex, so it depends on who you are and what you want.

Men and women who want to have a romantic relationship will put effort into making this happen – for example, by learning their potential partner's favourite things, wanting to spend time with them and replying to messages. If you are unsure whether someone is putting effort into building a relationship with you, think about what you have done for them and what they have done for you.

2.19 Sexual partners who are controlling

Some people are opportunistic – they think that you can be controlled and decide they will control you – whereas other people plan and manipulate you over a period of time.

Sometimes men or women may appear to want to have a romantic relationship with you and be very caring, when actually they just want to have sex with you. Below are some of the warning signs:

- Being told what to do, rather than being asked what you want, is a sign of abuse, unless you are playing a game that involves this (there is more information on sex games in section 2.20).

- When you say you don't want to have sex, your sexual partner tries to make you feel bad or says things such as 'Well, everybody else does' or 'You're fat and nobody else will want you' or other negative things. In this situation, if the person does not stop, you should end your relationship with them.

- When your sexual partner physically hurts you or threatens you if you say no or tell anyone about your relationship.

Don't let someone try to persuade you to have sex with them if you do not want to be persuaded. No means no, and you have every right to assert your choice not to do something.

Pornography can give people a distorted view on what their sex life will be like. For example, some men who have not had a great deal of sexual experience expect a woman not to have pubic hair or want them to shave it off. You do not have to do anything you are not comfortable with to meet someone else's sexual expectations.

Remember that you do not have to have any kind of sexual relationship if you do not want one, even if you have had sex with that person before. There are several reasons why you may want to choose to be abstinent (not have sex), including:

- prevention of pregnancy

- prevention of STIs/STDs

- waiting until you're ready for a sexual relationship

- waiting to find a well-suited partner

- having fun with romantic partners without sexual involvement

- focusing on college, career, travel or self-development

- supporting personal, moral or religious beliefs and values

- getting over a breakup

- healing from the death of a partner

- following medical advice during an illness or infection.

2.20 Sex games

Sex games are games people play to make sex more exciting. These are not like games you may have played with other people in the past that do not involve sex. These games may involve one of you taking a controlling role. However, there should always be a way to stop the game (as discussed below) and the roles in the game usually do not carry on outside of the bedroom.

Sex games do not include the concept of winning and losing. They consist of things such as dressing up in outfits and playing particular roles such as nurses or teachers (this may seem very confusing to you and it's important to understand that these are just games), or blindfolding your partner while you touch them or have sex. It is important to know that if you do not find what your partner wants to do appealing or interesting, or you just do not want to do it, that's OK. They should respect you; if they do not, do not have sex with them. Any games that take place during sexual activity should be with consent from both people (i.e. both people should agree they want to do it). Sometimes people agree a safe word/code word that either person can say to stop the game. They don't just use the word 'stop' because some games involve saying 'stop' but not meaning it. You could also agree an action such as clapping your hands twice, to mean stop, if your mouth was going to be covered.

Only play sex games with someone who has demonstrated that you can trust them. Ask yourself what the person has done to make you feel that you can trust them. Is their behaviour consistent? If their behaviour is not consistent (with regards to respecting your choices, feelings and opinions) this could be a warning sign of an abusive relationship (see section 3.8).

2.21 Physical pain

Some people on the autistic spectrum find that they are hypersensitive (more sensitive than other people) to tactile stimulation. If this is true of you, do not panic. It does not mean that you cannot enjoy sex.

First, rule out any physical causes for the pain by discussing the issue with your family doctor.

Once you have ruled out any physical cause, ensure you are psychologically and physically relaxed during sex. If you are having sex with someone who is inexperienced, it may be that they need to be more gentle or alter the angle that they move in. One of the reasons people use foreplay is to relax. If the muscles in your vagina are tense, this could be a cause of discomfort.

You need to understand how your own body works and responds. For example, some people find that tickling (gentle touch) is horrible, whereas others enjoy it. Other people prefer firm touch, which can range from a tight hug to being punched. Be careful, because even though you may not feel pain, your body may still get damaged. So be vigilant for signs of any reddening of skin or bruising if you enjoy firmer touching.

Explore what kind of touch on different parts of your body feels good and what doesn't. Do this by touching different areas of your body with different levels of firmness. By knowing what you do and do not like, you can assert yourself when talking to a sexual partner.

You may enjoy the feel of textured condoms/femidoms. It may be helpful to go to a store such as Ann Summers, either by yourself or with a sexual partner, to investigate sex toys and other things such as lubricants (used to make it easier for a penis or sex toy to fit into a vagina or anus). See what is available and what you might enjoy using. It's OK to try something and decide you don't like it. You do not have to do it again.

> The way many women explore what they like and don't like sexually is to use a sex toy such as a vibrator. These are also often used for fun and sexual relief. There are many different kinds of sex toys which can be used to masturbate, so you can explore what you do and do not like.

When you first start having sex, you may find that it seems a bit difficult. Like any skill, you have to learn how to do it. To start with, you may find that it is hard to relax, or that you need to use a lubricant to help the penis/sex toy enter your body. Ensure that you chose a lubricant that is suitable for the sex toy or condoms/ femidoms you are using.

If you are having anal sex, be especially careful to use enough lubricant.

2.22 Sex in relationships

Everyone has different sexual needs and times at which they want those needs met. Sometimes your romantic partner may ask to have sex with you when you do not feel like it.

However, having sex can lead to a closer relationship (i.e. the two people understanding each other better). So, even if you do not feel like it, you may consider having sex. This should be your choice and the decision about the type of sex you have or don't have should be by mutual consent.

Rather than doing something such as touching your partner's breast or penis, say, 'I want to touch your...' If they respond by saying yes, then you can touch; if they say no, then you don't touch. They should do the same for you; if they do not, then they are being disrespectful. Over time you will learn what your partner does and does not like, and it will become unnecessary to ask every time. You should discuss this issue with your romantic partner.

Top 10 things to remember from Chapter 2

1. People are asexual, heterosexual, homosexual or bisexual. It is OK not to have sex or to stop having sex with a partner you have previously had sex with.

2. Porn films and magazines are not realistic portrayals of sex (e.g. pubic hair is a very normal part of a woman's body, but many pornographic materials portray women without pubic hair).

3. Only condoms and femidoms protect against pregnancy *and* STIs (sexually transmitted infections) and STDs (sexually transmitted diseases).

4. You can always say no to sex. Just because you say yes to one kind of sex (e.g. oral sex), it does not mean you have to have any other kind of sex. You can also tell your partner to stop during sex.

5. Some people flirt to communicate that they are interested in having a romantic relationship or sex with another person. Flirting is a range of behaviours that are used as an alternative to more direct communication (e.g. asking the person if they would like to have a relationship or sex with you). Flirting is often preferable because you can be rejected or you can reject someone in a far less hurtful way, with less embarrassment for both people.

6. You should show your sexual partner respect by asking what they do and do not like, and they should do the same for you. Ensure that you avoid doing the things they do not like when having sex with them.

7. There are many reasons why people have sex. These include expressing feelings of love and affection towards a sexual partner.

8. Lust is a common emotion that is different to love. Lust is often just about desiring someone, not knowing the person as a whole.

9. Having sex with someone does not mean you are in a relationship with them or that they love you.

10. Some people on the autistic spectrum have sensory issues that can make sex difficult. Doing a sensory profile may help you identify what your sensory needs are.

Resources

Websites

NHS Choices
www.nhs.uk

The NHS Choices website provides information on health-related matters, for example contraception. There is a A–Z list of medical conditions, and also a search box where you can type in key words to find out more information about particular health-related topics.

Planned Parenthood
www.plannedparenthood.org

This site provides information on contraception as well as other related topics such as body image and sexuality. Planned Parenthood are one of the USA's largest affordable health care provides.

Cherry TV
http://cherrytv.com

Cherry TV is a website which contains videos of women talking about sex-related issues. It is not graphic and does not contain nudity, but aims to inform women about sex and related topics (e.g. masturbation).

TLC Trust
www.tlc-trust.org.uk
The TLC Trust is a UK charity. One of the things they provide is an online directory of sex workers, who are CRB checked and work with disabled clients. This means they have been checked against a computer database to make sure they don't have any criminal convictions. This is a sign of professionalism. Be aware that you may well still have an emotional reaction to having sex with a prostitute or sex worker. They are doing a job, so they will be caring and polite (if they do their job properly), but there is unlikely to be any after-care (i.e. they won't call you the next day to make sure you're OK) or support (unless you pay for it).

Touching Base
www.touchingbase.org
Touching Base aims to help people with disabilities find sex workers who are prepared to work with clients with disabilities. They are based in Australia.

Book

Valetta, D. (2011) *50 Things to Do with a Rabbit and Other Sex Toys.* London: Carlton Books. ISBN: 1780973683
This book explains how to use sex toys, including the Rampant Rabbit (which is a sex toy and not an actual rabbit).

3

ROMANTIC RELATIONSHIPS

In this chapter

3.1 Introduction

🔍 In this chapter, **partner**, unless otherwise specified, means someone you are in a romantic relationship with.

> Before I discuss this topic, as I explained in Chapter 2, some people are asexual, which means that they do not want to have sex and/or romantic relationships with other people. It is OK to be asexual; many people are asexual and live happy lives. Please do not feel that I have included this chapter because I think everyone wants romantic relationships, because I know that not everyone does. It is included for those who do, in order to provide information on staying safe. If you do not want to enter into a relationship, it is still important to understand the impression (what other people may think you are communicating) you may be giving – for example, that you are flirting with another person.

3.1.1 Why I included this chapter

Romantic relationships can be an integral part of a person's life, can be a great support and can fulfil many emotional needs that people have. There are many people on the autistic spectrum who have romantic relationships and are very happy. A romantic relationship can improve your own safety, because your romantic partner is someone who will care about you and can warn you of dangers, as well as love you, which can improve your feelings of confidence and self-worth. This works both ways. You can help your romantic partner stay safe by being someone they can talk things over with, and you can improve their confidence and sense of self-worth.

However, a lot of people on the autistic spectrum have experience of abusive romantic relationships, often not recognizing the abuse and not knowing how to leave the relationship or feeling too scared to do so. These issues are often not discussed because some people find them upsetting to talk about or think about. However, it is important that they are discussed so that people can gain the skills they need to be able to recognize a bad situation and get themselves out of it or ask for help.

3.2 Worrying about being single

Lots of women, non-autistic and on the autistic spectrum alike, worry that they will be single for ever. You could look at being single as a journey, with getting married being the destination. Not everyone wants to get married and this is OK. Therefore, if you do not want to get married, you will have a different destination.

Some people find journeys very exciting and you can make them fun. Of course, this means you are not benefiting from having a long-term relationship, but you can go to singles events and you can learn about friendships, and the skills you learn when you are single can help you to build romantic relationships. Going on dates with different men or women also allows you to meet new people whom you may not otherwise have met, and it may lead to becoming friends with some of the people you have been on dates with.

3.3 How do romantic relationships start?

The two people who become romantic partners are often but not always friends to start with. (Sometimes people are simply attracted to each other sexually or romantically and therefore become romantic partners without being friends first.)

Over a period of time (there is no standard amount of time), some friendships become romantic relationships, when the two people who are friends realize that they love or are romantically attracted to each other. Or they may find that they are sexually attracted to each other and do not just want to have casual sex, but want to have regular sex with each other and spend time together when not having sex. Later in the relationship they may decide that they love each other. Romantic relationships also require both people to agree that they are in a relationship.

Some people choose to have open relationship (see Chapter 2). There are many people who do not want an open relationship and that is OK. If your partner says that they will leave you if you do not want to do this, it is better to be alone than made to feel unhappy by someone else. At least if you are single (not in a romantic relationship), you have the chance of meeting a new partner.

To **leave** a person, in the context of romantic relationships, means to end the romantic relationship.

3.4 What does it mean to love someone romantically?

I discussed the difference between love and lust in Chapter 2. Love is an emotion that people interpret differently, so some deeper personal analysis on what love means to you may be useful because understanding this will give you more information to make better choices.

To love someone means different things to different people. It is important that you define what love means to you. Below is my definition which can be used as an example. If your definition is different to mine, that's OK – everyone is different.

Robyn's definition of love

Love is the most intense feeling of adoration you can have for another person, when you know and accept the negative aspects of their personality (but not ones that are harmful to you, e.g. it is not OK to accept someone being physically violent towards you or calling you names or abusing you in some other way). An example of a negative aspect of someone's personality might be stubbornness.

3.5 Having crushes

A crush is when you like someone a lot and you might fantasize about having a relationship with them or having sex with them. You don't think about how feasible this is and the person is often unobtainable (e.g. a teacher, boss or pop star). Often crushes can be quite intense. You might feel that you desperately want to spend time with the person you have a crush on, but crushes do pass. It is natural and normal to feel embarrassed or awkward about a crush.

Crushes are normal, but it is important not to think that anything will happen romantically between you and the other person. Quite often when someone has a crush on a person, they attach attributes to the person that they think are attractive but which the person may not have at all (e.g. being thoughtful). Sometimes when someone has a crush on a person, it's not romantic at all; the person who has the crush wants to be like the person they have a crush on.

If you find yourself thinking a lot about the person you have a crush on, it may be sensible to choose something exciting to think about instead. Every time you think of your crush, think about something else you're excited about instead, because if you focus on your crush, you are likely to be disappointed – unless, of course, they also have a crush on you.

Many girls and women have crushes on professionals such as teachers who work with them, and it would be dangerous to enter into a romantic or sexual relationship with a professional who works with you. There is a section later in the chapter about this.

The rest of this chapter is split into two parts. Part 1 is about abuse and warning signs of abusive relationships, and Part 2 is about positive romantic relationships.

Part 1: Abuse and warning signs of abuse

3.6 Abuse in romantic relationships

As I was researching this chapter, I found that many people had been abused and had been loyal to the person abusing them (i.e. stayed in the relationship). Many of these women felt unable to leave the relationship or prevent the abuse. I have made a lot of reference to this, but I want you to know four things about abuse:

- Not everyone gets abused.

- The impact of abuse is probably greater for many women on the autistic spectrum because they are loyal, feel unable to leave the relationship or do not know that what is happening to them is not their fault. They may think that nobody would love them if they left the relationship, or that nobody would believe them. It is common for women in this situation to feel they could not manage alone, or that if they told someone about the abuse, they would not be believed. However, the truth is that abuse is only the fault of the abuser, and many people leave abusive relationships and live happy, successful lives. The abuser tells you that nobody else would have you because they want you to stay; they think that telling you that nobody else would want you will make you more likely to stay with them and not leave the relationship.

- The majority of relationships are not abusive, but this book is about safety and what seemed to come through very clearly in my research was that women had been manipulated and felt unable to leave an abusive relationship. Please do not be too scared to have a relationship, but remember that this chapter can be re-read if you feel the information could be useful or applicable to you in the future.

- A romantic relationship can be one of the best things a person does in their life. If you want to, and if you have the chance, I would recommend trying it, even if it doesn't work. Non-autistic people also have relationships that do not work and so they leave their partner or try to repair the relationship.

Please remember that if you have relationship difficulties, this does not mean you have failed or are incompatible with people, or that you are a bad person or anything else. It is a fact of life that some relationships don't work. It is not evidence that you are incapable of having a relationship ever. Most people have a few romantic relationships before they find someone they want to marry or spend their life with. Some people do not want to spend their life with someone and instead have many short relationships throughout their life.

When a romantic relationship **doesn't work**, it means that the two people in the relationship find it hard not to argue or they make each other feel unhappy.

If a relationship does not work, it is OK to end the relationship. If you want to try to resolve the problems you are having, tell your partner that you feel that your relationship is not working. Sometimes just discussing the problems together and agreeing a solution can work. There are also professionals who can help you, such as relationship counsellors and sex therapists. If your partner does not want to seek help or you can't agree on a resolution to your difficulties, then consider if you really want to be in the relationship. If you are scared when you think about ending the relationship, ask yourself: Are you scared of the unknown or are you scared of leaving the relationship and not being in a romantic relationship with someone you love? If you are scared of the unknown, then see the section on leaving relationships later in this chapter.

3.7 Relationships with professionals working with you

It is almost always unacceptable for a professional working with you to have a sexual or a romantic relationship with you.

There are some professionals who offer sex as a service. They would be described as prostitutes or sex workers. If you decide to use a professional who offers sex as a service, this is OK, but it should be agreed before you start working with the professional that sex is a service they will provide to you, and this should be a service that they provide to other people. If you want to go down this route, use a responsible contact – for example, the TLC Trust (see the resources section at the end of Chapter 2). The sex workers on this site are all independent escorts who are highly professional, and most are good at their job.

Professionals working in the fields/professions of education, care and medicine cannot offer sex services, nor can they have a romantic/sexual relationship with their clients as they have to register as a practising (working) professional with a board of certification or association which forbids this behaviour.

A professional is someone who provides a service to you, which you pay for either with money, insurance or by others means (e.g. you volunteer time to their organization), or the government/state pays for their services. As a person receiving the service, you would be referred to as the client (or service user) – the person who is seeking help from a professional.

If a professional is working with you, they have a duty of care to you. This means they must ensure that the way they behave towards you is in your best interests, and if they hear of any safeguarding risk to you, they must inform the appropriate authorities to keep you safe.

To **behave towards someone**, in the context of a professional working with a client/patient, means the way a professional behaves that impacts on your care. For example, if a professional was late for an appointment and did not apologize, then their behaviour towards you is not professional, because professionals should attend appointments on time and apologize if they are late for any reason.

In your **best interests**, in the context of a professional working with a client/patient, means that a decision is made that will benefit you as much as possible. For example, it would not be in your best interests for a professional to encourage you to eat junk food every day just because it might be cheaper than fresh food. The reason it is not in your best interests is because you would be likely to gain weight and develop health conditions such as problems with your heart as the result of following this advice. It would be in your best interests for a professional to encourage you to eat a healthy, balanced diet.

Many professionals belong to professional organizations such as the BPS (British Psychological Society). Particular professions may require regional qualifications, particularly in the US. A professional may need a licence to work as a psychiatrist in Nevada and a separate licence to work in Texas. If you are looking for a professional to work with you who is not part of the NHS in the UK, then look for which board certification or qualifications the professional has. You can also check with the board to be sure that the professional is really registered with them. In a situation in which you and a professional who has been or is working with you as a client want to have a romantic or sexual relationship, always check (even if the professional says it is OK or that they have already checked)

with the board or society the professional is registered with the rules about professionals having sex or romantic relationships with their clients. It is almost always unadvisable. However, some boards of certification completely forbid sexual or romantic relationships between professionals and clients, while others have rules about the relationship that would not necessarily mean the professional losing their job. If, for example, a counsellor falls in love with their client, a board might stipulate that the counsellor must stop working as a counsellor for two years and must stop seeing the client professionally.

If a professional does not belong to a board or professional organization, it does not mean they can treat you in a hurtful/abusive way. They still have a duty of care towards you.

> ⓐ A **duty of care**, in the context of a professional working with a client, means that the professional must keep the client safe and must not do anything that would put the client in danger.

Be very cautious of any professional who feels it is appropriate to have sex or a romantic relationship with a client. If they tell you not to tell anyone, then the relationship is almost definitely abusive, and you should tell someone you trust what has happened. If the professional has asked you not to tell other people, even if you wanted to have sex or a romantic relationship with them, still tell someone.

You may not be sure whom you could trust. People you might be able to talk to about this could be your parents, a close friend or the police. Do not worry: you will not get into trouble for reporting a professional who is behaving in this way. What they are doing is wrong. Some professionals deliberately target people with Asperger's and other forms of autism and/or learning disabilities, because it is likely that they may be desperate to have friends and romantic partners, and the professional may think this is a good opportunity for them to abuse someone. People on the autistic spectrum are also often good at sticking to rules, so the professional might also think this will allow them to abuse their clients without anyone else finding out.

Sometimes when people have been abused or had inappropriate things said to them, they feel uncomfortable or confused about saying anything. In this case, you could ask someone you trust if they think what the professional did or said to you was appropriate.

Remember that if you report an abusive professional, you may be stopping them from abusing other people.

If you find it hard to talk about what has happened, this could be because you are unsure if it is abusive. If you are concerned about the consequences of reporting abuse, use the 'Record sheets for reporting abuse' in Appendix A of this book, where you can also find instructions about how to fill them in.

If you approach the professional (who wanted to have a sexual or romantic relationship with you) about their behaviour, they may tell you that you are making it up or lying. This is because they do not want to get into trouble. It is best to discuss the issue with someone else. Sometimes people misunderstand or misinterpret someone's intentions or what someone says. Discussing what happened with someone else should help you to understand whether the professional was being abusive or if you just misunderstood them.

3.7.1 Why it is wrong for a professional to have sex or a romantic relationship with a client

It is abusive for a professional to have a sexual or romantic relationship with a client because the professional has more power and influence and therefore control over the client. For example, the professional's opinion of what you do probably matters to you. Many people on the autistic spectrum want to please other people, so you may not want to have sex with the professional but you want to please them, they say it is the right thing to do and you trust them. Because they have authority and you are likely to do what they say, you might have sex with them. But having sex with a professional would be the wrong thing to do. In this scenario, the professional would have manipulated you for their own personal gain. As previously discussed, a professional should always prioritize what would be best for you, and sex or a romantic relationship with them is almost always not the best choice. In this situation, the professional could also lower your self-confidence by being discouraging, and this could mean you feel you cannot leave the relationship because you do not believe anyone would love you. Or you may start to believe you are a bad person.

Professionals have what are known as boundaries (boundaries were discussed in Chapter 1). Professional boundaries are like rules. Professionals have parts of their life outside work (their personal life) that they do not talk about with clients. They also do not demonstrate their full personality. For example, they could be a very selfish person, but at work they could be very good at listening to clients because that is their job. Similarly, if someone worked in a factory assembling vacuum cleaners and made sure their work space was always tidy, this does not necessarily mean that they keep their home tidy.

I'm a professional; I mentor clients. I have a set of boundaries when I am working. For example, I will only shake hands (if my clients want to shake hands) with my clients. I would never hug them or kiss them because this is a sign of familiarity and affection and would be inappropriate.

Any good professional will have boundaries. Not having sex would be an example of a physical boundary, whereas not having a friendship or a romantic relationship with a client would be an example of emotional boundaries.

Boundaries are not only for the client's safety; they are also for the professional's safety. If you did not have a physical boundary of not hugging clients, then a client might misinterpret a professional hugging them as being sexual in some way. They might then report the professional to the police or their board of certification for sexual harassment.

If you are a client, you are vulnerable, particularly if you have shared personal details, even if you do not consider these details to be personal. Personal details could include:

- previous relationships
- abuse you or your family have experienced
- medical problems.

The professional's job is to take into consideration what the client has told them – for example, how abuse might affect the client – and provide appropriate support as specified in their job role or described in information literature or their website.

Because you have shared this information, it is the professional's responsibility not to use that information to hurt you. For example, if you told a professional about an abusive relationship, and the professional thought that one of the problems you had had was that you could not tell when you were being manipulated (controlled by another person), the professional could then start manipulating you if you had a romantic relationship with them. If the relationship stays professional (i.e. you just see the professional for their job role such as counsellor or psychotherapist), then the professional has nothing to gain and therefore would not want to manipulate you.

This topic is confusing and may be upsetting to some readers. It makes me sad to know there are professionals who enjoy abusing people. If you meet one, please talk to the police or your parents, a close friend or relative. Do not let someone hurt you. It is also important to remember that if this abuse has happened to you, it is not your fault; the person intended to hurt you. They did not intend to hurt you because you deserved it or because you are a bad person; they were simply looking for people to hurt. This is known as predatory behaviour.

> ⦿ **Predatory behaviour** means that someone is looking for people they consider to be vulnerable or weak and then they isolate them from other people in order to get them alone and then hurt them.

3.8 Warning signs/red flags that a romantic relationship may be abusive

> 'It wasn't until I was out of the relationship that I realized how much he had manipulated me. He used my anxieties and insecurities against me. He made no efforts to understand me and criticized me constantly, making me feel that I was worthless. He wanted me to change, to be someone else. I was so desperate to be normal and have a relationship that I stuck with it. That's

not what anyone should do. Have the courage to realize that if someone wants you to change, that's their problem not yours. You are worth more than that.'

Beth, research participant

If someone really cares about you, then they will learn about who you are as a person and how being on the autistic spectrum affects you and what they can do to help you. They will be generally consistent with how they treat you, although everyone argues with their partner occasionally. If something goes wrong, when they are calm and you are calm, they will talk to you about it. (Some people find this hard to do face to face and prefer email or letter. This applies to non-autistic people too.) However, if they do not bring a topic up in conversation that is important to you, such as an argument you have had, then you can bring it up and discuss it. It is important for people in romantic relationships to discuss what is important to them; otherwise, your partner might not know how upset you were about the argument.

To **bring something up** in a conversation means to talk about a particular topic. For example, if I started to talk about the argument I had had with my romantic partner, I would be bringing the argument up in conversation.

Often it's not until the relationship has ended that you realize you were manipulated or abused. A warning sign or red flag is something that may indicate that you are being abused or hurt. If you recognize any of the following, speak to someone you trust about your relationship:

- Your partner wants to take control of your money. Your romantic partner wants you to do things that will give them control, which you do not want to do or cannot change your mind about. For example, many couples have a shared/joint bank account. This means that they can both put money into the bank account and both take (draw) money out of the account, as well as have access to other services the account may offer, such as the facility to set up direct debits or pay companies. Both people should also be able to choose if the money they have (through work or benefits) goes into the joint account. This is fine as long as you are both happy with this arrangement. However, it would not be OK if your romantic partner spent your money without your permission, or if you could not make choices about what happened to your money, or if there wasn't a way out of having a joint bank account. Before you sign anything at the bank, make sure you ask how you could take back control of your money if you needed to. For example, if your romantic relationship ended, you would no longer want to have a joint bank account with your former romantic partner (ex).

- Your partner is verbally abusive.

If someone is **verbally abusive**, it means that they make derogatory (negative) remarks about you. Verbal abuse could also be swearing or saying words deliberately to upset you or make you angry. If you have asked your partner to stop and they do not, then this is verbal abuse.

A partner might be verbally abusive because you have said no to their request to do something (e.g. have sex) or behaved in a particular way they do not like. For example, if you had got home late and your partner was angry and said something rude to you, this is something to be concerned about. It is important to remember, however, that people sometimes say things when they are angry that they later regret. A caring partner in this scenario would apologize later and deal with the situation in a rational manner (i.e. asking you why you were late). You should do the same for your partner. You may get frustrated with something your partner has done, and it would be important to tell them calmly how you feel about the situation and see if there is something that could prevent it happening again.

If the above information seems unclear, think about the frequency of the negative things your partner says. If it is frequent (e.g. once a week), then be concerned about this behaviour and ask someone who knows you and your partner for advice.

- Your partner tells you what you can and can't do (e.g. you can't go to the shops alone).

- Your partner forces you to do things or threatens you by saying that if you do not do the things they ask, they will leave you. This is emotional blackmail. Threatening to leave you or kick you out of the house is just a way to make you feel bad and control you.

- Your partner does not make time for the relationship. Your partner is always putting you off. For example, you might tell them that you really need to talk to them about a particular issue, but they almost always say they will talk about it later or at a particular time, but then on the time they specified they go out or don't discuss the issue. If the issue is money or something else important (as opposed to something trivial such as planning a birthday party) and they repeatedly put you off, this is a sign that they may be abusive.

To **put someone off** means to postpone doing something you have said you will do with them. People put things off when they don't want to do things.

- Your partner won't let you have time alone.

- Your partner says what you can and can't say about your relationship with them.

- Your partner doesn't want you to speak to your friends and family without their permission.

- Your partner does things of a sexual nature which you have asked them to stop and they have ignored you.

- Your partner hurts you. Even if it looks like an accident, if it keeps happening, this could be a sign of abuse.

- Your partner makes horrible unnecessary comments which lower your self-confidence. They may think that by lowering your self-confidence you are more likely to stay with them.

A **healthy relationship** is a relationship where both people are happy to be in the relationship and where both people are making efforts to ensure the relationship stays healthy.

Everyone has needs. Many people need solitude, for example – sometimes for part of the day or sometimes less frequently. Your partner should respect your needs just as much as you should respect their needs.

Romantic relationships take work, which means that you have to make an effort not to annoy or upset each other, but the consequence of this should not be that one of you becomes overwhelmed by trying so hard or unhappy if you are scared of your partner.

Just because there is no physical abuse in your relationship, it doesn't mean it's healthy.

3.8.1 What might a healthy, non-abusive relationship look like?

Here are some of the behaviours you are likely to see in a healthy relationship:

- Your partner respects you and your individuality.

- You are both honest and open (you tell your partner about your life and they tell you about theirs).

- Your support each other's choices even if you disagree with each other (except choices that affect both of you, in which case sometimes you both have to compromise).

- You both play an equal part in making decisions that affect you both.

- You respect each other's boundaries.

- Your partner understands that you need to study or meet up with friends or family.

- You can communicate your feelings without being afraid of negative consequences.

- You both feel safe being open and honest.

- A good partner is not excessively jealous and does not make you feel guilty when you spend time with family and friends. (It is hard to define what is excessive and so you will need to discuss this with someone who knows you both, e.g. a couples counsellor or a friend you trust, if you feel this is an issue.) A good partner also compliments you, encourages you to achieve your goals and does not resent your accomplishments.

- You do not physically hurt each other.

- Neither of you is inconsiderate, disrespectful or distrustful.

- You both communicate your feelings. There may be some topics (not to do with the relationship) that you or your partner decide you don't want to share with each other. This is OK, but it is important to share your feelings about each other and the relationship.

- Neither partner tries to control the other emotionally or financially.

- Neither partner stops the other from getting a job or does anything to get the other partner fired.

- Neither partner humiliates the other in front of other people or on social media (e.g. Facebook).

Everybody deserves to be in a healthy relationship free from violence. Knowing when you are in a healthy or unhealthy or abusive relationship can be hard. If you think your relationship might be unhealthy, use the list above. If you are still unsure, talk to someone you trust (see the resources section at the end of the chapter for contact details for Women's Aid in the UK and similar organizations in the US and Australia).

There are many types of abuse, and although you might think some of them are normal behaviour, they are not. You should take violence or abuse in your relationship very seriously.

If you think you are in an abusive relationship, you're probably feeling confused about what to do. You may fear what your partner will do if you leave or how your friends and family will react when you tell them. If you are financially or physically dependent on your partner, leaving may feel impossible. You may also think that the police and other people won't take you seriously.

These are all understandable reasons to feel nervous about leaving your partner, but staying in the abusive relationship isn't your only option. This is discussed later in this chapter.

3.9 Before marriage

For someone on the autistic spectrum, marriage can seem a very attractive option as it offers predictability and stability. However, marriage is a big lifetime commitment, and although divorce is possible, this can be a very stressful and expensive process. Marriage can also affect benefits such as (but not limited to) social security and housing benefit. If you do get divorced, please do not feel this is just because you are on the autistic spectrum; many non-autistic women get divorced. There are times – for example, if your partner has become abusive or hurt you – when divorce is necessary.

However, before you get married there are some issues that should be considered:

- Is it possible for you to live with your partner before you get married so that you can ensure that you are able to live together happily?

- Sometimes when people are married, they stop making an effort to maintain their relationship. This is something you could discuss with your partner and come up with ideas and solutions as to how you can both maintain the relationship.

To **come up with ideas** means to think of ideas to solve a problem.

3.10 Feeling scared to leave a relationship

'It's better to be alone than to end up getting hurt like I have in the past.'

Jenn, research participant

It's natural to feel scared of leaving a relationship and, understandably, most people are scared of the unknown. If you feel you have difficulties with predicting other people's reactions, then of course leaving a relationship will be hard. Below are some ways that might help you leave:

- *Write down your needs.* Write down the things that you feel you need your partner for, and start to think about how you could do these things or meet these needs without them. You could discuss this list with a friend or therapist.

- *Get space to think.* Stay with a friend or relative or, if you can afford it, at a hotel. Stay for a few days, as this will give you time to think about whether you really want to leave the relationship. During this time do not speak to your partner, but let them know before you leave that you need some time away from them.

- *Talk to someone you trust.* Even if you have been told not to tell anyone, tell someone about your experiences. The reason you have been advised not to tell anyone (by the abuser) is because they do not want to get into trouble. If you feel bad for getting them into trouble, think of it this way: you may well be saving someone's life. Abusers are likely to abuse more than one person, and this could result in the person killing themselves or being hurt by the abuser (depending on the type of abuse).

'Don't keep secrets, tell a trusted friend about your experiences.'

Jennifer, research participant

Part 2: Positive romantic relationships

3.11 Needs and wants

When you are in a romantic relationship, you do not have to change your personality, but you may have to change some behaviour if it upsets your partner. For example, there may be particular phrases your partner does not like you to use, or they may feel strongly about where a particular piece of furniture is put or that the washing-up is done before you both go to bed. But making a change to your behaviour should always be your choice; any change should not result in you feeling unhappy. If you find a change has made you unhappy, you should discuss the change with your partner. If the problem cannot be resolved, perhaps you should consider seeking help from friends or even professional help.

If you find it difficult to know how upset or angry you are, there are some strategies described in Chapter 9 which might be helpful.

A romantic relationship is a partnership, so although you have to make accommodations or changes in behaviour, so does your partner. It should never be that one person tells the other person what to do all the time. It is important to understand some changes are big and some changes are small, and some changes might be in the middle. There have been many people on the autistic spectrum who have lived unhappy lives because they were trying so hard to please other people by changing things in their behaviour, which meant they found life very hard to cope with. I am not advocating for these kinds of changes. If your romantic partner asks you to change something, you must explain either the effects the change will have or has had on your life. For example, if you notice negative effects because you are trying so hard to make the change your partner has asked for that you don't enjoy activities that you used to enjoy, you must explain the effect of the change to your partner.

3.11.1 Do I feel I could accommodate someone else? Would I want to? What accommodations would I need?

Perhaps it is difficult to imagine the answer to these questions right now, particularly if you are not in a romantic relationship. It might be helpful to discuss with other women what changes/accommodations they have made, and what changes/accommodations have been made for them.

Many people live without romantic relationships. They have friends who they spend time with, and they meet their sexual needs themselves or they have casual sexual relationships or use prostitutes.

If you are using prostitutes, it's important to know that it may be illegal in your state or country, and that it could be dangerous. See Chapter 2 for more information on prostitutes.

3.11.2 Deciding your needs and wants

Write down below what you want from a romantic relationship. Examples might be companionship, love, affection, someone to spend time with.

> **What I want from a romantic relationship**
>
> 1
>
> 2
>
> 3
>
> 4
>
> 5

Write down what you need. Needs are different to wants. A need is something you could not do without. For example, we need food, but we can live without fast food such as McDonald's. We may want McDonald's but it is not essential. Examples of needs could be a hug, time spent with me, someone who understands me.

> **What I need from a romantic relationship**
>
> 1
>
> 2
>
> 3
>
> 4
>
> 5

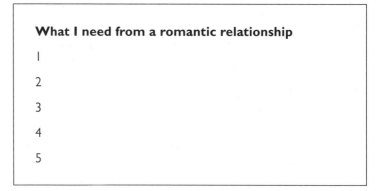

Write down what you do not want or need. For example, 'I do not need people emotionally burdening me, telling me all their problems, making me anxious.'

What I do not want or need from a romantic relationship

1

2

3

4

5

Are there current relationships (not necessarily romantic ones) that meet the needs and wants you have listed above?

To be in a romantic relationship requires some flexibility. There may be some things that you do not need or want but which you are prepared to put up with (accept). For example, sometimes it can be very hard emotionally (e.g. it could make you anxious) if your partner is going through a period of unemployment. Some people feel that it is worth feeling anxious and not leaving the relationship because they get a great deal of benefit from being loved by another person.

You should also consider that some of your needs listed above may be met in other ways.

3.12 Thinking about having a relationship

Fifty-five per cent of women in my survey said they had felt 'unloved romantically' and as if they would 'never find a partner'. If you want to have a romantic partner and felt that there was a chance that you could get married, it is logical that you would want to take the opportunity to have a romantic relationship. Even if things didn't seem perfect or you weren't sure the person was right for you, you would take the chance of a romantic relationship. In the same way, if you see an advert for your favourite food, you don't want to wait till next week to take up the offer and buy the food – you want to buy it now. But the advert does not explain the full consequences of eating that food – for example, how many calories it contains and that it could make you fat if you eat too much of it or don't exercise enough. Choosing a romantic relationship with someone you do not love or someone who is abusive will not provide you with your needs of feeling loved and may make you feel lonely and hurt.

When people talk about having children, they often say it is a life-changing experience. It's very important to know that a romantic relationship can also be a life-changing experience.

Regardless of the length of the relationship, people in my survey explained that it was important to know their partner. You can get to know your partner by going on dates or by being friends with them before you begin a romantic relationship.

Are there things that are important to you which your romantic partner does or doesn't do? For example, if you follow a religion, is it important to you that your romantic partner follows the same religion? Is it important to you that this person is calm? Does it matter that they yell when they are angry? The reason these questions are important is because if you meet someone and you are romantically interested in each other, but they do things that you feel are unacceptable (e.g. not following a particular religion) or are painful (e.g. yelling), then your relationship won't be stable if you end up arguing about these things. Nobody is perfect, but what are the things that are important to you which the person must or must not do?

It may be helpful to answer the question below:

What qualities/characteristics is it important for my romantic partner to have?

What qualities/characteristics is it important for my romantic partner *not* to have?

> ⊘ **Getting to know someone** means understanding who they are in terms of what they think is important in life, whether they have religious beliefs, what they expect from a relationship and so on. Getting to know someone is part of building a relationship.

3.13 How going on dates helps you get to know them

One way people get to know each other is by going on dates.

> ⊘ A **date** could be any activity you and a potential romantic partner (usually called **your date**) want to do together. Usually dates are time spent between two people.

Although a date is usually time spent with just the other person, sometimes it is really helpful for your date to meet your friends, and for you to meet their friends. Meeting each other's friends may give you some indication of what kind of person they are. For example, if their friends are mostly criminals, there's a good chance your date is a criminal too. Your friends could provide very useful feedback (information) about what they thought of your date (the person you went on the date with).

Going on a date with someone does not mean you are their girlfriend; it just means that you have spent some time together. Over time you will see what kind of reaction your date gives – for example, if they get angry easily – and you can both decide if you want to have a romantic relationship with each other.

3.13.1 When is a date a date rather than just spending time with a friend?

There is no easy way to know when a date is a date, as opposed to simply spending time with a friend. When someone invites you to do something, it is OK to ask them, 'Is this a date?'

If someone invites you to their house and you are not confident about going there, then why not suggest going to a place you are comfortable? It is perfectly acceptable to say that you do not feel comfortable going to their house yet.

If they are unhappy about this, perhaps they might respond, 'Oh, don't you trust me?' or they might call you negative names. In that case, it is likely that they just wanted to have sex with you and did not care about your feelings. If this happens to you, do not spend any more time with the person and don't respond to their phone calls or text messages.

If they respond well to your request – for example, 'OK, no problem, we can do something else' – then over a period of time your confidence is likely to increase with that person and you will be able to make a more informed decision as to whether you want to have a romantic relationship with them.

If your confidence does not increase, then they are probably not someone you should have a romantic relationship with.

3.14 Sharing your thoughts, feelings and experiences on dates

Some topics are very personal. These might include:

- past relationships
- sexual experiences
- abuse
- the deaths of people close to you

- how much money you earn

- health

- religion (unless you met in a religious context).

When you first start dating someone, I recommend avoiding these topics until you feel safe. If you feel safe immediately, then wait until your date talks about something very personal before sharing something personal yourself. Information exchange should be approximately 50-50 – in other words, you share the same amount of information as they do. It's best to avoid discussing the topics listed above because they are things that may offend or upset your date and may cause your date to disrespect you or potentially hurt you. As you build your relationship, you will be able to make a judgement as to whether you trust this person to respect your opinions. If you are unsure, ask a friend to meet you and your date and see what they think.

3.14.1 Talking about being on the autistic spectrum

It is sometimes hard to know when to talk to your date about being on the autistic spectrum. When and if you do so is a really personal decision and everyone is different.

When they start a relationship, some people choose to explain the traits they have. For example, instead of saying they have meltdowns, they explain this by saying, 'Sometimes I get emotionally overwhelmed. If this happens, please leave me alone.'

'My single most common mistake is to be too trusting at the start of a relationship and then get very attached. Even if I am dating somebody, I will tend to get overly attached and then feel hypersensitive and hurt when things don't work out. The occasional meltdowns and emotional overloads that come with being an Aspie girl have often been the catalyst for the end of my relationships. One strategy going forward would be to be much more open about the potential for meltdowns, so that if they happen, the person that I'm dating doesn't make the situation worse by breaking up with me right away. Sadly, this has happened over and over again in my life. Most meltdowns have been horrible experiences where the men in my life walk away from what they perceive to be "drama".'

Yas, research participant

At the beginning of a relationship and on dates, it's important:

- not to be too trusting

- not to get too attached

- to consider people's perceptions of autism.

It is a common assumption people make that because they are honest and trustworthy themselves, others will be the same. By telling someone about autism on your first date, you might make yourself vulnerable. If people think you are disabled, they may try to take advantage of you; when they know and care about you, they are less likely to do this. Other people may perceive autism as being 'drama' (i.e. difficult for them to cope with); once they know you, they can see what being on the autistic spectrum means in your life, how it affects you, if at all, and what they can do to help. Some people are scared of autism when they don't understand it, because it is something unknown to them.

3.15 Building up slowly

'I would encourage everyone to take time to get to know someone *before* starting a romantic relationship, regardless of whether someone is on the [autistic] spectrum or not. If I had adhered to this advice, it would have saved me quite some trouble and fears.'

Carol, research participant

To understand if a romantic relationship will meet your needs or not, it is important to get to know your potential partner before you decide to have a romantic relationship with them. If you know them, you will be better equipped to tell whether they will be able to meet your needs and if you will be able to meet their needs. From a safety perspective, this is likely to help you maintain your mental health, because if a romantic relationship made you unhappy, this could lead to you becoming depressed.

When people talk about romantic relationships, they often talk about building relationships. To build a relationship means to make a relationship. Someone you meet for the first time will not instantly be your best friend, because you both need to know if you like each other, understand each other's opinions, enjoy each other's company, respect each other and trust each other. The process in which you learn these things and many other things about a person is known as building a relationship. This term can be applied to any kind of relationship.

In this chapter we are focusing on romantic relationships. The way in which someone builds a romantic relationship with another person may be slightly different to the process of building a platonic (non-romantic) relationship (friendship). This is because a romantic partner is someone who you are likely to be much closer to (tell more intimate/private things to and rely on more). A romantic partner is also someone you are likely to spend more time with (in terms of hours) than a platonic friend.

3.16 Why do I want to be in a relationship?

If a person is just nice to you – perhaps they are polite and hold the door open for you, or they stop someone bullying you – you may feel very grateful to them, but this is different from being in love with them or fancying them. Sometimes people just admire each other. When you experience these feelings, it can be confusing and you could mistake your feelings for wanting a romantic relationship with that person. For a romantic relationship to work, you both need to relate to and understand each other, as well as like each other in a romantic way and want a relationship with each other. When you think you might want a relationship with someone, question whether your feelings are just admiration or gratitude.

3.17 How to avoid over-attachment

It can be very easy to get over-attached to someone you might have a romantic relationship with. Some people might not be as keen as you are or may be put off by your enthusiasm or feel overwhelmed by it. Ways of overcoming this could be to make yourself some rules/boundaries of how often you will contact the person and try to avoid fantasizing about what your relationship could be like. It is always easier to do this when you have things in your life to keep you busy, such as work and other interests. If you fantasize about a relationship, then you will be disappointed if it isn't as you imagined.

3.17.1 Signs of stalking behaviour in yourself

It is important to try to identify when someone really doesn't want to have a romantic relationship with you. If you contact someone a lot or go to places where you think they will be (deliberately, in order to see them), then this is stalking.

Stalking behaviours include the following:

- Some women lie to a man they have sex with that they are using contraception. Their aim is to get pregnant because they think this will give them a lifelong connection with the man who got them pregnant. Getting pregnant will not necessarily provide a lifelong connection with the man whose child it is.

- Going to places you would not ordinarily go or at a time you would not ordinarily go, just to see a particular person (unless they are pleased to see you). If they are not pleased to see you, then this may well be stalking.

- Googling them or searching social networking sites for them several times a week.

- Continuously calling them and leaving messages, and they don't call you back.

- Following the person around (for no reason other than wanting to spend time with them).

- Not adhering to their request if they ask you to leave them alone.

- Giving unwanted gifts to them.

- Continuously sending emails or letters to them.

How do you know if someone wants to be your friend? Ask them what they would like to do when you next meet up and when they would next like to meet up.

3.18 Contact at the beginning of the relationship

Contact could be face to face or by telephone, email or text messages, or any other way of communicating with someone.

When you do not know someone well, it is advisable to wait for them to contact you after you have contacted them. If you have sent them a text message, wait for them to reply before sending them any more messages. Also think about what the person says in their communication with you. For example, if they aren't asking you questions but you are asking them questions, then it may be that they don't want to communicate as much as you do.

There is a strategy for this in Chapter 10.

3.19 Sex in romantic relationships

'The right guy will value you whether you are having sex or not. Don't let guys use you. You deserve better. If you're afraid if you don't give him what he wants sexually he will do it with someone else, cut him loose. Women get STDs from husbands and boyfriends who sleep around. Don't put up with it.'

Beth, research participant

🔎 **Cut him loose** means not talk to him or be in a relationship any more.

(?) **Sleep around** means to have sex with someone when you are in a romantic relationship with someone else. Or it can mean to have sex with lots of people as opposed to just one person.

Only have sex when you are ready to have sex. This is not just a rule that should apply to losing your virginity. This is a rule that should be applied to new romantic relationships too.

If the person values you, then they won't mind waiting to have sex. If they do mind, then they are probably only interested in having sex with you and not the romantic relationship. Or they are not the right person for you. If someone is not romantically right for you, don't think of this as a personal failing. We are not romantically right for everyone, and the same is true of non-autistic people.

Sex may give you different feelings – for example, some people feel much closer emotionally to their partner when they have sex with them. But everyone's experience will differ.

3.19.1 Safe sex in a romantic relationship

When you are in a romantic relationship, it is fine to ask the man to use a condom. Even if you are using another form of contraception (e.g. the pill), it is perfectly acceptable to ask your partner to do this, since no form of contraception is 100 per cent reliable and only condoms and femidoms protect against sexually transmitted diseases. Some men on the autistic spectrum have sensory issues that make touching a condom difficult; however, you can put a condom on a man's penis for him. If they will not use a condom, then are you sure you want to be in a relationship with them? Although it is true that men don't get as much sensation in their penis when wearing a condom, if it makes you feel safer, then that shouldn't matter. You are also more likely to be relaxed, which will make it easier for the man to put his penis inside you. If using condoms becomes a problem, then ask the advice of your family doctor, a close friend or sex therapist.

If you are asking the man to wear a condom because you do not trust him or do not believe that he has not been sleeping with other people, then this could be a problem. Although it is perfectly acceptable to ask a man to wear a condom, romantic relationships work best when both people trust each other and if you have agreed that you will have closed relationship.

A **closed relationship** is when two people are in a romantic relationship and commit to only sleeping with (having sex with) each other.

If you feel that your romantic partner is sleeping around, then this will cause you anxiety and may cause problems for the relationship. People like to feel that other people trust them, particularly if they are honest and genuine, and can become offended if they are not trusted. In these circumstances, it would be important to seek help from your friends. Talk honestly with your partner about how you feel, and work out together what you can do about it. This may mean that you go to couples counselling, which is when you see a counsellor together (as a couple).

In this context, to **work out** means to decide on a series of actions, such as attending couples counselling, which will help you to overcome a problem. In this case, the problem is that your partner is unhappy because you do not trust them.

In this context, **actions** means anything you could do in your behaviour or activities that could help to solve the problem.

3.20 Maintaining romantic relationships

'Communication with your partner is everything. Your partner does not have mind-reading capabilities.'

Oceana, research participant

Being able to maintain a romantic relationship is very important. If you have chosen to be in a romantic relationship in the first place, you are likely to care deeply for your partner. Therefore, if you want to stay in the relationship, you need to maintain it. This is much like doors or mechanical devices that have to be looked after by adding products such as WD40 or oil to their hinges or repainting them. Of course, people are not mechanical and are therefore somewhat more complicated. There are many different ways of maintaining a romantic relationship, but below are some ideas:

- It is important to *let your partner know how you feel about them*. If you do not love them any more, it is important that you think about whether you still want to be in the relationship. Sometimes people express their love for someone through actions – that is, doing something that their partner will really like such as baking them a cake or taking them (booking and then going with them) to the theatre or cinema.

- *Verbal expression*. It is also important to verbally tell your partner how you feel about them. Sometimes having a romantic relationship with another person, seeing them a lot and living with them can be a challenge. Letting the person know you love them is really important, because it makes the effort seem worthwhile.

- *Communication*. Communicating about what is good and what isn't working so well in your relationship is also important. You don't just have to do this verbally – lots of people in romantic relationships communicate via email, text or Facebook message, as well as verbally. You might also consider having a communication book. This could be a notebook which is placed in a communal area such as on the kitchen table or the coffee table. If you feel upset about something or your partner feels upset, you could write in the book. You may also need a way of notifying each other that one of you has written in the book. For example, when you write in the book, placing a bookmark sticking out of the top of the book or placing the book somewhere else (where you have agreed you will both look for it) might be good ways of indicating that one of you has written in the book. Make sure you both know how you will notify each other that there is something in the book; simply telling each other verbally may be enough.

- *Wanting and being willing to have sex.* There is a big difference between not wanting to have sex at all and being willing to have sex because your partner wants to have sex. Regular sex can help to strengthen a relationship. Some people find it makes them feel closer emotionally to their partner, but you should not accept being blackmailed into having sex. It should always be a choice and should never be painful. You should also not make choices that make you very unhappy.

- *Change what you do.* For example, sometimes people change the position they use when having sex. Other changes might be going to a different cafe or having a certain meal on a different night of the week (rather than always having steak on a Friday, for example). Change can be good because it can give you a new experience, but it can also help you to appreciate what you have. Sometimes people enjoy change because it can be interesting and exciting. You should consider change, but do not let others force you to change if you do not want to.

3.21 What is the value of a relationship?

The word 'value' is used within the context of material possessions, normally to describe monetary value – for example, the value of a house might be £120,000. An alternative phrase could be the worth of something – how much the house is worth. When used in the context of romantic relationships, the meaning of the word 'value' is different.

As a result of being in a romantic relationship, people may feel loved or cared for, and this may be very important to a person and help them to feel happy. These things are known as values, because you value them (i.e. they are important to you).

So although having a relationship is difficult at times – because you might argue or because sometimes it might make you feel sad (when something goes wrong) – many people feel (a) that they want to have a romantic relationship and (b) that even though there are bad things about having a relationship, the good things (the things they value, such as being loved) make them so happy that they would not want to stop having a romantic relationship.

People who are abusive will try to make you feel that an abusive relationship is all you are worth – that you have no value. Having no value means they think you could not make someone happy and you are not good for anything. But everyone is worth more than being abused. The abusive person has chosen and intends to make you feel worthless because they enjoy abusing you and want to control you and continue to abuse you. If someone makes you feel worthless or without value, leave the relationship.

> 'If someone is forcing you to stay with them or emotionally blackmailing you, then you have to walk away. No matter how much they beg or plead or threaten to hurt themselves/ kill themselves, you have to walk away. That is not a loving relationship. If he constantly runs you down and makes you feel that no one would want you because you are different or a slut or fat or whatever he uses to manipulate and take your confidence, you need to be strong and walk away. Don't let anyone emotionally abuse you.'
>
> *Therese, research participant*

3.22 Equal relationships

When you are in a romantic relationship, it is important to have what is sometimes described as give and take. Another way of putting this is to call it an equal relationship.

This is because if only one person in the romantic relationship puts a lot of effort into making the other person happy, the person putting in all the effort will become unhappy and feel rejected or used. The other person is not putting in equal amounts of effort to make their partner happy.

Being used means when someone only wants to be friends or in a romantic relationship because you will do things for them, such as give them money or let them abuse you.

An equal relationship is when both partners put effort into caring and loving each other. This could be expressed in a number of ways such as:

- spending time together doing each other's favourite activities (a non-autistic person may not enjoy their partner's favourite activities but they may enjoy doing them because they get to spend time with their partner)

- talking and listening to each other

- cooking dinner for each other

- sharing chores (if you live together).

3.22.1 How to work out whether your relationship is equal

'Learn your values and boundaries before getting into a relationship, and if you feel that something is "wrong", listen to your instincts.'

M, research participant

A way to conceptualize and help you work out if your relationship is equal may be to draw a pair of scales or a seesaw (see Figure 3.1). You could do this alone or with your partner.

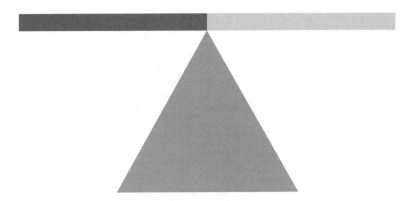

Figure 3.1 Equal relationship seesaw

Write down the things you do for each other in a list. Then decide a maximum weight (e.g. 100kg). Or you could use a numerical score (e.g. points out of 100 – more points means more effort). Write on the list how much each of the items is worth (see below for an example).

The greater the weight (or the higher the number), the greater effort you or your partner are putting into doing that item. Then add up each person's score.

Alfie
Cleans dishes – 2 (not much effort)
Listens – 9 (a lot of effort)
Walks the dog – 4 (some effort)
TOTAL – 15

Florence
Doesn't swear – 9 (a lot of effort)
Listens – 5 (fairly easy)
Vacuums – 2 (not much effort)
Comes home from work on time – 9 (hard work)
TOTAL – 25

Draw these on the scale/seesaw. If your partner is doing more things than you or fewer but heavier things, the scale will tip to one side. If you and your romantic partner are happy with how things are, that is OK. But if you want things to be more equal, then perhaps you could ask your partner what you could do for them. If the scale tipped the other way and you were putting more effort in, then you should also discuss this with your partner.

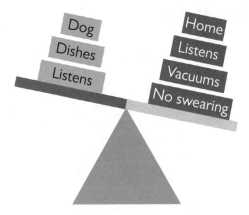

Figure 3.2 Unequal relationship seesaw

3.23 Arguments

Sometimes it can be very hard to see another person's point of view.

To **see a point of view** means to understand another person's opinion. For example, in an argument within a romantic relationship, if you see the other person's point of view, then you understand why they feel a particular way – for example, if you felt you had legitimate reasons not to go to a wedding, but your partner disagreed with you because they felt that it insulted their religion. If you understood why your partner felt it insulted their religion, this is being able to see their point of view.

In a romantic relationship, this can be a problem because you probably spend more time with your partner than anyone else and the relationship is likely to last longer, whereas platonic friendships come and go.

So here are some useful tips:

- Sometimes when you have an argument, you need some time away from each other. This may mean one of you sits in the bedroom while the other sits in the living room. The time away from each other can allow you both to process what has happened and decide what you should do next. Sometimes people recommend that you sleep on it.

To **sleep on it** means that if you have had an argument (or any kind of experience) or need to make a decision, you do not make any more decisions on the subject until you have been to sleep. When we are asleep, our brain processes information, and this can make it easier to make decisions the next day.

- If the argument was your fault, you need to say you are sorry. Do this verbally or write it down, or show it in your actions. But if you show it in your actions, make sure your partner knows and check their understanding of what you are trying to communicate to avoid confusion. This point may seem obvious, but many people, including non-autistic people, forget to say sorry. You should also expect your partner to say sorry. People show they are sorry in different ways. If you are not sure, ask your partner how they show they are sorry, or agree that they will verbally tell you they are sorry.

- Rate how important the subject of the argument is to you and ask your partner to rate how important it is to them. Do this when you are both calm. You could do this numerically, on a scale of 1 to 10 (10 being very important and 1 being least important). If the issue is between 5 and 10, perhaps a compromise could be found. If it is very important to your partner, you might be able to consider trying to put up with the cause of the argument. You might be able to do this by asking for help or strategies from someone outside the relationship (e.g. a trusted friend or relative). You could also consider consulting a marriage counsellor (even if you are not married) or, if the problem is of a sexual nature, a sex therapist.

  Alternatively, you could represent how important the issue is visually. Use the image of a thermometer, either by imagining this in your head or by drawing it on a piece of paper. Place three marks on it at equal distances apart and either colour them or imagine them in red, amber and green. When you have an argument, decide if this argument is very important to you (the thermometer goes to red), not so important (amber) or not important and can be ignored (green). If you have drawn the thermometer, you could place post-it notes with the subject of the argument on the appropriate part of the thermometer.

- You could also consider how important the argument or disagreement is to you, compared with how important the relationship is to you.

- You could list possible solutions and see which ones might work. You could even use a scale to rate which would be your preferred option (e.g. 10 being most preferred, 1 being least preferred).

An example of this last idea might be the following. (Note: This is a simple example so that you can understand the concept of compromise. If I had made the scenario less simplistic, then the idea of compromise might have got lost in the details of the story.)

Justin and Mary are a married couple. They have decided to go out to dinner, and Justin wants to go to the steak house across the street. Mary wants to go to the burger restaurant, which is also close by. They both rate how important it is to them. Justin says on his scale it is 5, and Mary says for her it is 6.

They think about what a possible solution could be. They both understand that they have a difference of opinion about where they should eat and decide that there are three options:

1. They eat at home.

2. They go to one of their choices. Since Justin's score on the scale of importance was lower, he would be prepared to go to Mary's choice, as long as the next time they eat out, they can go to the steak house and agree on a date when they will do this. (They both accept this date may need to change, e.g. if one of them has to work later than usual.)

3. Since both restaurants are close to home, they go for their starter at the burger restaurant, have main course at the steak house and pick up ice cream from the store on their way home for dessert.

This argument was just about where you go for dinner, but the above strategy of listing three possible options and deciding which is most appropriate could be applied to many arguments – for example, which DVD to watch or what to cook for dinner.

Of course, many arguments are more complicated and matter much more to each person, as in the scenario below.

Mark and Suzanne have been in a romantic relationship for three years. Mark's workplace is holding a party. This is something that Mark finds very hard and Suzanne has promised she will go with him to support him.

Suzanne forgets this on the day of the party, because her boss has given her a lot of work to do. Mark has to go to the party alone. He is scared and very upset that Suzanne has not shown up. When he gets home, he calls Suzanne and is very angry. He shouts a lot and starts to cry; this in turn makes Suzanne very upset.

Sometimes when we argue, just the fact that we are arguing can be very upsetting. This is true for non-autistic people too. In this scenario, it may be that both people need time out.

Both Mark and Suzanne are tired and less able to process what has happened. In a romantic relationship, it may be helpful to agree with your partner that if you are ever in this situation, it is OK to ask for time out, and you could have an agreed amount of time (e.g. ten minutes or until morning) and agree when you will talk again.

If you find it hard to speak when you are upset, perhaps you could agree to communicate via text.

One possible outcome of Suzanne and Mark's situation would be as follows.

> Suzanne apologizes that she forgot to go to Mark's work party, explaining clearly that this was not intentional. After sleeping, Mark can appreciate it is possible that Suzanne made a mistake.
> Suzanne offers to take Mark to dinner (this means she will pay for his dinner) at his favourite restaurant. She is demonstrating that she is sorry through her behaviour.

3.24 Everyone makes mistakes

An important point I would like to make from this story is acceptance. Mark accepted that it was a genuine mistake and accepted Suzanne's apology. Mark's feelings were still hurt, and it does not mean that Suzanne did the right thing in not showing up, but the incident is now in the past and cannot be undone. Accepting that someone has made a mistake and that they are sorry is very difficult.

But what if the person does not accept they made a mistake or does not say they are sorry that they made a mistake. Sometimes a way to accept that someone else has made a mistake is to repeat three times that they have made a mistake and to say, 'It is OK, I will feel better soon. Everyone makes mistakes sometimes.' Do this every morning and every evening for a week and you may feel better. If you love your partner, you have to learn to accept that people make mistakes.

If your partner keeps doing things that upset you, especially if they are deliberately doing things to upset you, and you have both tried or your partner is unwilling to try to resolve the situation, you may need to question if this is the right relationship for you to be in.

3.24.1 Agreeing to disagree

Sometimes you also need to learn to agree to disagree. This means that you and your partner have differing opinions on a topic and you agree that you do not have the same views.

Top 10 things to remember from Chapter 3

1. It is OK not to want to have romantic relationships.

2. Many women, regardless of whether they are on the autistic spectrum or not, experience being single. This can lead to opportunities to meet new people.

3. Abuse within a romantic relationship is never OK. There are many different types of abuse, including emotional, financial and sexual abuse.

4. A professional, if you have been their patient/client/student, should not have a romantic or sexual relationship with you.

5. Some people on the autistic spectrum can become overly attached to a person, and the other person can find this overwhelming. Setting yourself rules/boundaries may help you to manage this.

6. It is important to understand value in a relationship. What are you gaining? What is the other person gaining?

7. You can leave a romantic relationship at any time. If you are experiencing abuse, it may seem very scary to leave. But if you do leave, you have the opportunity to make a happier life for yourself.

8. Everyone makes mistakes and they can be overcome.

9. You do not have to have sex with someone just because they are your boyfriend/girlfriend.

10. People normally go on many dates and have several romantic relationships before they find someone they want to marry. Just because one romantic relationship does not work, it does not mean that all your romantic relationships will fail.

Resources

Books

Aston, M. (2008) *The Asperger Couple's Workbook: Practical Advice and Activities for Couples and Counsellors.* London: Jessica Kingsley Publishers. ISBN: 1843102536
This is a practical book for people on the spectrum and their romantic partners. It contains activities which couples can work through together with the aim of strengthening their relationship.

Stanford, A. (2002) *Asperger's Syndrome and Long-term Relationships.* London: Jessica Kingsley Publishers. ISBN: 1843107341
Ashley Stanford is married to a man who has Asperger's syndrome, and in this book she gives her advice about how to make a long-term relationship work. Ashley knows a lot about people on the spectrum and I think her perspective is helpful.

Organizations

Women's Aid
www.womensaid.org.uk
Women's Aid is a UK charity for women who are experiencing or have experienced domestic violence, including sexual violence. They have a website and a helpline.

The National Domestic Violence Hotline
www.thehotline.org
The National Domestic Violence Hotline is a US organization that provides 24-hour support to anyone affected by domestic violence, including through advocacy and safety planning resources.

1800 Respect
www.1800respect.org.au
Australia's national sexual assault domestic family violence counselling service offers online support through instant messaging, and information and links to other services that can provide support.

4

DRUGS, ALCOHOL AND OTHER SUBSTANCES

In this chapter

4.1 Introduction

There is not a great deal published on drugs and alcohol in relation to people on the autistic spectrum.

There are four main problems that people on the autistic spectrum encounter with regard to drugs and alcohol:

1. *Peer pressure/wanting to fit in.* Because people on the autistic spectrum often feel very lonely and want to make friends, they may do things that they don't really want to do but which they feel will help them to fit in and be liked by other people.

    People on the autistic spectrum may be more susceptible to peer pressure than non-autistic people. Resisting peer pressure requires social skills that are normally learnt from other peers, which may not have been learnt if you have limited social networks. People on the autistic spectrum may have processing difficulties which make it hard to pay attention to relevant information or form a response quickly.

Peer pressure is when people try to encourage you to do or make you do something you do not want to do, by making you feel bad or by repeatedly asking you.

2. *Coping mechanism.* Many people on the autistic spectrum find social situations difficult and overwhelming and may use drugs or alcohol to help them cope with particular situations. Many non-autistic people do this too. However, using drugs or alcohol as a coping mechanism can mean the person does damage to their body and experiences physical and psychological dependence, which could interfere with daily life and lead to losing their job, home and social/ family connections.

    Alcohol, in particular, is a socially acceptable and frequently used coping strategy. Using alcohol can be dangerous because it slows down reaction times. Alcohol can also change your behaviour. For example, if you are less inhibited, you might be more willing to argue with someone, which could result in them physically attacking you.

3. *Addiction.* If a drug or alcohol is used as a coping mechanism, there is a risk of addiction. This can damage physical and psychological health.

4. *Spiking.* As with non-autistic people, people on the autistic spectrum are at risk of spiking (when a drug or alcohol is added to a drink). The drug used to spike you can affect the way you behave and make you drowsy or confused. It can also make it difficult for you to move or speak, and, as spiking is usually done deliberately by someone wishing to take advantage of you, it can make you vulnerable to being attacked or robbed.

You may have already learnt some of this information at school, but please remember that this book tries to cater for a wide variety of readers and not everyone had this education in school. Please do not take any of this information as an insult to your intelligence – surely it is better to have information than not.

Part 1: Preliminary information about drugs, alcohol and other substances

4.2 Types of drugs and substances

There are different categories of drugs and substances. Drugs are often referred to using other names, because the chemical compound name might be long and hard to remember. Some of these alternative names can also denote types of the same drug, such as different strengths of the drug. Cannabis, for example, has several different strengths such as hash and skunk.

If you hear people talking about drugs or you read information people have written about drugs, or there are two useful websites in the resources section at the end of the chapter, which may help you identify what the person is talking about.

I have not listed names of drugs because those names might only apply to your country and there are so many of them. Also, this is a book and therefore static, whereas a website can be updated more frequently with the names that are currently being used.

4.2.1 Drug classification

Below is information about drugs and substance types. Some drugs are less dangerous than others. Dangerous drugs are classified in systems. In the UK there is what is known as the class system (class is short for classification). Class A is the highest class a drug can be assigned (i.e. most dangerous).

Many factors are considered when deciding which class a drug should be put in. These include the harm caused to a person taking the drug and withdrawal problems.

> ⑦ **Withdrawal** is the process of coming off a drug. For example, if you are addicted to alcohol, when you stop drinking alcohol, your body has to get used to not having regular doses of alcohol. Withdrawal from many drugs can cause side effects, such as headaches and sickness.

> ⑦ **Abusing a drug** means to use a drug for the wrong reasons – that is, not using the drug in the way it was intended. Using drugs in the non-intended way could kill you.

In the USA the drug classification system is known as the Schedule system (Schedules 1–5). Schedule 1 drugs are the most dangerous. As with the UK class system, there are clear police actions to be taken if the drugs are used or sold without a prescription (or if the prescription is forged).

4.2.2 Pharmaceutical drugs

Pharmaceutical drugs are made in laboratories or factories by companies. There is a very high safety standard which companies must maintain to allow them to produce the drug legally. These drugs are prescribed by doctors and nurses. Some can be bought in pharmacies or supermarkets or other shops. A drug that can be bought at a shop is known as an OTC (over-the-counter) drug. If taken without following the directions/instructions or without advice from a qualified doctor, nurse or pharmacist, they can be dangerous. If you need a prescription-only drug (one that cannot be bought over the counter), you can only get a prescription from a doctor or a nurse. Whether a drug is over-the-counter or prescription-only, it is important to follow carefully any instructions a professional gives you and check that the dosage you are given is the same as the dosage on the packet and your prescription. Make sure the medicine has not been tampered with (i.e. the packet has not been opened by someone else).

(?) **Legal status**: Some drugs can be prescribed that would otherwise be illegal. For example, morphine is a class A substance, but it can be legally prescribed for pain relief by a qualified doctor.

4.2.3 Illegal drugs and street drugs

(?) If a drug is described as a **street drug**, this does not mean you find it lying on the street. **From the street** is a phrase used to refer to drugs that are not bought from a pharmacy or other shop that sells drugs legally.

There are some drugs that are considered to have no medical use, such as LSD (lysergic acid diethylamide), although sometimes these drugs are made legally available for specific clinical trials (for which a licence is required). Apart from this, they should not be being made or taken.

(?) A **clinical trial** is when scientists do an experiment in a clinical environment (e.g. a hospital). Patients must agree to be part of the experiment to find out what the effects of a drug are and if it can be used to help people.

Some drugs, however, may be legal but become illegal because they are being used by someone without a prescription or being made in someone's kitchen rather than a safe laboratory or factory. These drugs are illegal when sold or given to you. These drugs can be harmful and may be contaminated with other chemicals which might be harmful. They could also be addictive.

Often, drugs not made in laboratories or factories are laced.

(?) **Lacing** is when other chemicals or drugs are added to the drug you think you are buying. For example, cocaine might be mixed with talcum powder. Drug dealers (the people selling the drugs) do this so that it appears that the people buying the drug are getting more cocaine than they really are. This allows the drug dealers to make more money, because they are using less cocaine than the person buying the drugs is paying for.

Street drugs, even if they are pharmaceutical drugs but being sold without a prescription (therefore a street drug), can cause many ill effects such as stroke and death. These drugs often have strange nicknames such as P, smack and Charlie (see the resources section at the end of this chapter for websites that have information on drug names).

4.2.4 Legal highs

There are some newer drugs known as legal highs. Sometimes these are products that are labelled as other things – for example, plant fertilizer – when they are not plant fertilizers at all but a drug used to get high.

> **Getting high** means to become intoxicated by a drug. Note that this term is not usually used when referring to legal drugs or drugs used in medical settings.

Like illegal drugs, these drugs are often referred to by nicknames (e.g. meow meow). They can be very harmful. Drug legislation changes frequently and some of these drugs have or will become illegal.

4.2.5 Alcohol

Alcohol is widely available in lots of different forms. In most countries it is not illegal, although there is usually a minimum drinking age or a minimum age at which it is legal to buy alcohol. For example, in the UK this age is 18. Drinking age only refers to alcohol (i.e. not other types of drinks such as cola). Sometimes people younger than the minimum drinking age may drink alcohol in their homes. Like the other drugs listed, alcohol can be addictive and harmful to the body in large quantities. Often when people talk about drinking alcohol, they may say simply 'drinking'. This is context-specific. For example, if you went to a meeting in an office, you might be asked if you would like a drink, but the person does not normally mean an alcoholic drink. If you were at a party and asked if you would like a drink, then this would probably mean alcohol. If you find it difficult to know which context you are in when you are asked if you would like a drink – formal (such as an office) or informal (such as a party) – then one way to overcome this is to ask, 'What have you got?' (meaning 'What are the choices of things to drink?'). Or if you are at a pub or bar, ask the person what they are having. If they are having an alcoholic drink, then it's OK to ask for one if you want one too.

Write down in the space below the slang names used for alcohol. Be aware that some countries, cities and even communities might have their own words for alcohol. You could ask a friend or colleague at work to help you write down what would be said in your locality.

Slang names for alcohol

Cocktails (a mix of spirits, such as vodka, with juice, cola or other drinks) can have strange sounding names such as snake bite. Do not take these names literally. Most bars or restaurants will have a drinks menu or a drinks list; ask for a drinks list or Google the name of the cocktail.

4.2.6 Uppers and downers

An upper is a drug that gives you more energy or makes you happier; this could be described as your mood going up. A downer is a drug which makes your calmer; this could be described as your mood going down. See Chapter 9 for more on types of emotions.

4.2.7 Cigarettes and cigars

Cigarettes and cigars are legal in most parts of the world. As with alcohol, there is usually a minimum age to be able to buy them, although many people do start smoking at a younger age. Cigarettes and cigars contain nicotine which is addictive, and smoking cigarettes or cigars is harmful to the body.

There are lots of slang terms used to refer to cigarettes and cigars. Write some that apply to your locality in the box below. Ask a friend or colleague to help you.

Slang names for cigarettes and cigars

4.2.8 Diet pills, sport nutrients / supplements and fat burners

These substances may be legal, but they all change the way your body works, so it is very important that you seek a qualified doctor's advice before taking them. You also need to research how to be sure that the supplements, fat burners or diet pills are genuine. Many companies now sell these substances through the internet, but the products may not be genuine and can do you harm. So be sure you know how to check or use high street shops.

4.2.9 Caffeine

Caffeine is a legal drug normally found in coffee and some soft drinks. It can make the body alert and increase the heart rate. Most people do not consider caffeine to be addictive or harmful. However, some people do become dependent on it. It can also be problematic if you consume a drink containing caffeine in the evening, as it can make you feel alert so you may find it more difficult to get to sleep. Some people also wake up in the middle of the night with a faster than usual heart rate, which can be caused by late-night caffeine consumption.

4.2.10 Gluten and casein

These are not drugs, but I felt it important to mention them because they can have a negative effect for some people on the autistic spectrum. Many people eat a gluten-free and casein-free diet. See Chapter 9 for more about gluten and casein.

4.2.11 Flower remedies

Some people on the autistic spectrum find flower remedies very helpful. They are derived from flowers. Other people question whether they work or not.

4.3 Making choices

Some drugs are OK – in fact, some are essential and can save lives (e.g. insulin if you are diabetic). Other drugs can be helpful but in moderation. Drugs prescribed by doctors, nurses and pharmacists can be essential to keep you alive and healthy.

Many people are prescribed drugs by their doctors or nurses. The doctor or nurse should then monitor the drug's effects. If you buy medicines from a pharmacy, these will come with instructions.

Illegal drugs are illegal for a reason – they can be harmful.

It should always be your choice what drugs you take. An exception to this would be if you became mentally unwell and were sectioned under the Mental Health Act in the UK or committed in the USA. Another exception would be a life-or-death situation – for example, if you were rescued from a car accident. You would be given drugs because you would not be able to make decisions for yourself and doctors would want to keep you alive/out of pain as much as possible.

The doctor treating you will only give you the drugs they feel are right for you. Even so, finding out more information can be useful so that you understand what changes may happen within your body. If you are considering taking drugs recreationally, it is important that you understand that this is a risk to yourself and others. There may also be risks to your life and health even after the effects of the drug have worn off.

4.3.1 Decide for yourself

'You need to decide for yourself how much alcohol or drugs you drink/take and whether you do them at all.'

Jenn, research participant

Many people in my survey recommended that people on the autistic spectrum should just say no to drugs and alcohol.

People have many different reasons for deciding not to take drugs or drink alcohol. For example:

'In the end I just decided to stay away from alcohol and drugs. Using them does not add to the quality of life. It clouds my mind's eye.'

Fushin, research participant

Also, if you are young, consider this:

'Alcohol use as a teenager will affect your abilities to grow and learn. It may feel like confidence in a bottle, but in the long term it will do more long-term damage to your self-confidence.'

Oceana, research participant

You own your body. Therefore, if you have capacity, you can choose what happens to it, and that includes choosing if you are going to drink alcohol or take drugs. (As I mentioned earlier, if you are sectioned or committed, then you cannot make these choices.) Be sure you make the choice that is best for *you*, not one that is best for someone else.

4.4 Limits and boundaries

'I set boundaries for myself for drinking alcohol in social situations. I've never been drunk in my life, because I need control. For me, in social situations I drink three Breezers OR two gins at most, but only if my basic mood is OK or good. If I feel sad, I don't drink at all, because alcohol tends to intensify my mood, whether I feel good or bad.'

Carol, research participant

Carol explains above that she sets boundaries for herself. Carol's boundaries are: three Breezers (a type of alcoholic drink) or two gins (a type of alcoholic drink), but only if her 'basic mood is OK or good'.

Carol mentions that alcohol 'intensifies' her mood. This statement demonstrates that Carol has self-awareness – an awareness of what happens to her when she drinks alcohol. It is important to be self-aware when making these decisions.

Self-awareness is an understanding of how you feel about particular topics and how you respond and think.

Be aware that a measure of alcohol in one country won't be the same in another (it may be larger or smaller), so watch carefully when your drink is poured for you to see how much alcohol is being added. Or research the country you are in to see how large the measures of alcohol are. Be aware also of the volume of wine glasses as these can vary, whereas beer is normally measured in half-pint and pint glasses.

What effect does alcohol have on you? Fill out the answers to the questions below to help gain self-awareness.

1. Alcohol in small quantities (alcohol is measured in units, so a small quantity might be two units) affects my mood (i.e. it intensifies whichever mood I'm feeling) in the following ways:

    _____

2. Alcohol in larger quantities (specify quantities, e.g. 4–6 units) affects my mood in the following ways:

    _____

3. Alcohol in large quantities (specify quantities, e.g. 8+ units) affects my mood in the following ways:

    _____

Now ask yourself similar questions about drugs.

4.4.1 The effects of drugs and alcohol

You might not feel the effects but that doesn't mean that a drug or alcohol has not affected you.

Sometimes people cannot tell when they are drunk. Being drunk is another way of describing when their body is affected by alcohol. It is very important to know how drinking alcohol or taking other drugs might be affecting you, either physically or emotionally. The effects of the drug or alcohol may cause you to act in a way that you would not normally. For example, you may feel more confident, less anxious or more persuadable.

Persuadable means that it is easier for other people to convince you that something is a good idea.

Before you get so drunk that you are unable to think clearly, you need to stop drinking so that you can get home safely. This is why it is important to understand how alcohol affects you and therefore how much you can drink and still be able to get home safely. You might want to try drinking alcohol at home or with friends in order to learn how much alcohol you can drink before you can no longer think clearly. Everyone has a different tolerance.

Tolerance is dependent on how regularly you drink alcohol, the type of alcohol you are drinking, how much you have eaten, your body weight, how fast your body's metabolism is, whether you have taken other drugs, or whether you are ill.

4.4.2 Side effects

It is important to make a distinction between the side effects from a drug being prescribed by a doctor who is keeping a person safe and the side effects being caused by a drug not prescribed by a doctor and therefore not monitored correctly, potentially risking the person's life.

Antipsychotic drugs such as Risperidone and Olanzapine are given to people who have psychosis which can include what are known as positive and negative symptoms. Psychosis is a mental illness that can cause hallucinations and paranoia. This can mean that someone with psychosis perceives the world in a totally different way to other people, and this can cause the person to harm themselves or other people. Because the symptoms of this illness are so debilitating, people are given antipsychotic drugs to keep themselves safe (from harming themselves or others), and taking the medication also helps them to continue their normal everyday life activities. Antipsychotic drugs can make the person taking them gain weight and have other side effects, but a doctor will ensure that patients have the correct dose to minimize these effects. Sometimes side effects happen, but if taking the medication could save your life or prevent you from hurting yourself or others, it is better to be alive and safe with some side effects than be dead.

🔍 **Positive symptoms** could include hallucinations and hearing voices. **Negative symptoms** might include slowing down of speech.

If the side effects of medication worry you, sometimes it is possible to write an advance directive. This is a document that says what medications or treatments you want and do not want if you are sent to hospital.

'I drank to try to fit in, in social situations. I often had no off-switch to know when to stop drinking. This led to some bad situations where I was taken advantage of, or allowed myself to be taken advantage of or did things that I shouldn't have. Please be very cautious when it comes to drinking. Think twice about doing drugs. Asperger's syndrome allows us to be too trusting.'

Deb, research participant

4.4.3 Setting your own boundaries

✎ Create a table similar to Table 4.1 below.

Table 4.1 Setting boundaries

What I will do	What I will not do
Example: I will drink up to two units of alcohol with friends I know and trust.	*Example:* I will not smoke marijuana around people I do not know well.

4.5 Peer pressure

'I have often been offered alcohol during social events because it is somehow expected of you. But I don't like to drink alcohol so I always decline. Nobody should feel pressured to drink alcohol or smoke or take drugs. I do neither. I can just advise other girls to decide before the event how much they want to drink and stick with it.'

Nicky, research participant

Many people find peer pressure very difficult to cope with. Sometimes this might be because you believe/perceive that everyone else is drinking alcohol or taking drugs, or that you can see that everyone else in the room appears to be drinking alcohol or taking drugs. Sometimes you might be encouraged to drink alcohol or take drugs by people you know.

If you perceive that everyone is doing something, ask yourself these questions:

- Have you inspected or asked each person in the room exactly what they are doing? For example, cola/soda can look a bit like lager (a type of alcoholic drink), so maybe some people are drinking non-alcoholic drinks.

- What about the people who are driving home? They cannot drink and drive safely, so they will not be drinking alcohol. You may think they are drinking, but do you really know this?

- If you are in a small room, maybe you are the only person who does not to want to smoke a joint (cannabis) or another drug or drink alcohol. You are not the only person in the world to decline. You could only say you were the only person in the world to say no if you had asked everyone in the world. If you have not asked everyone in the world, then you can't know how everybody will react.

- Many people want to fit in and make friends. True friends won't care whether you drink or take drugs. You are an individual. If you try to do things outside of your values, you will end up unhappy.

A person's **values**, in this context, are the things a person feels are important. For example, if you are a person who thinks taking drugs or drinking alcohol are things you don't want to do or you feel you don't like them, this is known as a value.

If the people around you are drinking alcohol and/or taking drugs and you don't want to do that, perhaps these aren't the right people to spend time with; maybe there are people out there in the world who are like-minded in their attitude to drugs and alcohol. There is more in the world than what is in front of you.

Decide what you will and won't do before you go out somewhere or before your friends come to your home. Use the websites in the box at the beginning of this chapter to educate yourself. Understand how different drugs affect people. As someone on the autistic spectrum, you may feel the effects of drugs more acutely than non-autistic people.

4.6 How to say no and still be accepted

People on the autistic spectrum are often desperate to fit in.

🔍 **Fitting in,** in this context, means to feel like everyone else or feel accepted by other people.

It is also very important to many people on the autistic spectrum to have friends. However, if taking drugs makes you a person's friend, then this person is likely to be using you. For example, if they were a drug dealer (someone who sells drugs), they may give you free drugs until you become addicted and then start charging you for drugs. The drug dealer does not care about you (even if they pretend to). Often drug addicts only care about getting their drugs, and nothing is as important to them as satisfying their addiction. Because of this, people who are addicted to drugs do not make good friends. Sometimes people may also put pressure on you to take drugs so that they can laugh at you or get you into trouble.

Sometimes friends may be occasional drug users. This is rather different. They may offer you drugs such as ecstasy, because they want to share the experience with you, but be aware of the dangers that can come with this. A true friend is someone who would not put pressure on you and will like you even if you do not drink alcohol or take drugs.

If you are with a group of friends who are trying drugs such as cannabis or cigarettes or alcohol, they may offer these to you. In this scenario, you might be encouraged to try drugs not because people want you to get addicted but just because they are being polite or want you to share the experience.

In these situations, what can you do to say no and still be accepted? These strategies can be applied to almost any drug, alcohol or smoking:

- Say 'No, thanks, I don't smoke' or just 'I don't smoke.' Keep the tone of your voice calm. If you do not know what your voice sounds like when it is calm, ask a friend to demonstrate with their voice what they sound like when they are anxious and what they sound like when they are calm. Ask them to help you to practise this and record it on a dictaphone or your phone, so that you can listen to it until you are able to keep your voice calm.

- If you are standing in a line and a joint or drink is being passed down the line or you are sitting in a circle with other people, you could either:

  □ just step out of the line, before it is passed to you

  □ or take the packet of cigarettes, joint or alcohol and pass it straight to the next person in line or in the circle.

  In these situations, having relaxed body language (i.e. not having tense muscles) is important, because it gives other people the impression that you're not judging them (i.e. thinking that what they are doing is wrong) and that you are confident.

- If you can see a joint or alcohol or pills being passed around, you can leave the situation and then rejoin your friends after it has been passed around.

- If you know your friends take drugs or drink alcohol and you don't, before you go out you could tell them that you do not want to take drugs or alcohol. You don't have to mention that you are on the autistic spectrum, but you could say something like 'My neurology is a bit sensitive and I tend to react badly to them'.

- Ask a trusted friend for their advice. If you are going out with a close friend, you could agree a code word that you will say if you need help. This doesn't have to be something obvious (i.e. something you wouldn't normally say) – it could just be something such as 'Hmmm'.

Sometimes people don't want to just say no. For example, when being offered alcohol, they might say, 'I think I have had enough alcohol for tonight' (even if they have not been drinking). In this situation, it is OK to say this. What you say here does not necessarily have to be the absolute truth. For example, you may feel you could drink another drink or two, and if you go on to do that later, then the person offering you the drink will just think you have changed your mind.

It's important to know that not all non-autistic people drink or take drugs.

4.7 Trust

When your friends are offering you drugs or giving you advice about it, ask yourself how reliable their advice has been in the past. Are they a carefree person or do they normally think about the consequences of their actions? Would they gain or benefit from misinforming you? Do they know a lot about the topic they are telling you about? There is no need to distrust everyone, but be cautious and ask questions until you are satisfied you have enough information to make a decision. If you are at all uncomfortable or worried, say no.

4.7.1 On an evening out

If you are standing at a bar and have ordered a drink, it's unlikely to be spiked or tampered with by the barman/woman, but watch as they make it for you. If you are at home, then mix/pour your own alcoholic drink. If you are at a friend's house and they offer you an alcoholic drink, and if you don't feel safe or don't know whether you are safe or not, offer to help them and follow them into the room where they are making the drink.

4.8 What to consider if you decide to try recreational drugs or alcohol

> 'Never change your behaviour to impress others; they should be impressed that you stay yourself.'
>
> *Judith, research participant*

I do not condone taking illegal drugs, but I appreciate and respect your decision as an adult to choose what to do with your life. Below are some things to consider.

If you do decide that you want to try drugs or alcohol, do not do it to impress other people or make them like you. Nobody will be impressed or like you any more just because you do or don't take drugs. As Judith says above, they should be impressed that you stay yourself. This means that you are strong.

> *(?)* A **strong person** is someone who makes a decision to do something and goes and does it and doesn't just think, 'Well, it's hard, I won't bother.'

To be strong in this situation is to decide something and then to do it – you decide you don't want to take drugs and you don't take drugs. There are many people, non-autistic and on the autistic spectrum, who only do things because they think it will make them more popular. Because they put so much effort into trying to do things that they do not really like, they are putting less effort into the natural qualities that they have (e.g. being good with animals or art, music, listening and caring for others). The smart thing to do is stay strong. You may feel very low or depressed and think you do not have qualities and skills, but every human being has qualities and skills. This is just the way you feel perhaps because nobody has ever given you the opportunity to find out what your qualities or skills are. Or perhaps people have just wanted you to be like everybody else. Many great people in the world were or are high achievers because they were strong as a person. They did not try to be like other people.

There may be people who say they don't want to hang out (spend time) with you because you don't want to drink or do drugs, but these people are not worth spending time with. They may well get you into trouble and do not have your best interests at heart.

> *(?)* **At heart** means what the person most cares about. If a person has your best interests at heart, then they will do what is best for you, but if they do not have your best interests at heart, they will not think of the consequences to you of them making a decision about something. For example, they wouldn't consider that another person has sensitive neurology and that taking drugs would therefore be bad for them. (Not everyone has sensitive neurology – this is just an example.)

As an adult, you can make your own choices about what you do to your body and whether to break the law or not.

Below are points you should remember:

- Be sure you know what you are taking/drinking.

- Think not only of the effects now but also the side effects and if there may be a crash.

🔍 A **crash**, in this context, means when you have felt euphoric and then you feel very depressed due to a drug. The depressed feeling is called a crash.

- Find out as much information as you can about what you are going to do.

- Be aware that many drugs are addictive. Many people will tell you that you will not get addicted, but that's just their opinion. Seek advice from drugs charities for accurate information.

- Talk to a close friend or relative whom you trust. Tell them what drug you are trying, when you are planning on doing it and where you will be. If you can, it may be helpful to use drugs or alcohol for the first time with people who have experience.

- Remember that some drugs (and, in certain countries or circumstances, alcohol) may be illegal, not only to use them, but to buy them or to be given them, or sell them to other people.

- If something goes wrong and you feel very ill, go to A&E (accident and emergency – known as the ER or emergency room in the US) at your local hospital. The staff there are not police and they will treat you medically.

You also need to think about how you will recover from the after effects of the alcohol or drugs:

- *Why you want to take drugs.* If you want to take drugs because you are very anxious or very depressed, then it would be safer for you to talk to your doctor about these feelings. There are medications and therapy that can help you with these feelings. Recreational drugs can be addictive and this can lead to committing crimes to get the money to continue taking the drug. This also means there is a risk you won't be able to get the drug, and this will mean you may start withdrawal which can be very harmful and could even kill you.

- *How you feel emotionally.* With a drug such as LSD which causes hallucinations, it is anecdotally documented that if you take it when you are unhappy, anxious or worried, you are more likely to have a 'bad trip'.

  After the drug has stopped working you might have flashbacks.

A **bad trip** is when you take a drug such as LSD and have a bad experience; for example, seeing hallucinations that frighten or upset you.

After a drug has stopped working, you might experience the hallucination you saw while on the drug. This is known as a **flashback**.

On a drug means your body and mind is affected by a drug.

- *Your sensitivity to drugs.* Some people are very sensitive to drugs. When you are prescribed pharmaceutical drugs by a qualified doctor, the dose you receive can be controlled very carefully and lowered if necessary. You can ensure that the active ingredient (the chemical part of the drug that has the effect) is always the same amount in each preparation (pill, capsule, liquid, etc.).

Preparation is the way the drug is prepared. For example, pills, capsules and liquid are examples of preparations of Prozac.

Part 2: Self-medicating

4.9 Using drugs as a coping mechanism

'Alcohol and drugs can reduce your inhibitions but you need to be careful you don't become reliant on them.'

Therese, research participant

Sometimes people use illegal drugs and alcohol as a coping mechanism. This means that they use alcohol and/or drugs to help them cope in particular situations. For example, alcohol can reduce a person's inhibitions and make them less anxious. However, alcohol is also addictive and can make a person irresponsible. It also has health risks such as liver damage.

However, in moderation and within the recommend intake of alcohol, this is OK.

Many governments around the world publish advice on recommended daily intake of particular foods or nutrients. Often these guidelines include alcohol.

However, there is a risk of addiction, particularly if you are using alcohol to try to cope with anxiety or mental illness, so you need to be aware if your alcohol intake is increasing and why you are doing it.

Many drug addicts also started using drugs as a way of self-medicating.

Self-medicating is not solving the problem. An alternative way would be to use antidepressants that are carefully controlled and monitored by a doctor, so as to minimize any harm to the body, and to use talking therapies such as CBT (cognitive behavioural therapy) to understand why someone feels depressed and what they can do to make life better. Once they had some effective coping strategies, they could come off the antidepressant and would be a far happier person than if they had self-medicated with alcohol or drugs.

If you meet drug addicts and they want you to take drugs and you don't want to, or if they keep asking after you have said no, then it is probably best for you not to socialize or spend time with them. They may say that they are no longer using (drugs) or that they are clean.

🔍 In this context, **being clean** means the person is not taking drugs.

Be cautious. They might just be saying this to make you feel more comfortable. Unless they have been on a rehab (rehabilitation) or withdrawal programme, or to a rehab centre or hospital, it is unlikely that they are no longer addicted. Sometimes people do undertake withdrawal alone, but it is very dangerous. The effects of withdrawal can kill you, and you need a doctor who can prescribe medication to counter the effects of the withdrawal.

This is not to say that all drug addicts are bad or liars, but if they are offering you drugs, they are likely still to be using drugs themselves.

4.10 If alcohol or drugs become a problem

'I told my GP [family doctor] about my realization that some days you just can't drink enough – he put me on antidepressants. Now I don't have the added worry about extra weight gain from the alcohol and coping is just that bit easier!'

Georgie, research participant

For many people, drinking alcohol or taking drugs as a coping mechanism can result in developing an addiction. Georgie explains that some days she felt she couldn't drink enough. This does not mean that everyone will feel that way. Many people say this kind of thing to mean they couldn't drink enough alcohol to feel better emotionally. Georgie's GP (family doctor) gave her antidepressants, and one good thing about this, as well as helping her cope, was that she doesn't have to worry about the weight gain that alcohol can cause.

Many people in my survey talked about using AA (Alcoholics Anonymous), an organization that helps people who are alcoholics (people who have an addiction to alcohol); they do this in a number of ways including support groups. There is also NA (Narcotics Anonymous) for people addicted to other drugs.

> 'Using alcohol to deal with social situations is BAD. I know from experience. It might feel better at the time but it won't be helping you in the long run.'
>
> *Hannah, research participant*

🔍 **In the long run** means in the future.

If you are having problems with alcohol or drugs, speak to your family doctor.

If it is hard to speak about it, it might be easier to write down what you need to say and then read or show what you have written to the doctor. If your doctor offers a telephone service, it might be easier to talk to the doctor on the telephone. (I am aware that this is not the case for everyone.)

You could also do a Google search for Alcoholics Anonymous or Narcotics Anonymous and attend one their meetings.

4.10.1 Pharmaceutical drug problems

Some drugs prescribed by your doctor can be addictive – for example, some painkilling drugs such as codeine. If you feel that this is a problem for you, talk to your family doctor.

Also, some pharmaceutical drugs can do you a great deal of damage if you take too many. For example, taking more than eight paracetamol in 24 hours can damage your body's organs, although you may not notice it or feel it at the time.

If you are using 'as and when' medication, make sure you note down if your need for these drugs changes; if your need increases, tell your doctor.

🔍 **As and when** medication is medication you only use when you need it – for example, for anxiety, sleep or pain.

4.11 Strategies for coping without alcohol and/or drugs in social situations

'I found myself partying far too much as part of "socializing". Eventually I realized that there were far better ways to have fun with far fewer damaging consequences.'

Audra, research participant

As Audra mentions above, 'partying' (going to lots of parties) is not something everyone enjoys. If you do enjoy partying, that's OK. If you don't, there are many other people who feel the same way. It does not mean you are boring, that there is something wrong with you or that you can't have friends. One coping strategy may be to stay out of social situations that are stressful, so that you won't need drink or drugs to cope.

Perhaps there are particular events you feel more comfortable with. For example, I do not like clubbing because I hate being physically close to so many people. I do like going to gigs/concerts and I find I can cope better when there is a main focus (i.e. the band).

If your friends only want to do the social activities they enjoy, you could explain you find these social situations stressful and suggest a different activity – your friends might enjoy trying something new.

Some people find it very helpful to use ear plugs. If you are hypersensitive to sound, they can help to reduce anxiety and confusion and make hearing less painful. For some people, using ear plugs makes it easier to distinguish between different sounds. They are often given away free at a club or gig/concert venue's bar.

If you are hypersensitive to light, sunglasses might be helpful when there are bright lights. Coloured lenses make it easier for some people to see clearly.

Agree an exit plan with the person you're going with (i.e. what to do if you become overwhelmed) and the signs that your friends can look out for that might indicate you are feeling overwhelmed. The exit plan could also include what the people you are with can do to help and how you will leave the venue if you need to and meet up with people you went with. Sometimes just having the plan can make you feel better.

If you are at a noisy, busy club, bar or another kind of venue, go outside for 5–10 minutes to take a break. Even if you don't smoke, you could stand outside in the smoking area.

Using websites such as www.meetup.com might enable you to find other people or groups interested in similar things to you. There are many people who enjoy quieter activities.

Kristina wrote the following about friendships. I thought it would be helpful to include here.

'If someone doesn't respect your decisions, then they are not a true friend.'

Kristina, research participant

4.12 Trying to end your life with drugs and alcohol

Sometimes people use a combination of alcohol and drugs when they are very low and depressed and feel that they want to die. Large doses of alcohol and/or drugs can be lethal (i.e. they can kill you) but it is more likely that you will end up with a visit to the A&E department or ER. The alcohol and/or drugs can have very bad side effects and do damage to your body. These effects can be long term (i.e. last for the rest of your life).

If someone feels they want to kill themselves, sometimes this is a cry for help. This means the person wants to help rather than to die, but feels unable to ask for the help they need. There are other ways of getting help. Many people have overcome depression and suicidal feelings. It is not impossible! Below are some suggestions for how to get help if you are considering ending your life.

- Phone a helpline. In the UK, there is a charity called the Samaritans which offers people the chance to be listened to. They offer telephone, face-to-face and email support. It may be helpful to email them if you find speaking hard, but sometimes people find it easier to speak to someone they do not know, as they feel less judged. Samaritans volunteers are very well trained and will not judge you. In the USA, there are similar organizations, including the National Suicide Prevention Lifeline which also has a phone number for people who are deaf and an online chat service. (Details of these organizations are included in the resources section at the end of this chapter.)

- Write a letter to your doctor.

- Nobody will be angry with you or feel that you are any less of a person if you ask for help. If it is difficult to talk to a member of your family or a friend, an email or letter might be easier. Explain how you are feeling and that you want help. If you cannot describe how you are feeling, you can tell them you cannot describe how you are feeling.

- If you are a member of a church or other place of worship and you trust your pastor/priest/rabbi, if might be helpful to speak to them.

Remember, these feelings are likely to pass.

Top 10 things to remember from Chapter 4

1. There are many different types of drugs, alcohol and other substances that you may come across. It is important that you decide what you do and do not want to do with regard to drugs, alcohol and other substances.

2. Some drugs are safe, such as those given to you with a prescription by a qualified doctor or nurse.

3. It can be hard when you desperately want to be liked but the people around you are doing things you do not want to do. However, there are strategies that can allow you to say no to drink and drugs without being looked upon badly.

4. Be aware that when you first take a drug or drink alcohol, it can take some time for the effect of the drug or drink to be noticeable. However, the drug or alcohol is still travelling through your bloodstream, so it is important to be cautious.

5. Some people on the autistic spectrum have been known to self-medicate, which means to take drugs or drink alcohol to make themselves feel better emotionally. This can have many health dangers and there are better ways of helping yourself. If you feel you might be using drugs or alcohol to cope with life, consider talking to your family doctor who can advise you on alternatives.

6. Some people have tried to end their life with drink or drugs. This can cause long-term damage to the body. If you are feeling that you want to end your life, there are free helplines that you can call to talk about your problems (see the resources section at the end of the chapter). The Samaritans in the UK also has an email service. Talking about your problems may help you feel better and more able to cope.

7. If you want to take a health supplement, diet pills or a fat burner, make sure you check that the company that you are buying it from is reputable. Also check that the product is suitable for you by asking your family doctor.

8. Sometimes people will put drugs or more alcohol into a person's drink. This is to make the person drinking the drink less able to perceive danger, sleepy or less able to react. This can allow an attacker to harm the person. Make sure you cover your drink and always watch it being poured.

9. If you do decide to take illegal drugs (I don't condone this), then make sure you have researched what you are going to do and tell a friend what you are going to do in case you need help.

10. Be true to yourself. People should respect you for who you are. If you are someone who does not want to drink or take drugs, then that choice should be respected. You most certainly are not alone. Many non-autistic people as well as many others on the autistic spectrum do not drink or take drugs.

Resources

Books

Tinsley, M. and Hendrickx, S. (2008) *Asperger's Syndrome and Alcohol: Drinking to Cope?* London: Jessica Kingsley Publishers. ISBN: 1843106098

This book is written by a man with Asperger's syndrome and looks at how some people on the spectrum use alcohol to cope.

Organizations

Samaritans

www.samaritans.org

Many people find it helpful to talk to someone they don't know when they are upset or emotionally distressed. The Samaritans provide 'listeners' – people who are trained to offer anyone contacting them someone to listen to them, and will keep the information confidential.

National Suicide Prevention Network

www.suicidepreventionlifeline.org

A US organization which offers support if you are in emotional distress or feeling suicidal.

Talk to Frank

www.talktofrank.com

Talk to Frank is a UK organization which provides information about drugs. Written in an accessible way, this is a useful resource to find out key information such as the names of street drugs, so you can understand what people are talking about.

Websites

National Library of Medicine – Drugs Portal

http://druginfo.nlm.nih.gov/drugportal/drugportal.jsp

This website allows you to search for names of drugs and find out more information about them.

5

PREPARING TO GO OUT

In this chapter

5.1 Introduction

I felt that it was important to include this chapter because women on the autistic spectrum should be able to access their local community. Being able to access local community services, both recreational and businesses, creates the potential to widen social networks and have fun, which in turn increases overall wellbeing and improves mental health.

Also, many people fear for people on the autistic spectrum and worry that something bad will happen to them if they try to live an independent life. As a person on the autistic spectrum, I can tell you that taking risks is important. Sometimes bad things will happen, but this is true for all people. However, there are ways to overcome fear and learn from experience. Simply being protected by someone else all your life will not keep you safe, because nobody can offer that kind of protection indefinitely. What happens when the person is no longer able to keep you safe? The only solution is to learn about things that have affected other women and what they have done to live independent lives and learn from your own experiences. Analyse what went well and what didn't go well, and what information from this experience can be applied/generalized to help you in other situations.

5.2 Pre-planning challenges

When going out, many unexpected things happen. You cannot plan for every eventuality – sometimes things do go wrong.

It is therefore useful to write down, from your own experience, what bothers you (e.g. loud sounds, getting lost). Then write down what you can do to avoid, prevent or cope with those things that you bother you. See Table 5.1 for an example.

Table 5.1 Pre-planning table

I don't like...	If this happens, I need to...	So I should bring... with me
Loud sounds	Listen to music	MP3 player headphones

The 'So I should bring...with me' column can be used like a checklist of things to take when you go out.

Rather than use a table as above, you might find it easier to process the information if you draw it in a flow diagram, as shown in Figure 5.1.

Figure 5.1 Pre-planning flow diagram

5.3 Planning what to do if you need help

'When I have to go to unfamiliar places, I check on the internet which ways I have to go and stick to those. Shortcuts always confuse me and I don't use them often.'

Nicky, research participant

Before you go out, plan who you can ask for help. For example, if you go to a cinema, you could ask someone at the ticket desk/box office for help.

If you are going to a music venue, there will be stewards (people who ensure you find your seat) and possibly bouncers (people at the door who make sure that people adhere to dress codes and rules).

Some venues providing entertainment have a list of permitted and non-permitted items of clothing, which is called a **dress code**. Sometimes these rules are to maintain an appropriate standard of dress, but they can also be there for practical reasons. For example, if people were allowed to wear hoodies (hooded sweater/jumper), it would be difficult to identify people on CCTV because the hood could cover their face. If a fight happened in the night club and it wasn't possible to identify some people on CCTV, the police would not know who to arrest.

You could decide what you might need to ask for. For example, you could ask if there was somewhere quiet you could go.

If you were feeling overwhelmed, one solution would be to go outside of the venue. You could stand on the edge of the smoking area or in the smoking area (if you smoke). If you don't smoke, nobody is likely to take much notice of you standing in or near the smoking area. Other people might think you are waiting for a friend or have come outside for some fresh air.

Try to avoid standing outside in the dark alone, and go back inside the building if there is any fighting or drug dealing happening.

If you are at a music venue and find the sound too loud, some venues have ear plugs kept at the bar (behind the bar).

There is no need to give the ear plugs back to the venue when you go home. If you find sound to be a problem, it would be better for you to get your own ear plugs, which are made specifically for your ears. They will be more comfortable and will probably give your ears better protection because they will fit properly inside your ears.

Before you go out with friends, agree a meeting point should any of you get lost (non- autistic people sometimes get lost too). It is perfectly acceptable and reasonable to tell your friends that you are concerned you will get lost. For example, you may agree to meeting at the ticket booth. Because this is a clearly defined place, you can ask people in the venue where it is and use visual landmarks such as a fire exit signs or the type of flooring to help you remember how to get to it.

Many people I have met who are on the autistic spectrum cannot recognize faces, even those of familiar people. This is a condition called prosopagnosia, which means that the part of your brain that processes visual information does not link, or has problems linking, to the part of the brain that stores memories of faces. If you think you may have prosopagnosia, one thing that may be helpful is to remember the clothing people have on (both their sweater/jumper and T-shirt as they might take their sweater/jumper off) or remember their shoes. From a safety perspective, you may mistake a stranger for someone you know, and this could lead you into a dangerous situation.

5.3.1 Technology

Many women and men on the autistic spectrum – and many non-autistic people too – find technology immensely helpful for staying safe. Below is a summary of the ways people use technology, I know that most readers are probably aware of technology, but this section may help some people.

COMPUTERS

Throughout this chapter I have made reference to Google, which is what is known in tech speak (technology language) as a search engine. A search engine is a website that allows a person to type in words (terms) and then search the entire internet for references/instances of those terms.

Google Maps is an excellent maps website. Not only can you see maps of many towns, cities and villages around the world, often in great detail, but you can also plan journeys and view many streets as photographs. You can walk (virtually) from a subway station to a library, for example. This can be very useful for ascertaining whether a street is well lit (well-lit streets are safer at night, as people can't lurk in the shadows) because you can see from the photographs if there are many street lights or none at all.

MOBILE PHONES/SMARTPHONES

Mobile phones and smartphones have become much more affordable and versatile over the last few years. Many phone manufacturers now either create or allow for the creation of apps (applications) which can be installed and used on the phone, much like a computer program on a computer. These apps can do all kinds of things – for example, convert text to speech. If you were unable to speak, a text-to-speech app could allow you to communicate with others.

Smartphones also often incorporate a map system and GPS (global positioning service) which allows the phone to show you on a map exactly where you are. Some map programs can even tell you how to get to a particular place with directions for walking, driving or public transport. Of course, phones also allow you to text or call other people for help.

In-car GPS system/satellite navigation

This allows you to have a computer inside your car that shows your position on a map and can guide you to particular destinations.

However, be aware that in some large cities the signal is often not good.

5.3.2 Things to remember with technology

- Make sure it is charged.

- As far as possible, avoid becoming completely reliant on technology and have an alternative method for overcoming the problem that technology helps you with.

- Some devices can use an emergency battery so it would be a good idea to purchase one.

- Make sure the device is insured in case it is stolen/breaks.

- When using any device, try to be vigilant of who is around you.

5.4 Being aware of the area you are in/are going to

Within any geographical area, there are likely to be particular areas where there is a greater risk of crime. Therefore, if you go to these areas, you may need to change your behaviour. For example, it would be advisable to stay away from areas where drug dealing was taking place. Should you encounter this behaviour, however, it would be unadvisable to look shocked. People might attack you if they considered you a threat – if, for example, they assumed you were going to tell the police.

Many people on the autistic spectrum find it hard to control their facial expressions. In the scenario described above, one solution would be to chew some chewing gum. Nobody will consider this unusual, and your facial muscles will be being used to chew the gum and therefore you will look less shocked.

If you are planning on going somewhere new, even within your own city, do your research first to find out if the area is safe. Use websites such as Google to learn about the neighbourhood.

Follow the steps below:

- If you are unsure of the name of the neighbourhood that the place or venue you are going to is in, go to a website such as www.wikipedia.org and type into the search box the name of the venue and city, for example 'Great American Music Hall San Francisco'. (I am very dyslexic and find it easier to use Google for this because Google can spell better than me and better than Wikipedia.) The description should say which neighbourhood the venue is in. Because Wikipedia can be added to by anyone, some of the information may be biased.

  This means that people will add their personal opinions; however, if you need a brief overview of something, such as which neighbourhood a venue is in, it can be very helpful.

- Next, Google the name of the neighbourhood and read the websites available to help you judge what kind of neighbourhood it is. (TripAdvisor can also be a good source of information since it often contains reviews of places, but be aware that some people post negative comments because they have unrealistic expectations or enjoy complaining. It is better to judge what a place is like by whether there is mostly positive feedback.)

- Use online forums. You can make a judgement about what kind of area you are going to by asking questions such as 'Is this area safe for a lone woman at night?' and reading the replies you receive. If you are still unsure if an area is safe or not, then ask the tourist information office.

Be sure to plan your journey. This may help reduce your anxiety. Do not prevent yourself from doing things because you are scared. If you do some research about where you want to go and list the risks and how you can overcome the risks, you can still enjoy life. But you need to face your fears.

To **face your fears** means to do the things you are scared or fearful of.

Anna, a professional working with people on the autistic spectrum, recommends writing down what it is you are scared of – for example, travelling by bus – and writing down all the small steps it takes to ride the bus. Here is an example:

1. Leave the house, close the front door and lock it.

2. Walk to the end of the road.

3. Turn left and walk to the bus stop.

4. Wait for the bus.

5. Get on the bus.

6. Ask for a ticket and pay for the ticket.

7. Sit down on the bus.

8. Ring the bus bell when you arrive at where you want to get off.

9. Get off the bus.

A **step**, in this context, is one instruction from a list of instructions or actions that go in a particular order. For example, each number in the above list is a step.

Anna goes on to say that you should write down how you think you will feel about doing each step, and recommends *The Incredible 5-Point Scale* by Kari Dunn Buron. I also like this book. Use *The Incredible 5-Point Scale* to rate how high you think your anxiety will be. Also, write down what you are scared of, for example 'I am scared people will laugh at me.'

After completing a step, write down your experience of it (or you could draw your experiences if this is easier). Anna stresses the importance of writing down what your anxiety rating actually was. Review the list of things you were scared of (e.g. 'that people would laugh at me') and write down what happened (e.g. 'nobody noticed I had gone outside' or 'nobody laughed at me, people were polite'). Do this for each step, and make sure you congratulate yourself for achieving each small step. It is important that you try to think positively. Rather than thinking, 'Well, everyone else can do this so easily and I can't – it's not fair!' you could think, 'By learning to overcome my fears, I will be a stronger person.'

If you simply allow yourself not to do things because you are scared, this will make life harder and you are likely to become less confident. Because you are almost agreeing with yourself that you can't do something without even trying, you may find yourself in a pattern where you think, 'I would like to do something,' but then you think, 'Oh, but I won't be able to do that.' It is far better for you to try to think 'How can I do that?' If anxiety is a problem for you, Chapter 10 has an anxiety strategy which may be useful. Also consider CBT (cognitive behaviour therapy); this is best provided by someone who understands autism.

5.5 When things go wrong and you need to let someone know you are on the autistic spectrum

'Go places with others or friends. Carry a small card that gives steps to take if lost and information about you.'

Jennifer, research participant

5.5.1 Autism alert cards

There may be instances where you will need help, especially if you know you become nonverbal (cannot speak) under a lot of stress or find it hard to articulate what you are feeling. You could consider carrying an autism alert card.

An autism alert card is the size of a business card or credit card. Sometimes it comes in a small plastic wallet. If your card comes in a wallet, you can also put in the wallet a folded A4 sheet of paper with detailed instructions on what to do to help you.

The card itself explains that you are on the autistic spectrum and what to do if you need help. It also contains contact information for someone who the person reading the card could get in touch with (e.g. your partner or parents).

Autism alert cards

- In the UK, the National Autistic Society and Autistic Rights Group Highland have created their own.

- In the USA, www.zazzle.com has a template for you to make your own.

- In Australia, Autism Victoria sells them.

See the resources section at the end of the chapter for details.

When adapting these cards for your personal needs, think about what could help you, such as someone prompting you to listen to music or do up your jacket. Are there things people should definitely not do (e.g. touch you)? This might be hard to think about, so it could be useful to ask someone who knows you well. This information could be added to the A4 folded sheet that goes into the wallet. Consider writing the information in bullet points which may be easier and faster to read.

5.6 Being vigilant

> 'Never leave a drink unattended. Stay with your friends when you go out. Don't let a strange guy isolate you. Don't take alcohol or other drugs from guys unless you know them very well. It might not be what they tell you it is and could be tampered with.'
>
> *Beth, research participant*

5.6.1 Being vigilant when out or at other people's homes

Although this is supposed to be a chapter about going places, some of these issues also apply to people in your home or in other people's homes.

In her advice above, Beth describes several useful tactics for staying safe. Below I have explained each point in more detail.

- Keep a hand over your drink when at a bar or outside your own home or a friend's home (unless at a busy party).

   When you go out to a bar or a restaurant, it is important to know that if you leave a drink unattended (e.g. if you go to the toilet, you might leave your drink on the bar), there are some people who might see that as an opportunity to put a drug or more alcohol in your drink. Sometimes people do this as a joke, but sometimes they want to make you more vulnerable so they can hurt you in some way.

   If you need to leave your drink unattended you could:

   □ ask a friend to look after your drink

   □ drink it before you leave

   □ in an emergency (e.g. if you needed to throw up), take your drink with you or do not drink your drink when you return if you have left it unattended.

- If you go to a bar or a club or another busy venue, make sure you stay near your friends or the people you go with.

   Don't just assume that since you can see them they will be able to see you, particularly if you are on the other side of a room to your friends. If you stay together in a group, you are less likely to be targeted by opportunistic people looking to hurt other people.

- Sometimes men and women may try to get you on your own – Beth describes this as *isolating* you.

   They might do this by standing in front of you with their back to your friends or asking you to come with them somewhere. If this is the first time you have met the person, this behaviour is cause for concern. They may just be drunk or intoxicated and not thinking about how their behaviour could be interpreted. If you are with friends, go and stand with them; if you are alone, go to where there are other people. You can also ask the person who is trying to get you alone to please leave you alone.

   How can you get away from someone you do not know in a busy environment such as night club or bar? Many women use this strategy. If you are somewhere other than close to the toilets, tell the person you want to get away from that you need the toilet. Ask them to wait for you where they are (e.g. you could say, 'I'm going to the toilet, just wait for me here'). Then when you have been to the toilet (you don't have to use the toilet – you can just go to the bathroom and come out again), you go somewhere else in the venue in the opposite direction to the person you want to get away from. This might seem very dishonest, but it is an acceptable strategy in this situation because it keeps you safe.

- Sometimes people offer you drink or drugs. Sometimes they may lie about what it is they are giving you, particularly if their intentions are not good. When you know someone well, you can decide if you trust them, but if you do not know the person well, the best thing to do would be to decline their offer politely. It is probably OK if they are offering you a drink from the bar, but you must watch the drink being poured.

- When you are not drinking your drink, place your hand over the top of the glass so nobody can drop anything in it.

- Before you go out, decide what you will do if you start to feel ill. If you start feeling dizzy, particularly if you don't feel you have drunk very much alcohol, drink some water. Ask your friends for help. If you are alone, call the relevant emergency number below:

  □ 999 UK

  □ 911 USA

  □ 000 Australia

  □ 112 Australia (mobile)

  □ 106 Australia (text phones).

Ask for an ambulance and explain what has happened.

Don't let the above put you off (stop you or make you too anxious) going out. Just be aware of what is happening around you.

5.6.2 Being vigilant while walking

'When you are in an unfamiliar and potentially dangerous place, never give people the impression that you are lost (by standing on the street and looking at a map, for example). You must always walk with confidence as if you know where you are going – this makes you less vulnerable to predators.'

Jay Blue, research participant

As Jay Blue explains above, it's important to look as confident as possible. Note that it fine to ask someone where a particular place is, but it's advisable to ask shopkeepers, rather than a passerby, as they are less likely to be a threat.

A **passerby** is someone just walking down the street.

5.6.3 Ways to look confident when walking

Practise the information contained in this section in front of a full-length mirror (i.e. one in which you can see your whole body) or with a friend or someone you trust.

- Remember that non-autistic people are frequently unconfident but pretend (act) that they are confident. If you find this concept difficult to understand or use, think of a favourite actor/character in TV or film who you think is confident (e.g. the Doctor in *Doctor Who*). If you are not sure or cannot tell who is confident and who is not, ask friends who have seen the TV series or film you are thinking about. The actor portraying this character may well be feeling nervous and unconfident about playing this role. Since it is so important for him to appear confident, however, there will be directions within the script and the director will tell the actor how to behave. In particular scenes he will be asked to act as if he is confident. It may help you to imagine that you are an actress. If this is confusing or difficult, that is OK.

- Before you leave to go out, list some calming thoughts that you can think of should you become nervous or anxious – for example, if you like dogs, you might think about dogs. Many people's facial expressions mirror their emotional state. If you're feeling calmer because you are thinking a calming thought, your facial expression is more likely to look calm. Be aware that things may look different to how you imagine. Keep your face as relaxed as possible (practise this in the mirror), don't hunch your shoulders, and walk with your head up (not staring at the sky). (Sometimes looking down at your feet is OK for a short period of time when avoiding a dangerous situation.)

    When you walk, don't take small tiny steps or massive big steps; just walk as you normally would (practise in the mirror). When anxious, some people tiptoe (walk on their toes rather than placing the sole of their feet on the floor); this could appear unconfident to other people. If you look confident, you are less likely to attract hassle or trouble from other people.

- If you have a smartphone with a map or GPS function, it is fine to look at this in neighbourhoods that don't experience a lot of crime (do your research online first as to what kind of neighbourhood you're in).

    If you do not have a phone with map capabilities, you may find it better to print a small A4 map which can be folded and carried in your pocket, rather than a large full-size map. You could obtain this map from a website such as Google Maps. Some websites also give you walking directions in many parts of the world.

- Chew gum (as previously discussed).

5.7 Having a plan B

'I never leave home without scouting out the route to a new location first. I use Google Maps to get me the right directions, and I print those for reference, even though I use my GPS system. The printed directions are there just in case the GPS doesn't work.'

Anouschka, research participant

🔍 A **plan B** is sometimes called a contingency plan or an alternative plan. It is a plan of what to do if your original plan goes wrong. For example, if you planned to walk to the store on White Oak Street, and White Oak Street was closed, plan B would be to go to a different store.

Anouschka uses a printed-out map from Google Maps as her plan B. Her plan A (the first thing she will do) is to use her GPS system.

Sometimes, just having planned out a plan B can make you feel more confident and self-assured. Using visual landmarks such as subway stations or particular shops may also be helpful for remembering a route.

Don't underestimate the effect that visual stimulation can have on cognitive processing. If you are someone who finds it hard to filter out information, then perhaps you could consider sunglasses, tinted glasses or coloured lenses.

Common visual difficulties

Lots of people on the autistic spectrum have greatly been helped by coloured lenses. Sometimes this is because they have Irlen syndrome. (More information can be found at www.irlenuk.com or, in the USA, at www.irlen.com.)

One simple way to find out if coloured lenses help you is to go to a sunglasses shop and try on different coloured lenses (e.g. pink, blue or yellow). If you find your vision is improved, you could buy a pair of inexpensive sunglasses. If you feel you might have Irlen syndrome, make an appointment to see a specialist.

5.8 What to do if strangers are bothering you

If you find yourself in a situation where a stranger will not leave you alone, or if they are following you or calling you abusive names, these are some things you can do to try to resolve the situation:

- If you can, look the person in the eye (don't do this if it is painful) and tell them that they are being disrespectful and to please leave you alone. Make your body as straight as you can and speak in a loud, clear voice. Try not to let your voice sound too high-pitched (as you would if you were anxious) or flat.

- Walk away from the person, but do not run unless you feel physically threatened.

- Go into a shop or other building that has staff and ask for help.

- Consider carrying a rape alarm. In the unlikely event that someone tries to rape you or attack you physically, the rape alarm's cord can be pulled and it will omit a high-pitched noise which, although unpleasant, will scare off most attackers.

5.8.1 Why people intentionally upset others

There are some people who enjoy making other people upset. This can be very hard to understand, particularly if you are a conscientious person and would not like to make others feel bad.

If the person who is being horrible to you is a stranger, it is unlikely that they are doing it because of who you are. It is more likely they've decided they want to be horrible to someone. They may think you are an easier target because you are a woman and because most women are not as physically strong as men due to their physiology. (This does not mean women are weak; they are often smaller than men and simply don't have the body mass for the amount of muscle some men have. This is a generalization, however, and of course there are women who are as strong as men, and men who are not as strong as the average woman.)

5.9 Deciding how much of your body others see

It is your choice how much people see of your body. But be aware that if you are wearing clothes that show part of your breasts or very short shorts (that go no lower than the top of your thigh), some men misread this as a sign that you are promiscuous.

The same is true of wearing shirts/tops which are see-through or very lacey with holes in them so you can see a lot of your skin.

Also be wary of wearing sexually suggestive slogans. It could lead some people to make judgements about you.

You should choose how you dress and be comfortable with what you wear. Just take into consideration what others may think. From a safety perspective, what you wear could cause men to come up to you and ask you for sex. If you feel confident in dealing with this, then that's OK.

The other point to consider here is that the rules are slightly different when you are with a group of women. For example, if you went to someone's hen party (a party for a woman before she gets married), and you all decided to wear short pink tutus, revealing tops and a fake penis on a chain around your neck, then this is safer than behaving this way on your own.

5.10 Public transport

Public transport can be accessed by anyone. Some of those people will be people you are comfortable with; others may not be. Below is a summary of things it may be useful to think about when using or planning to use public transport.

- Buses and trains may stop at certain times during the day or night, so make sure you check that your service will still be running when you are going somewhere or going home. Do this by looking at the service's website or by calling the service provider. If you are unsure of how to contact the correct person, then the tourist information office in your locality may be able to help, or ask someone you know who is familiar with the local area. Some bus stops and most stations will have timetables.

- It may be helpful to sit near the driver or conductor (this may make you feel safer). Being on the autistic spectrum is perceived as a disability by most people in society. If you feel you would benefit from using the disabled priority seats, then do so. Some transport authorities require you to have a disabled permit to use the priority seats; contact your transport provider to ask about this. In the UK, you can apply for a freedom pass.

- If you are on a bus or train that has double seats, choose a double seat that is empty or sit next to someone in the first empty seat you see, or stand up. Note that some modes of transport (e.g. minivans) may not permit you to stand.

- Do not sit in a carriage alone or just with a man. If you feel unsafe, get off at the next stop and change carriage.

- If someone starts talking to you and you do not want to talk to them, say, 'I'm sorry, I do not feel like talking now,' or ignore them and get off at the next stop and change carriage, or get the next bus.

- Do not give your phone number to someone if you do not want to. You can say, 'I don't know my number' (even if you do) or just no.

Top 10 things to remember from Chapter 5

1. Planning a trip away from home, as opposed to going spontaneously, even if it is just to the shops, can help to make you feel less anxious and more able to cope.

2. If you are going somewhere new, especially at night (when it is darker and therefore there are more opportunities for people to hurt others), research what the area near the venue is like (e.g. is it an area with a lot of crime? Is it well lit with lots of street lights?).

3. There are a lot of dangers, but many people go out of their homes and do all kinds of things and never have a problem.

Being vigilant and planning as much as possible will reduce the likelihood of problems you might encounter while away from your home.

4. Always have a plan B (i.e. an alternative plan). If plan A is to take the bus home, but there are no buses, then plan B would be to take a taxi home.

5. Make sure your mobile/cell phone is fully charged. A checklist of things you need to take with you might be helpful. You could place this by the door or where you will see it before you leave the house.

6. To manage effectively when you are out of your home on your own, you need to understand what your triggers are (i.e. what upsets or overwhelms you) and have a plan of how to overcome or avoid those things.

7. Some people have a condition known as prosopagnosia which affects the person's ability to recognize faces (even of familiar people such as family).

8. Google Maps (www.google.com/maps) has a street-view function, allowing you to 'virtually' walk from one place to another (e.g. from a public transport stop to a wine bar). This can be a useful tool for identifying visual landmarks to help you navigate. Also, when you are looking at Google Maps, there are fewer stimuli than if you were there in real life, and therefore less information to process.

9. It is important to act confidently even if you do not feel confident. If you look lost or scared, this can make you a target for people who are opportunistic and choose the easiest target available. Someone who looks lost is an easier target than someone who looks as if they know where they are going. Someone who is lost might be disorientated or overwhelmed and not notice a thief, for example.

10. If someone keeps talking to you and you don't want them to (particularly if they move closer to you), say you don't

want to talk right now. If you are on public transport that is frequent, get off at the next stop and get on the next carriage (if on a train or subway) or wait for the next bus.

Resources

Book

Buron, K.D. and Curtis, M. (2003) *The Incredible 5-Point Scale: Assisting Students with Autism Spectrum Disorders in Understanding Social Interactions and Controlling Their Emotional Responses.* Shawnee Mission, KS: Autism Asperger Publishing Co. ISBN: 1931282528

Don't be put off that this is a children's book – it is a fantastic resource with many useful strategies in it, which are simple to implement. There is also a version for adolescents.

Autism alert cards

The following organizations supply autism alert cards in their respective countries.

US

zazzle.com
www.zazzle.com/autistic_alert_card_business_card-240121816207249757

UK

The National Autistic Society
www.nas.org.uk

Scotland

Autistic Rights Group Highland
www.arghighland.co.uk

Australia

Autism Victoria
www.amaze.org.au

6

INTERNET, MOBILE DEVICES AND DIGITAL INFORMATION SHARING

In this chapter

6.1 Introduction

Devices able to make use of the internet have become more common and more affordable. Many websites, apps and programs have been designed for people on the autistic spectrum, often *by* people on the autistic spectrum. Via the internet, people have been making contact with each other, enjoying shared interests, gaining new interests and even meeting romantic partners.

The internet and devices that use the internet have many advantages, but there are some safety issues to be aware of.

6.2 Viruses and other online parasites

The internet is full of confusing jargon (terms used to describe things). Some of this jargon is used to describe things that can damage your computer. If you are using the internet, being aware of what these words mean is very important, because it means that you can protect yourself from them. Below are some examples.

6.2.1 Virus

A virus is a program that has a negative effect on a computer. Effects could be deleting files or making the computer stop working. Viruses are designed to replicate by attaching themselves to programs or other computer files and then being copied or downloaded on to another computer.

6.2.2 Trojan horse

A Trojan horse is a computer program that is often downloaded either as part of what appears to be or is pretending to be a legitimate program. Once the Trojan horse is installed on your computer, it allows a 'hacker' (someone who controls other people's computers without the owner's consent) to use a program to control your computer. They do this via the internet or via the network if you are part of one (e.g. in a library or university). Hackers can also copy and then use the personal information (e.g. bank account details) that may be stored on your computer or information that you type.

6.2.3 Worms

A computer worm is a program that replicates itself. The replication creates added network or internet traffic, which, if replicated enough, can slow down connections so much that the internet or network could become unusable.

6.2.4 Links and downloads

Some people will set traps on the internet so that you download viruses when you think you are downloading something else.

Here are some things to look out for/be aware of:

- Pop-up ads are boxes that appear on the screen when browsing/viewing the internet. They may contain a cancel or close button: ignore this. Close them in the same way you would any other window.

- Sometimes a friend may send you a link in an email – for example, www.gobledeygoop.com/hello. If you were not expecting to be sent a link, or the way the email is written isn't the way your friend would have written it, or this link doesn't seem like something that would interest you or your friend, do not click on it. Create a new blank email. Email your friend and ask if they intended to send you the link. Also be aware that there are now what are called tiny URLs. These are short web address. Again, be sure that the person intended to send it to you.

- Make sure you keep your virus checker (anti-virus software) and/or security systems (such as a firewall) up to date.

- If you want to download a program, make sure you trust the website.

Trusting a website means that you think it is legitimate (i.e. you think that the website is real).

- If you are unsure as to whether you should trust the website, use Google to search for the name of the website. Look through the search results for online forums/message boards where people have talked about the site, or for other references. References (mentions) make it more credible and therefore more likely to be trustworthy. If the search results have postings and messages from people who say the website you want to use is not trustworthy, then do not use it.

- Be wary of pop-up boxes that say they have scanned your computer and that you have viruses. They recommend you should buy their products to get rid of the viruses. These are often scams. As above, use Google to research the name of the software the pop-up box is trying to sell you. If you decide you want to buy the software, Google the manufacturer of the software and download directly from the manufacturer's website, instead of following (clicking on) the link in the pop-up box.

- Sometimes you may see an offer to download a computer pet or animal. These are quite often a disguise for spyware.

Spyware are computer programs that record information such as websites you have visited. This information is then sent to another person so that you can have advertising targeted at you – so that the pop-up boxes that appear on the screen might be things you would be interested in.

- Sometimes they are also used to disguise viruses. If you are unsure, Google the name of the program or animal/pet and see what comes up. If there are lots of websites on which people say how much they love their pet and seem not to be experiencing problems, then it is probably OK to download it. But if there are websites where people have commented that their computer has stopped working or files have gone missing, don't download the program. If you cannot find any information about it, don't download it.

6.2.5 Trolls

A troll is a person who posts on a website deliberately to upset others and spoil a website for other users. Trolls are often found on 'in memory of' pages. On social networking websites such as Facebook, these pages are set up in memory of someone who has died so that others can post messages to the family or memories of the person. This can be very comforting for family and friends, and help them cope with the sadness when someone dies. A troll leaves disrespectful or hurtful messages, with the aim of deliberately causing hurt or offence, or of annoying people. They do this because they find it fun.

6.3 Lying

Be very aware that people who you do not know in real life can lie on the internet and may well do so. People may lie because they want to convince you to do something (e.g. meet them or give them money). Particularly if you are a teenager, be aware that there are some adults who deliberately pose as children in order to befriend children and then hurt them.

6.3.1 Paedophiles

A paedophile is an adult who enjoys having sex with children. This is illegal and very damaging to children. It can be very difficult to know if someone is a paedophile (if you do not know the person in real life), but often there are patterns in their behaviour which may include grooming.

6.3.2 Grooming

Grooming is when an abuser is nice to someone so that the person will want to spend time with them. This then gives the abuser the opportunity to abuse the other person.

6.3.3 Adult sex abusers

People forget that adults can also be sexually abused. Some people are very convincing and can make you think you want to do something when you do not. They also groom people in the same way as paedophiles; they are nice to you because that will make you want to spend time with them and trust them. This allows them the opportunity to abuse you.

6.4 Online etiquette

When communicating with people online, there are a few things that people do to be polite to others. Below I have listed some things that may be useful to know from a safety perspective. Being polite will help you stay out of arguments.

- Using CAPITALS means you are SHOUTING (metaphorically). People will interpret this as if you were having a face-to-face or phone conversation with them and think you were shouting. This can be considered rude. However, there may be some websites that specify capitals; in these circumstances, it is fine to use them.

- If someone is doing well and says this on a social networking website, it is rude to reply to their comment in a negative way. For example, if they said, 'My dad's just bought me a new car,' and you replied, 'Well, some of us have to earn our cars,' this would be considered rude. If someone is happy about something in a message, unless you feel there is a danger or threat that may happen as a consequence of this, reply in a positive manner or not at all.

- Do not tell others what they should do or pass judgement on their life.

To **pass judgement** on someone means to tell someone what you think of what they are doing with their life. Most people are glad to receive compliments, but unless they are directly hurting you or someone else, then do not say they are doing a bad thing unless they ask for your opinion. Also do not tell people what they should be doing with their life. Make suggestions but don't dictate, as this offends people because they feel as if what you are really saying is 'I know better than you'.

This is considered disrespectful and will result in you losing friends. Other people may do things you do not agree with, but they are entitled to their decisions as long as they are not abusing you in anyway.

- Normally, people expect you to wait for them to reply to a message you have sent. If they do not reply for some time (e.g. a week), you could send them one more message, but no more until you receive a reply. If they continue not to reply to you, then it is unlikely that they are your friend, unless something has happened in their life which means that they have spent some time away from the internet. Or perhaps they are someone who does not check their messages often.

Unfortunately, you will come across rude and disrespectful people on the internet. It is best to ignore these people and try to be as respectful to others as you can. Everyone makes mistakes. Nobody is expecting you to be perfect, and you do not have to actively engage with rude people or try to make them behave in a more polite way.

If you are finding that you keep meeting people who are disrespectful, go to other message boards, Facebook groups or other places on the internet to meet people.

6.5 Online friends vs. real-life friends

'I used to join groups and trust that the people I had around me were as upfront and honest as me. Then I learned to see that they were a community of individuals, much like any community – plenty of people you shouldn't trust.'

Aspergirrl, research participant

There are many different kinds of people online (i.e. using the internet). There will be people with good intentions and people who do not have good intentions. It would not be right not to trust anyone, as this would prevent you from building relationships with people. Always be cautious and know that there are trolls and other disreputable people using the internet, but there are also many nice people. Use the ladder of trust from Chapter 1 as a way to think about the information you share with someone else.

(?) **Virtual friendships** are friendships with people you do not see in real life but communicate with via the internet.

(?) A **real-life friend** is someone you see face to face.

Virtual friendships often work a little differently to real-life friendships. For example, being friends with people on Facebook is not the same as being friends with them in real life – supporting one another emotionally, spending time together, enjoying each other's company. Sometimes someone will 'friend' you (i.e. add you as a friend on a website such as Facebook) because they want to read your status updates and find out what you are doing in your life. In real life, someone would become your friend because they liked you and wanted to spend time with you. Essentially, friending someone on Facebook does not mean that the other person necessarily cares about you (although it is possible that they do); a friend request is not confirmation that this person is your friend, because friends share mutual interests, time together and actively care for each other (i.e. they will help you and you will help them). A real friendship is built over time and a friend request alone does not mean that the person is a friend.

Refer to the information on types of friends in Chapter 1.

> Remember that having lots of friends or being liked by many people may not be as important as being loved and cared about by a few friends who know you well and whom you know well. What is more important to you? Lots of friends or friends who know you well and care about you?

6.5.1 Pretending to be your friend because they want something

Unfortunately, there are people who would like to hurt other people's feelings or take other people's belongings or money away, and people who like embarrassing or humiliating other people via the internet.

Sometimes they may try to befriend you. This could be via email. For example, they may email you and write, 'I saw your profile and I would really like to get to know you.'

If people contact you and you do not know them, these people may want to scam you. A scam is when someone tells you a lie to make you give them money or other possessions. Scamming is a type of manipulation. People wanting to scam you may offer you business deals, special offers or loans, or ask to transfer money to your bank account. These kinds of emails are almost always scams – ignore them!

6.6 Boundaries online

Elsewhere in this book I have talked about boundaries (see Chapter 1). Just as with real-life friends, online friendships need boundaries. Boundaries are like rules for what you will and won't do.

> 'I once read the advice: "don't put any information online that you wouldn't want your mother to know".'
>
> *Carol, research participant*

Some people will follow the advice Carol has quoted above literally and will consider whether they would want their mother to know the information they are posting online. If you take it literally, the advice above depends on your relationship with your mother; some people get on well with their parents and can be very open (share anything) about their interests, hobbies and even their sex life. Other people would not like their mother to know certain information about them, but they are happy for their friends to know.

Other people would not take this advice literally and would interpret it as suggesting that you should always be aware that other people will read what you write.

Sometimes it is very helpful to decide your boundaries and write them down before you come across a situation that requires you to make a decision about whether information should or should not be shared. Doing this beforehand enables you to make decisions when you are not under any pressure. For example, it is easier for most people to decide they will not share photographs of themselves when someone is not asking or demanding that they do this at the time.

When deciding your boundaries, you could have two categories: physical and emotional. Physical could include things like naked photos of you, photos where you are wearing revealing clothes (i.e. clothes that show off your body) and internet sex (this can be done over a webcam and involves participants masturbating and watching each other do so). Emotional could include particular aspects of your life such as details about deaths, sexual experiences, sexuality, autism and anything else that is very personal to you.

Also, your boundaries may change depending on which username/screen name you are using. For example, on Facebook you may be using your real name, but you may be a member of forums where you use a username/screen name (a made-up name).

Decide at what point in knowing someone you will share different types of information.

6.7 Information that you share

Certain information posted on websites such as Facebook could have very negative consequences. Use the ladder of trust in Chapter 1 to help you think about what information you want to share.

In this context, **posted** means information written on a website.

'Be careful who you consider a friend. I now am careful of who I give my phone number out to because I can get harassment down the phone. Just ignore the ones who are looking for attention.'

Karina, research participant

The advice below is only meant as guidance. If you feel strongly that you want to share any of the types of information described below, that is your choice.

You may feel that this list seems obvious or common sense. But many people, including non-autistic people, have given out information on this list without considering the consequences. This is not because they are stupid but simply because the person asking for the information has been very convincing (e.g. saying they go to your school) or the person sharing the information did not anticipate the consequences. You may build relationships with people and want to share this information, and that is OK if you have decided to trust the person.

Some of this information is very similar to the ladder of trust in Chapter 1; however, the information below specifically concerns internet and mobile devices and that is why it is included here.

- *Your name.* If people know your name, they can search for you. Use a screen or username (these are discussed later in this chapter).

- *Exact location.* It is acceptable and reasonable not to be exact about where you live. For example, when I was a teenager I lived in a small village in Suffolk, 30 miles away from three large towns, so I would say I lived near one of those towns. If you were to say you lived in a particular village or town, if the person knew your surname, they could use a telephone directory to find your street address. This would mean they could come to your house and may hurt you or try to persuade you to do particular things (e.g. have sex) or damage your home.

- *Telephone number.* You shouldn't give your home or mobile/ cell number to people you do not know. People could keep calling you, or call you but convince you they are from a company and need to take some personal details, which could result in them scamming you.

- *Bank details* (e.g. account number, branch) as these could be used to take money out of your account.

- The name of your *school, college, university* or *work place.*

- You should give consideration to sharing personal details such as:

     □   *The fact that you are on the autistic spectrum.* People may use this against you. For example, if they know you cannot lie, they might ask you very personal questions and then tell other people what you have said. This could be embarrassing for you and result in teasing from other people. This is why people use screen names so that they can tell people that they are on the autistic spectrum without being identifiable.

     □   *Sexual history.* People could see this as an opportunity to bully you, or they might see it as an opportunity to manipulate you into a situation in which you are forced to have sex with them.

     □   *Things that have gone wrong in your life* (e.g. divorce). People might use this against you or share this information with other people who may bully you because of it.

     □   *Religious or political and moral beliefs.* If others have opposing views, they could start an argument with you. If you want to discuss these issues, go to websites that support your views (e.g. if you are a Christian, go to a Christian forum).

- *Naked or semi-naked photographs.* People might laugh at these and send the photographs to other people. Sharing photographs of yourself with people you do not know, particularly if you are under 18, is not a good idea. Photographs can be used to identify you. Also, you may not want someone to be thinking about your breasts or having sex with you, or laughing at your picture with their friends. Remember, even if you think someone is female, if you do not know them, you cannot know for sure that they are who they say they are.

- *Mother's maiden name.* This is often used as a security question (a question websites ask to identify you), so telling someone your mother's maiden name might give them access to other personal information, because they can pretend to be you and log in as you on websites and change your password.

- *PIN* (personal identification number) for your bank cards as this could mean someone could use information they obtain online to steal money from you.

- *Passwords.*

- *Name of your teachers, boss or other people you know.* Their first name is normally OK, but telling another person's last and first name could allow them to find out which school you are at or where you work, and this would allow someone to stalk you. When you know someone well and trust them in real life, it is OK to tell them the names of your teachers and boss. If you don't know your teacher's first name, then you can say the subject they teach (e.g. my art teacher).

- *Names of places that are unique to your location.* For example, McDonald's are all over the world, but Bar 39 may only be in San Francisco, so telling someone this kind of information could allow them to track you (follow you).

6.7.1 Ways of sharing information safely

'I always use nicknames on the internet.'

Nicky, research participant

Of course, there may be times when you want to share some of the information on the list above. For example, you may want to discuss autism or politics. There are safer ways of doing this than using your real name.

Many people decide not to use their real name, even on websites such as Facebook. You may also want to have an email address or separate email accounts for usernames you create. If your email address that is associated with your username or screen name is yourname@emailprovider.com, then people can still work out your name, and, as previously discussed, your name could allow them to find you.

If you find it hard to think of a nickname (nowadays these are usually referred to as usernames or screen names), then one solution would be to think of two favourite movies or two favourite music albums and take one word from each. For example:

Movies: *Jurassic Park* and *Along Came a Spider*

Username: parkspider

Albums: *California 37* and *Dark Side of the Moon*

Username: californiamoon37

It is also important to have a robust password – that is, a password nobody would guess. Good passwords normally have letters and numbers that are not in an intelligible sequence. So rather than having a password of robyn8891, which is my first name and potentially significant years to me (1988 and 1991), I might make my password r8n9yb1o8. Passwords should also include some capital and some lower-case letters. For example, Hh0Tlng76f would be considered a robust password. You should also have different passwords for different websites. If someone found out that your login name and password for your Facebook account was the same as for your email account, the person (hacker) would have access to your Facebook and email, and could pretend to be you on websites. Because they have access to your email address, you would be unable to change your Facebook details. But if your password is different for your Facebook and email accounts, then even if they have your Facebook password, they could not imitate you as they would not be able to access your email address.

If you need a rule to know how frequently to change your password, I recommend every three months.

Even with a username, people could identify you by your photo. Be careful about which websites you put your photo on. Instead of their photo, some people use pictures of things they like as their picture (avatar) to represent themselves on websites.

Some websites offer privacy settings that allow you to limit who can see particular photos and other information.

6.7.2 What if I want to share personal problems?

Being a human being with problems can be very isolating. Being a human being on the autistic spectrum with problems can be even more isolating. It is natural that you would want to find out if others had had similar difficulties and ask for advice. It is fine to do this using a username/screen name or nickname. You need to understand that this can make you vulnerable (i.e. people can use this information to hurt you). For example, if they knew you had some bad relationship experiences in the past, they could tell you that they love you, when actually they just want to have sex with you. This works because they have told you what they think you want to hear – you have had bad experiences so it is a reasonable assumption to think you would want to be loved.

In real life, the way people deal with this is to build up a trusting relationship with a friend before sharing their problems. To do this, people share small amounts of personal information at a time and judge if they want to share more information by the other person's reaction. This is called building trust. Use the ladder of trust in Chapter 1 as an exercise to further your understanding of this topic. People may just be posting on a message board or forum online because they want to find out information about the problem they are experiencing. Therefore, the type of relationships you have with the people you only meet online will be less trusting than with those people you meet in real life, because you have not gone through the process of building trust with those people. This is why it is better not to use your real name, because using your real name means the person may be able to find out more information about you and contact you and potentially harm you.

6.8 Using webcams/Skype

A great number of people use Skype which is a program that uses VoIP (voice over internet protocol). Skype enables voice and video to be transmitted live over the internet to another program such as MSN.

Sometimes people use webcams as a way to hurt other people.

One thing to be aware of is nudity. People may ask you to take your clothes off as this is amusing or sexually arousing for them.

Or they may show you their naked body or masturbate in front of you (on the screen), or ask you to masturbate. It's important to understand that it is your choice if you want to behave in this way, but be aware that anything you do may be recorded and sent to other people. If it makes you feel uncomfortable, end the conversation and block the person if you want to.

> *(?)* **Blocking someone** means they will not be able to contact you or see when you are online, and you will also not be able to see them online. If you do this by mistake, you can unblock people.

If someone wants to talk to you on Skype, but you do not know them in real life and they won't show their face but they want to see yours, this is a sign either that the person is not who they say they are or that they are just trying to control you. End the conversation and do not talk to this person again.

6.9 Contacting people too much

It can be difficult to know how much to contact someone. Sometimes people may feel that you are romantically interested in them if you contact them too frequently. Others may think you are obsessive and others may not be bothered by it.

If you are unsure about this, you may find the contacting people strategy in Chapter 10 (section 10.1) useful.

6.10 Sexting

Many people raised sexting as a topic in my original survey.

Sexting is sending sexually explicit text messages. The messages could include photographs of your naked body (or receiving them from another person). In some parts of the world, sexting is illegal.

> *(?)* **Pornography** is images or written text depicting erotic behaviour (sexual acts or pictures that include sexual body parts) that is intended to cause sexual excitement. It can be in many forms, such as magazines, books, films, photographs, videos, written stories, the internet. Consider the laws that govern pornography in your country/state.

Not to be confused with making sex-orientated jokes via text message, sexting is about one or both people being sexually aroused and/or having an orgasm or getting close to one. This is because while people are exchanging the messages they often (but not always) masturbate.

> 'Be careful about sexting – it seems safe, innocent, anonymous, but I felt bad about it later.'
>
> *Jacinta, research participant*

You may feel bad about sexting afterwards because you have shared very personal information with another person whom you do not know. Some people feel that sex is something that people should only do if they care about each other, and using a piece of technology depersonalizes it for some people. How do you feel about this?

So consider your views on sex and how you might feel after sexting. Take particular care if you are under 18.

An example of how sexual behaviour via text message or over the internet can be breaking the law

- Sarah, 14, takes a sexual photo of herself (e.g. a photo of her breasts) on her mobile/cell phone and sends it to her boyfriend, who is 15 (called James). Sarah is now potentially guilty of distributing child pornography. James is potentially guilty of possession of child pornography.

- Sarah dumps James. Out for revenge, James sends the photo to his friends at school. James is now also guilty of distributing – and his friends of possession of – child pornography. Sarah is embarrassed as a sexual photo of her circulates school.

- James's friend uploads the photo to his social networking profile, where his photos are visible to the public. James's friend is in breach of website terms and guilty of distributing child pornography.

- Paedophiles browse profiles with loose privacy settings and find image of Sarah. Sarah unwittingly becomes the subject of child pornography for distribution among strangers and paedophiles. She is now at risk of being exploited by paedophiles and sexual predators through the use of blackmail.

In the UK, strengthened laws against possessing indecent images of children (i.e. under 18) ranges from Grade 1 (Facebook images) to 5 (extreme images: life-threatening, serious injury).

Sending indecent images of children/pornographic images via mobile phone is illegal.

6.11 If people are bothering you

Unfortunately, just as anywhere else, there are people on the internet who will bother you, be rude to you, bully you, threaten you or perhaps send you inappropriate images of themselves. Below is a list of things that you can do and remember:

- Often these people are just opportunistic. They do not personally want to hurt you (even if the comments are personal to you). They are just looking for people they can be nasty to and get a reaction out of. For example, if they were calling you a fat slag, then they are just assuming that you care about your looks (they would call you this even if you were thin) and calling you the most offensive name they can think of. They haven't considered your BMI (body mass index) to determine if indeed you would be considered fat; they also haven't reviewed your sexual history. They haven't actually thought their comments through. Do not point this out to them as they will laugh at you; just remember that these comments are factually incorrect. Please try to remember that they just want to be horrible to anyone. They have a problem, not you.

- Most websites now have reporting features. Reporting features are buttons that can report (send a message to people who run the website) a post, video or photo as offensive or inappropriate. If someone is horrible to you, consider reporting them. Do not suffer in silence. However, do not threaten to report people and do not tell them that you have reported them, as both of these actions will cause more arguments.

- If you are using a forum or group, there may be an admin. An admin is someone who makes sure that people respect each other and do not post offensive comments. They also ensure that users of the forum follow the rules. If you contact the admin and explain what is happening, they may be able to offer you some help. They may offer to delete posts or comments from people who are abusive to you and to block users if they are breaking the rules.

- Be careful not to 'bitch'. This is when you complain about someone to a friend who is not an admin, teacher, parent, sibling or another person who will help you. It's OK to ask for advice and it's important to share your problems with your friends; however, be aware that repeatedly complaining about the same incident or person may be perceived as bitching.

'If you are bullied on a certain chat room/website delete your account there.'

Judith, research participant

- If someone is putting pressure on you to tell them something or meet them and you do not want to, tell them to leave you alone. If they will not, block them (this will stop them contacting you). Use the help pages of the website you are using or Google to find out how to block people. If the website does not offer this feature, then close your account. You can always open a new account with a new username/ screen name.

- You may think that someone is stalking you. Stalking is when someone follows you – for example, if you unfriended them on Facebook and they made a new account and then added you again repeatedly or kept messaging you. Or they might be asking other people about you when you had clearly told them to leave you alone. Contact the police and explain you are being stalked.

- If someone has misunderstood something you have said, then reply with a message that states that you are sorry but they have misunderstood what you meant.

- You cannot control someone else's behaviour. If you don't like what they are doing, block them or unfriend them or ask them not to message you. If you keep telling them what to do, they are likely to become upset or angry. If what they are doing is not directed at you, then you can tell them to stop, but let other people fight their own battles and don't get involved with other people's arguments and disagreements.

- Remember that information on the internet isn't all true. Look for references to back up/validate what people write. Decide if you trust the source of information. For example, what your college professor says is likely to be true, but what someone you don't know says may not be as credible.

6.12 People misunderstanding what you write/type

This is a topic that affects both non-autistic people and those on the autistic spectrum.

71 per cent of non-autistic women and 80 per cent of women on the autistic spectrum said things they had written online had been misunderstood.

This can happen in all sorts of different situations.

'I've found I have a very broad sense of humour from slapstick to dry and sarcastic. People tend to think you have one type of humour and that's it. And the first joke you tell or laugh at is what you are. So if I said something silly and shocking and then leave a dry humour comment on their Facebook status, I am being mean or rude or something. The use of constant smileys is helpful (yet annoying).'

Jeni, research participant

Jeni's solution to the problem described above has been to use a smiley ☺ which is created by typing : and) with no space between. These are called emoticons (emotion icons), which are graphics of faces with particular expressions. When someone uses an emoticon, it can explain the emotion they are trying to express. For example, :D means laughing.

It's also important to learn about contexts. There are some contexts where humour would be considered inappropriate by many people.

Humour is not the only type of communication that can be misunderstood.

'I think that I write things very straightforwardly – I mean what I write and write what I mean. But often, others [non-autistic people] "read between the lines" and think I mean something that I have not written. I find this very frustrating and am not sure how to deal with it.'

Jenine Booth, research participant

Reading between the lines means to infer (understand) information that is not actually written. For example, 'I don't really enjoy soccer; it's not good for fat people.' Someone might infer from this that the writer thinks of themselves as fat, because they have said that they don't like soccer and, straight after this, that they do not think it's good for fat people.

'I'm pretty internet wise. It's a large part of who I am and I've come to realize since I was a teenager just how to "cope" with the internet. I'm calm, understanding and always think how I word something before I speak. I never use caps unless it's for a specific reason and I always try to see things from everyone's point of view. I now just ignore anyone who tries to "bully me".'

Stella, research participant

Everyone has their own rules for using the internet, and not everyone finds it easy to think of all the possible points of view someone may have. For example, someone could think about a sentence they have written and feel confident that it could not be misunderstood, but then someone misunderstands it. This happens to most people from time to time.

If you feel this happens to you frequently, or that it might happen to you, there are two options:

- You can tell your trusted friends that you are on the autistic spectrum and that sometimes others may misunderstand you and you might misunderstand them, and ask them, if this happens, to explain the misunderstanding to you as clearly as possible.

- You can do as described above but don't mention being on the autistic spectrum – just say you find understanding others difficult.

6.13 Meeting people from the internet

'If you ever meet anyone on the internet and you plan to meet them in real life, ALWAYS take your friends with you! If whoever you're meeting has a problem with that, then maybe they're not who you think they are. They should understand that you are a woman trying to protect herself. You could even meet more than once with your friends until you feel the person out and feel comfortable enough. ALWAYS meet in a public place. ALWAYS know how to find your way home. I have a horrible sense of direction, so I write down exact directions that get me home from school, home, friends' houses, etc. I have these directions on my notebook, my phone...'

Alex, research participant

As discussed elsewhere in this chapter, sometimes people pretend to be someone they are not. They may do this because they want to have sex with you, take money from you or hurt you in some other way.

It's important not to confuse people changing some particular detail about themselves online in order to keep themselves safe and people who do it to hurt you. For example, if you lived in Birmingham but said you lived in Manchester, then you have a valid reason to say this – so people do not know where you live and therefore cannot stalk you.

But someone who changes key details to make themselves appear attractive or to enable them to hurt another person is very dangerous.

Alex's advice is very good here:

- If you do want to meet someone alone, meet them in a public place, not at their house or your house or a friend's house.

- Meet them with a friend or several friends.

- If they say that they want to meet you alone, this is a sign they may not be who they say they are, so be very cautious.

- Have a route home planned.

Also, if you go alone:

- Tell a friend where you are going.

- Tell a friend who you are going to meet, what their online name is and which site you met them on. This way, if something bad happens to you, the person who you met will be more easily traced.

- Tell other people what time you are likely to get back home. If you live alone, text the friend you told about your meeting when you get home to let them know you're safe.

- Always take your mobile/cell phone with you and make sure it's fully charged.

- If you feel at all uncomfortable, leave and go home. You can say, 'I'm sorry, I need to leave now.'

- Never get into a car with the person or go to their home until you have decided you trust them, and certainly do not do this the first time you meet them.

- Get a friend to meet them and take your friend's advice on whether you should trust them or not.

Sometimes people will twist the truth a bit – for example, say they are 26 when really they are 30. This would be considered a small lie and probably, if the person had been truthful about other things, an insignificant one. However, if the person said they were 30 when they were really 50, this would be a big lie because the difference between the ages is so great. The bigger the lie, the more cautious you should be.

Note: It is the potential *consequence* of a lie that is most important. For example, lying about your age and saying you are 15 when you are actually 19 seems very minor as it is only a few years difference. However, if someone lied about their age because they wanted to have sex with someone under the age of 16 this would be a big lie, because their intention would be to break the law, and the consequence would be that they hurt someone who is younger than them and vulnerable.

6.14 Online dating

Many people use online dating to meet new people. There are now many different websites that cater for all kinds of different people, including people on the autistic spectrum.

As with any kind of dating, it is important to understand your expectations of a romantic partner. Most people have several romantic partners (there is no average number) before finding someone they want to spend the rest of their life with.

The things written previously in this chapter about information that you share are still valid when considering internet dating. There may come a point in your relationship/friendship with another person at which you want to give them your phone number.

If you want to give them your phone number but you are worried about the consequences of this, you could buy a pay-as-you-go (no contract/plan) phone and use this number for them to contact you. As you build trust in each other, you can start to share personal information.

People may try to pressurize you to do things. Only do what you feel comfortable doing; don't meet someone just to please them. Someone who respects you and cares about you will not put pressure on you. You can say to the other person, 'I feel you are pressurizing me.' If they do not stop, don't talk to them.

It is OK if you do not want to meet people in real life; some people have virtual romantic relationships, which are romantic relationships that do not involve meeting up in real life.

Important information

If you do decide to meet someone from an online dating website, ensure you follow the three steps below:

1. Make sure you arrange to meet in a public place.

2. Have an exit plan (i.e. if it goes wrong, plan how you will leave and where you will go).

3. Always tell a trusted friend where you are going, who you are meeting (screen name and website) and when you are likely to return home. Contact the person via text, Facebook message or phone (agree how you will do this before the date) to let them know you have arrived home safely.

You can follow these steps for more than just your first date with someone; you can keep using the steps until you feel comfortable.

If you have had nice time on a date, it is polite to message the person you had the date with to thank them for a nice time. You can also ask them if they would like to see you again. Or if you do not want to see them again, you could say, 'I had a lovely time with you, but I don't feel we have a romantic connection.'

You can also use this phrase if your date asks you if you would like to see them again.

The social rules for online dating are slightly different to other forms of communication.

If someone sends you a message and you decide you do not want to talk to them/message them back, you do not need to reply and this will not be considered rude.

The purpose of online dating is to meet potential dates (boyfriends/girlfriends), so if people do not think they will get on with you, they will not reply to your message. Remember, though, that since they do not know you, they have made a very quick judgement (they have not thought about it for a long period of time). This does not mean you are a failure, unlovable or will not get messaged or replied to by someone else.

Most women, regardless of being on the autistic spectrum or not, have these experiences. You may find you need to message at least 10–15 different people until you get a reply.

Also be aware that some people use internet dating for sex and don't want a relationship at all. Some people may ask you to chat with them via Skype instead of using the dating website's chat services. I would recommend meeting the person before giving them details such as your Skype name as this may be linked to your email address and therefore the person could find out other details about you that you may not want them to know.

6.15 Cyber-bullying

Cyber-bullying is being bullied online. Among other things, it might involve people spreading rumours about you, calling you nasty names online or posting photos of you that have been edited in some way to embarrass you. It is a huge problem for many people, regardless of whether they are on the autistic spectrum or not. But often people on the autistic spectrum have such low self-confidence that the bullying can have a larger impact than it would for someone with greater self-esteem.

6.15.1 What can I do if I am cyber-bullied?

- Tell someone you trust, such as a teacher, parent or close friend. Even though it might seem embarrassing, make sure you tell someone and get their advice on the situation.

- Ask the bully to stop once, but do not engage in a conversation that might make the situation worse. Some people are very good at thinking of comebacks, but this is often much harder for people on the autistic spectrum. If someone makes a comment about you or is spreading rumours, contact the website's admin and report it, but do not reply to the bully after you have asked them to stop.

A **comeback** is a clever reply to an insult, which makes the other person look silly.

- Block people who are bullying you on websites.

- Remember that if someone says something that is not true about you, people who know you well will be more likely to believe your side of the story than a bully's. Just because someone says something about you does not make it true.

- People do not die or have bad luck because they don't repost a message or forward an email that says you must. People write those messages to scare other people and for their own entertainment.

- Check the law in your part of the world with regard to cyber-bullying. What the other person is doing may be illegal.

- Keep a diary as evidence of the cyber-bullying. This may be useful if what the other person is doing is illegal or to show a teacher/therapist.

- Don't use your real name. Some people have several usernames/screen names or nicknames online and choose to keep their real-life friends separate from their online friends.

- Do not email or message someone (including text messages) information that you would not want shared unless you can ensure they will keep it private.

- Change your password for each website about once every three months to minimize the risk of someone finding out your password. Use strong passwords (i.e. ones with letters in both capitals and lower case and numbers).

- If someone is following you around online – for example, if you unfriend them from a site and they create another username and friend you again – and you have made it clear that you never want to hear from them again, this is cyber-stalking.

Make sure you do not become a cyber-bully yourself. It may be natural to want revenge on someone, but this could get you into trouble. Always respect other people's opinions on their own life; don't tell someone you think they are wrong. It is rude to post negative comments on someone's online space (i.e. their page or wall). Do not harass someone by sending them more than one email demanding a reply.

Do not pretend to be someone you are not. Although other people may behave in this way, that doesn't make it OK for you to do the same, and you could hurt others.

Top 10 things to remember from Chapter 6

1. Not everyone you speak to on the internet will be 100 per cent honest. Some people will lie to manipulate/control you, while others may lie to impress you or make you think they are something they are not.

2. Use a screen name/username/nickname to mask your identity so that people do not know who you are in real life. They are then less likely to be able to find your address, telephone number and other contact information.

3. Sexting is illegal in some parts of the world.

4. If you are meeting someone in real life when you have previously only talked to them via the internet, make sure you meet them in a public place. Go with a friend to meet them and/or tell someone you trust where you are going, who you are meeting, the website you met them on and their screen name/username, and when you will return home. Contact that person to inform them when you arrive home. That way, if the person you are meeting online has any bad intentions (e.g. kidnapping you) and you do not return home, the person you told can alert the appropriate people (e.g. your parents or the police). You can agree with them beforehand who you want them to alert.

5. Facebook friends and real-life friends are not the same. If you are friends with someone on a social networking website, this just means you are interested in finding out about each other's lives, but it does not have to mean you care about each other or would want to spend time with them in real life.

6. Decide upon some boundaries for yourself about the information that you will and won't share online.

7. Sometimes people misunderstand what others write/type. If you feel misunderstood, explain this to the person you feel has misunderstood you.

8. Cyber-bullying (i.e. bullying online) has increased in prevalence and is now illegal in some parts of the world. Use Google or a law information service to find out what the law is where you live.

9. Be aware that others may see your behaviour as bullying. For example, sending someone several emails demanding a reply might be seen as harassment.

10. Only download programs/information from trustworthy websites. Googling the name of the website and reading the information that comes up may be one way to ascertain if the website is trustworthy or not.

Resources

Websites

Internet Watch Foundation

www.iwf.org.uk

This is the UK hotline for reporting criminal online content.

Wired Safety

www.wiredsafety.org

This site has information on cyber-bullying and other internet-related problems.

MONEY

In this chapter

7.1 Introduction

Money management is an essential skill for anyone. When you have a job, money management allows you to save up for things you want and to provide yourself with security and continuity. For example, paying a mortgage ensures you will be able to live in the same place since you own it, rather than rent it. When you rent your home, your landlord (the person you pay your rent to) could sell your home and you would have to move. Some people would also consider that they have a social duty to work so that they can pay taxes. Taxes are used to pay for services such as refuse collection and schools. In some countries such as the UK, taxes also pay for healthcare and pensions.

It is important to note, however, that many people on the autistic spectrum do not have jobs or are unable to work. In the UK, only 15 per cent of adults on the autistic spectrum are in full-time employment. As a result, many adults on the autistic spectrum receive benefits and do not have large incomes (i.e. they don't receive a lot of money each month).

Without a job, you do not have the option of doing overtime (working more than your contracted hours for more pay) to pay off debts or save up for a holiday.

Incomes for people who are on (receiving) benefits/social security/pensions are fixed.

A **fixed income** means you only receive a certain amount of money every month.

For people on a fixed income, it is important to manage money effectively because it will be very difficult to rectify any mistakes, such as overspending on a credit card. However, money can be a very abstract concept to many people. You often don't actually see your money in your hand, and so it can be hard to conceptualize exactly how much money you have, how much will come into your bank account each month and how much you should and will spend and/or save.

7.2 If you find managing money hard

'I am useless with money. I would say I am an intelligent woman, but when it comes to money I lack the planning skills to spend and save responsibly.'

E, research participant

Many very highly intelligent people find money difficult and confusing. It is important to try not to feel that having difficulty managing money makes you any less intelligent, because it does not. People are good at different things.

If you find it hard to learn about money, it doesn't mean you are stupid, thick, unintelligent or anything else negative. It just means you find it difficult. There are probably things you find very easy that other people find difficult.

7.3 Budgeting

Budgeting can be a very hard skill to learn. In my survey, non-autistic women had as much difficulty with budgeting as women on the autistic spectrum.

First of all, it's important to understand what budgeting is.

7.3.1 What is budgeting?

Budgeting is the method used to plan out and calculate how much money you have coming into your bank account, how much money you have going out of your bank account (e.g. to pay bills) and how much money, if any, you will have left (and, if you want/are able to, how much of this money you will save). It also involves understanding what you have to buy and when. For example, your rent might need to be paid on the fifth day of every month (5 January, 5 February, etc.) and the phone bill may need paying on the thirtieth day of the month (30 January, 30 February, etc.). But other bills are less predictable. For example, your heating bill is likely to be higher in the winter months than in the summer months. Also, some bills do not come monthly; some come every quarter. This means the year is split into four parts and a bill is sent for each part, so it will come roughly every three months. This is often the case for energy (gas, electricity) bills, so ask your energy supplier about when their four quarters start and end.

Budgeting might seem scary as you may feel bad that you do not have much money coming in or you may have debts. Managing your money effectively through budgeting gives you the best chance of being able to pay off your debts and buy the things you need and want.

7.3.2 Tools to help you budget

Below are some of the tools that might help you budget. Each point is independent of the other points discussed, so if you look at one and think this will not work for you, move on to the next point.

Workbook and/or website

The National Autistic Society, a UK charity (not for profit), worked with an organization called CFEB (Consumer Financial Education Body) to create a website and a workbook about managing money. You can access the website at www.managingmoney.org.uk. There is a link to the NAS online shop where you can purchase the workbook if you would prefer to use it instead of the website.

Visual ways of representing money

If you have difficulty with the abstract concept of money, perhaps it would help to have it displayed visually. There are many ways to do this:

- If you like maths or have some skills in it, you could consider creating a table as shown in Table 7.1.

Table 7.1 Incomings and outgoings

Incomings	Amount £	Outgoings	Amount £
DLA	100	Rent	100
ESA	250	Electric	20
Total	350	Total	120

This is only an example. When you create your table, you may wish to leave blank rows to add more information.

Table 7.1 shows the total incoming and outgoing money. You could write on your table daily and add up how much you have spent each month and subtract it from the money you have coming in each month. Or you can add together everything you have spent each month and add it to the table. Or you could draw a graph such as a bar graph to illustrate this.

- The above strategy may seem very complicated, and it may be easier for you to work out your income and outgoings on a spreadsheet (a computer program designed for organizing mathematical data). You could use Google Docs (an online program which is free to use) to do this. Figures 7.1 and 7.2 give examples.

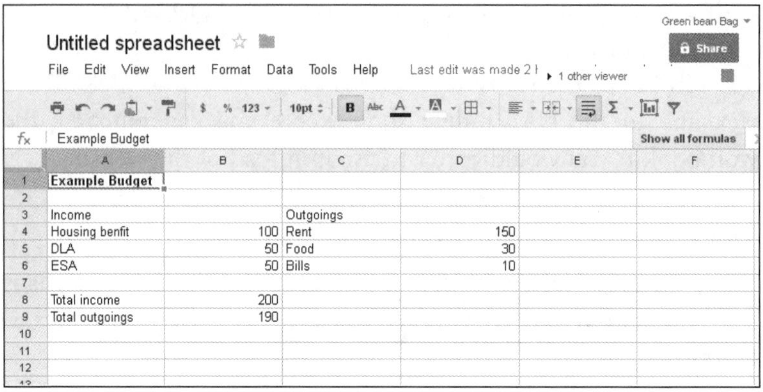

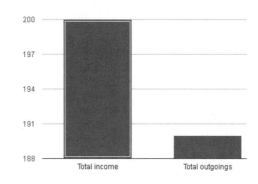

	A	B	C	D	E	F
1	Example Budget					
2						
3	Income		Outgoings			
4	Housing benfit	100	Rent	150		
5	DLA	50	Food	30		
6	ESA	50	Bills	10		
7						
8	Total income	200				
9	Total outgoings	190				
10						
11						
12						

Figure 7.1 Example of a Google Docs spreadsheet

Chart 1

Figure 7.2 Example of a Google Docs bar graph

You could edit (amend) your spreadsheet every day. You can do this from any computer that has access to the internet and where security settings don't prevent access to Google Docs. Although all the information is stored online, the program is safe to use because you need a username and password to access the information.

- You may need something simpler than the above suggestions. For example, you could try the following strategy:

  - Obtain a large jar or clear plastic container (up to 2 litres).

  - Fill it with water and some food colouring.

  - Decide if you are going to use this jar/container to work out how much you have spent daily, weekly or monthly.

  - Set a limit for the increment of time you have chosen – for example, I can spend £10 daily.

  - Mark increments of money on the jar (e.g. £10, £50, £100, £200).

  - When you spend money, write this down in a notebook.

  - At the end of each day, use a cup or spoon or pour out the water until the water remaining in the jar is at the same level as the amount of money that you have left to spend (e.g. if you had £10 left, the water would be at the £10 mark).

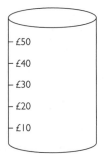

Figure 7.3 Money jar

- Ancient people of the world used to use different types of knots to help them calculate how much money they have spent. To some readers this may seem a little strange; however, to others it may make perfect sense.

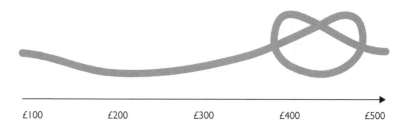

Figure 7.4 Money rope

- Obtain a piece of rope (choose your size, perhaps 1 metre) from a hardware or DIY store.

- Calculate how much money you have coming in this month.

- Choose the type of knot to represent incoming money and outgoing money and write this down.

- Place a knot near one end of the rope to signify the amount (e.g. £500) that you have coming in.

- Use a ruler to space out equal increments – five knots for £500.

- When you spend money, tie a knot in the relevant place on the rope.

- It can be helpful to quantify the amount of money you are spending in real terms (i.e. how many of a particular item can you buy for an amount of money). It's important to find a way of doing this that makes sense to you. You could use your special interest/obsession, as shown in the following example:

Rent	£50	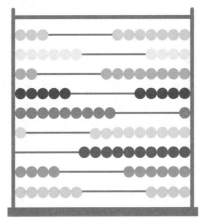

Figure 7.5 An example of how to use special
interests to understand money

Jenny's special interest is animals. In particular, she likes rabbits. She has three rabbits and has to buy 1kg of rabbit food per month which costs £25. When she is working out her budget for the month, she finds it useful to mark her budget with the equivalent of rabbit food. For example:

Rent is £50 per week. For £50 Jenny could buy two bags of rabbit food so she marks her budget like this.

Rent = £50 = 2 × rabbit food.

- Many phones now have apps which can be used to budget and are often free.

- Some people find using an abacus very useful.

Figure 7.6 Abacus

- Maths cubes are commonly used in schools. These are small coloured cubes that can be used to represent numbers. For example:

Figure 7.7 Maths cubes

- Blue cubes could represent £10 – 1 cube = £10, 2 cubes = £20.

- Green cubes could represent 50 (or 5 blue cubes) so 2 green cubes = £100 (or 10 blue cubes).

- You could build a wall or other structure with the cubes (they are small so would fit on a mantelpiece or table). Have the money you have coming in represented in cubes; when you spend money, you remove the relevant cubes.

Spending limits

It can be helpful to set a spending limit. This enables you to know how much you can spend and then work out what you want to spend it on. Follow the steps below to work out a limit:

- First, decide whether you want a daily, weekly or monthly spending limit.

- Step 1: Add up all of your incoming money.

- Step 2: Divide by:

  - 365 if you are calculating your daily spending limit

  - 52 if you are calculating your weekly spending limit

  - 12 if you are calculating your monthly spending limit

  Write down the result of this calculation – this is your daily, weekly or monthly income.

- Step 3: Add your essential outgoings together (e.g. bills, rent, council tax, food shopping, etc.).

- Step 4: Divide by:

  - 365 if you are calculating your daily spending limit

  - 52 if you are calculating your weekly spending limit

  - 12 if you are calculating your monthly spending limit

  Write down the result of this calculation – this is your daily, weekly or monthly outgoings.

- Step 5: Write down the results of Step 2 and Step 4.

- Step 6: Subtract the two numbers you have just written from each other (e.g. if you just wrote down 46.57 and 19.17 then the answer would be $46.57 - 19.17 = 27.4$).

  Write down the result of this calculation – this is your daily, weekly or monthly spending limit.

- Step 7: Each time you spend money, write it down in a notebook or in the notes section of your phone. Write down when you spend money, how much you spend, and what you buy.

- Step 8: Add your spending together:

  - add up what you've spent in one day if you are calculating your daily spending limit

  - add up what you've spent in one week if you are calculating your weekly spending limit

  ▫ add up what you've spent in one month if you are calculating your monthly spending limit

  Write down the result of this calculation – this is your daily, weekly or monthly spending total.

- Step 9: Write down the results of Step 8 and Step 6

- Step 10: Subtract the numbers you have just written from each other (your daily, weekly or monthly spending from your spending limit).

  Write down the result of this calculation – this is how much money you have left over from your spending limit.

- See Figure 7.9 for a visual example of this strategy.

- It might be helpful to have an emergency £20 per month. Use this if you overspend, but be sure to replenish it at the start of each month.

Remember that budgeting is a skill. Like any other skill, you will make mistakes to begin with. For example, you might anticipate being able to save 10 per cent of your earnings and find you can't do this because you are then unable to buy essential things such as food. If this happens, you need to think what you could do differently next time to avoid making the same mistake. If this is difficult for you, then perhaps ask the advice of someone else such as a relative, close friend or financial advisor.

There are also online tools available such as:

- https://budgetbrain.moneysavingexpert.com/budgetplanner

- www.moneyadviceservice.org.uk

See the resources section at the end of the chapter for other useful budgeting websites.

It is also important to spend money on things that make you happy as this will improve your quality of life and wellbeing.

If you take out a loan or borrow money in any other way, make sure you add this to your outgoings and adjust your budget accordingly.

7.4 Spending money on things to make you happy/improve the quality of your life

From a safety perspective, if you are unhappy because you never take a holiday (even though you have the money to) or you never buy a friend a drink at a pub or bar (which might make you feel good and be part of an equal friendship), then your emotional wellbeing may be affected. You may be unhappy because you are not using the resources you have available to you effectively.

> 'My parents were very pennywise, so I learned from an early age to save, save and save some more. When I got my own money, I still adhered to this and ended up still living as if I had nothing to spend. Friends called me tight and I never offered anyone a drink, for instance. I had to learn things like this. And also to spend money on my dreams (I love to travel), though it almost made me physically ill at first to spend so much money on a trip.'
>
> *Carol, research participant*

If you have been taught from an early age the importance of saving, then when you come to make a large purchase such as a holiday, it might make you feel sick, due to anxiety or fear.

Most people have dreams.

In this context, a **dream** is something you really want to do, as opposed to a thought you have while you're asleep. So, in this context, your dream might be to visit New York City or go to night school.

Some of your dreams may be obtainable and some may not. If you have enough money to fulfil (do) your dream, and as long as it is safe to do so and you will have more money coming into your bank account to sustain you, then living your dreams could make you really happy. Even if those dreams are small, they could have a positive impact on your mental health and increase your confidence.

If you have an income that allows you to consider not just buying store brands (e.g. supermarket's baked beans), you may prefer other brands, and in terms of quality of life it may be worthwhile buying other brands because you may feel that they taste better. This may seem obvious to you, but it is not an obvious thought to everyone.

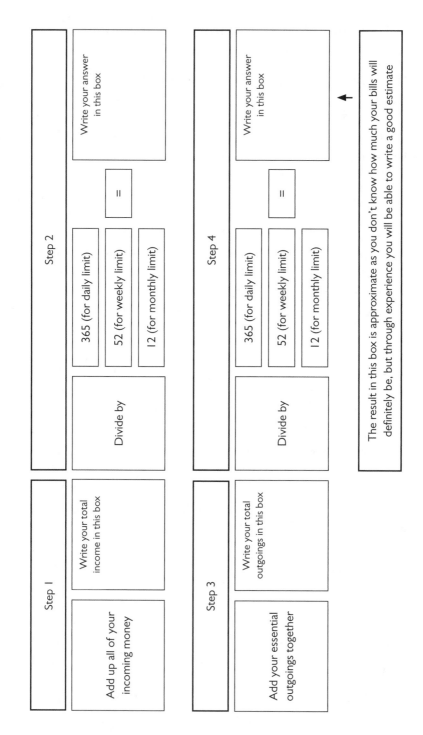

Step 1

Add up all of your incoming money

Write your total income in this box

Step 2

Divide by

365 (for daily limit)

52 (for weekly limit)

12 (for monthly limit)

=

Write your answer in this box

Step 3

Add your essential outgoings together

Write your total outgoings in this box

Step 4

Divide by

365 (for daily limit)

52 (for weekly limit)

12 (for monthly limit)

=

Write your answer in this box

The result in this box is approximate as you don't know how much your bills will definitely be, but through experience you will be able to write a good estimate

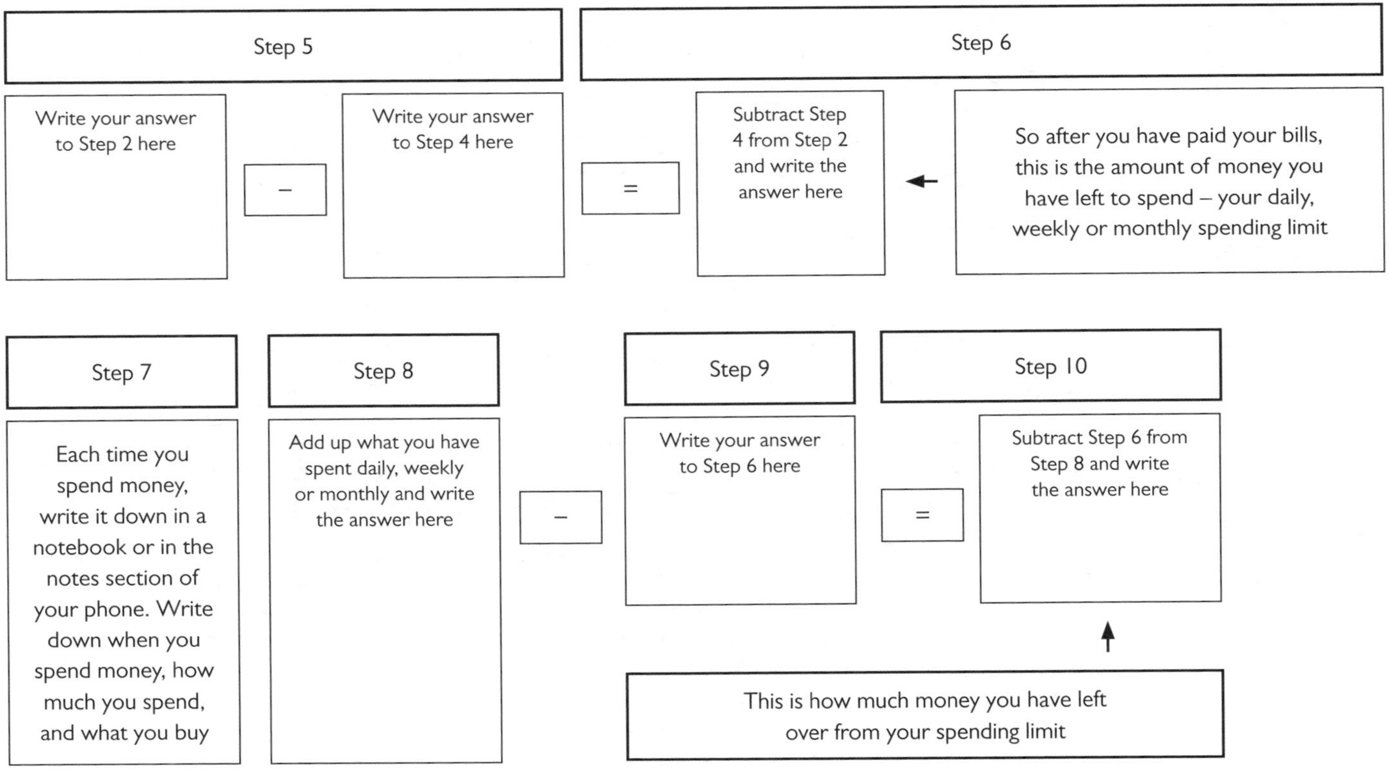

Step 5

Write your answer to Step 2 here

−

Write your answer to Step 4 here

=

Step 6

Subtract Step 4 from Step 2 and write the answer here

So after you have paid your bills, this is the amount of money you have left to spend – your daily, weekly or monthly spending limit

Step 7

Each time you spend money, write it down in a notebook or in the notes section of your phone. Write down when you spend money, how much you spend, and what you buy

Step 8

Add up what you have spent daily, weekly or monthly and write the answer here

−

Step 9

Write your answer to Step 6 here

=

Step 10

Subtract Step 6 from Step 8 and write the answer here

This is how much money you have left over from your spending limit

Figure 7.9 A visual representation of budgeting

7.5 Lending money to other people

'I never buy things I can't afford. I don't borrow money. I only lend small amounts to good friends and as long as they don't pay me back I don't give them more. That way it can't add up to a bigger amount.'

Nicky, research participant

Lots of people have difficulty knowing when to lend money to people and when not. Nicky's strategy of lending good friends money in small amounts (you can decide what you consider to be a small amount) and only lending the person more money if they paid what they borrowed in the past is sensible. However, you might not be able to tell if someone is a good friend or not.

Sometimes it can be hard to say no. You might be desperate to keep friends, or someone might be telling you about what seems like a desperate situation which you could solve for them. Or they promise that they will pay you back very soon.

Being a good friend does not mean doing whatever your friend wants you to do, especially if it causes you hardship (e.g. not being able to buy your weekly groceries) because you do not have enough money having lent it to your friend. A good friend is someone who is supportive, but this does not have to mean supporting your friends financially.

Friends **support** each other in many different ways. For example, listening to your friend is emotionally supporting them.

Throughout life, people have lots of problems and they have to learn to solve those problems for themselves. Sometimes this means that they need help from professionals, or they may need someone to talk things through with and decide on some action points.

To **talk something through** means to discuss an issue.

But this kind of support is very different to saying 'Here's £50 – now your problem is solved.' Your friend would not be learning from this experience, and if they encounter the same problem again, they will not know how to solve it and you might be unable to help them. Being a good friend involves helping your friend overcome problems, but not solving them for them.

You may decide that it is easier not to lend anybody anything (including possessions, e.g. DVDs). Many people don't lend possessions or money. If you set this as a rule, you could write yourself a script to act out if someone asks you for money (or anything else). For example, you could decide that if someone asks you for money, you will say, 'I'm sorry but I don't have any money I can give you.'

Another way to think about this is to remember that if you keep giving people money, then you will not have any money for yourself. Although you do have money that you could give to another person, you would not be able to cope financially and therefore you don't actually have the money to give another person. You do have money, but not money to give away to other people, because this will impact negatively on your life.

7.6 Keeping money safe

When you are away from your home, or when you are in your home with other people, it is important to store money so that other people cannot see it (apart from when you need to use it, of course).

You may have read in other books general guidance such as:

- Keep your pockets that contain money zipped up. Some change of a few pounds can be kept in your pocket as this is a small amount of money. If it is stolen, you will not have lost much. Also, if someone saw you putting only a small amount of money in your pocket, they would be less likely to try to steal it from you as it would not be worth their while.

- You might carry other money with you in a wallet or purse. Only have small amounts of money with you at any time (this could be £10 or £20 but it is up to you to decide). There may be times when you need to carry large amounts of money, but try to avoid this, and if you do carry a large amount of money with you, do it during in the day. At night, when it is dark and there are fewer people around, there are more opportunities for people to try to steal from you. Thieves often wait until night to steal, as there are fewer people around to witness the crime and they can take advantage of dark areas which are easier to hide in.

- When using a debit or credit card, place your other hand over the hand that is typing in your PIN so that nobody else can see it and so that a camera attached to the ATM or cash machine cannot take a photo or video of you typing your PIN.

- If you need to count money, do this at home alone or with someone you trust.

7.7 Being taken advantage of

'Not knowing when I was taken advantage of. This happens to me all the time. I think this is something that people should focus on. Teach people with Asperger's how to see when someone's taking advantage of you.'

Kesley, research participant

There are many ways in which someone can be taken advantage of financially. Below is a list of common ways people have been taken advantage of and some red flags that might indicate that you are being taken advantage of.

7.7.1 Red flags when considering lending money to people

- If the person asking you is an addict of any kind (e.g. drugs, alcohol, gambling), then it is likely, regardless of what they say, that the money they are asking for will be spent on what they are addicted to.

- If the person's story about why they need money seems a bit confused or overdramatic, do not believe them, or find out more information by asking people you know who also know the person asking for the money.

- If the person has not tried other ways to overcome the difficulty for which they are asking for the money, such as contacting their bank and asking for an emergency loan, you should be suspicious.

- If the person has a reputation for being 'flakey' (someone who says they will do things but then doesn't), you should be very wary of lending them money.

- If the person tries to make you feel bad – for example, if you say no, and then they say, 'Well, I am going to kill myself now' or 'I hate you' or 'You are a really bad person' – this is known as emotional blackmail.

Emotional blackmail means when someone says something to you intentionally to make you feel bad so that you will do what they want you to do.

- Be wary of:
    - being asked for large amounts of money (over £100)
    - being asked for money by a stranger or someone who claims to know someone you know
    - being asked via email or text message, particularly someone you do not know or do not know well
    - people who keep asking you and don't leave you alone, even after you tell them to.

- If you are being asked to give money for a business investment, people who do not have a clear and concise financial forecast (a plan of how much money they will gain in income and how this will happen, with clear marketing goals, etc.) are unlikely to be trustworthy.

- Say no to people who say the money has to be given today.

- Avoid lending money to people who 'play with your emotions' (e.g. telling you a very sad story to make you feel sorry for them).

- If the person arranges a time to meet with you to discuss money, but then doesn't turn up and this happens more often than they keep to an arranged date and time, they are unlikely to be able to manage investments effectively.

7.7.2 When you are not the only person in control of your money

You may have a financial guardian, or perhaps your civil partner or husband or friend who you live with may have taken responsibility of paying bills.

- If you have a financial guardian, it may be wise to read your bank statement with them once a month, so that they can explain when and where the money has been spent and why. Your financial guardian should be prepared to do this with you or to compromise (e.g. sending you an email when they have spent money on your behalf to explain why they have done this).

- If the person who is your guardian does not want you to see or access the bills, this may be a sign that they are taking advantage of you, unless they have a good reason (e.g. it causes you great anxiety).

You can check that money has been paid to a particular company by calling them. Usually, the company will want to know your account number (not your bank account number unless you are calling a bank, but your customer account number with that company) and possibly a bill reference number. These numbers should be on your bill.

You should be suspicious in any of the following situations:

- Your financial guardian tries to prevent you from checking that bills have been paid or that there are no unusual transactions (an unusual transaction is anything you think shouldn't be there) on your bank statements.

- The person avoids talking about your money. For example, when you try to talk about the subject, they change the topic of conversation.

- The person arranges a time to meet with you to discuss money but then doesn't turn up and this happens more often than not.

- The person agrees a time to discuss money issues but then something happens and they become unavailable at the time you agreed. If this happens more than once in a week or month, then be suspicious.

7.7.3 Things to be aware of when dealing with companies and banks

- Check your bank statement regularly for anything unusual. Things to look out for are:

  - companies you do not recognize taking money from your account or putting money into your bank account

  - money going out that you do not remember spending

  - bank or loan fees that you do not remember agreeing to.

- Any kind of pressure selling (when someone tells you have to do this today or you asks questions such as 'You wouldn't want to miss this deal, would you?'). These are signs that people may be trying to take advantage of you. When you first go to speak to a salesperson, say (even if you *are* intending to buy that day) that you are not intending to buy that day (so that they do not put pressure on you). If they start putting pressure on you or trying to convince you to buy things you do not want or need, leave the store and go to another one, or ask them to stop pressurizing you or ask for a different member of staff to serve you.

- If someone says you are guaranteed to make money from investing in a particular company, most of the time this is untrue.

- When buying anything electrical or worth more than £100, buy from reputable companies. Establish if they are reputable by reading reviews online. For any company there will be complaints, but if feedback/comments are 85 per cent positive, then the company is probably OK.

- When buying online, the payments page web address should say https:// as opposed to http:// – the 's' stands for secure. Insist on reading the terms and conditions of any agreement you sign and always take a copy home with you to file for future reference. If a company will not give you the terms and conditions and a copy of them to take away with you, do not sign the agreement.

- If you feel confused, tell the salesperson you will come back another day. Ask a trusted friend for advice or to go with you. Ask very direct questions such as 'How much do I have to pay per month including any fees or interest?'

    If the sales person cannot answer this question in a straightforward (easy to understand) way, do not sign any agreements or buy products from them.

A **fee** is an extra sum of money which is sometimes charged for things such as administration.

- If a company says they will do a job for you (e.g. fix your computer or mow your lawn), agree the sum you will pay them before they start and check that they have done the job they said they would do before giving them the money. If they haven't done the job and get upset that you haven't given them the money, remember that they did something wrong, not you. If they have a valuable possession of yours and won't give it back, call the police and ask for help.

- Look for credit and debit card signs on websites or pay using PayPal.

- If agreeing to a loan or credit card, ask what the cooling-off period is. This is a period of time (e.g. 21 days) in which you can change your mind about the decision to get the loan or credit card and cancel it. Check that there is no penalty (penalty, in this context, would be money to pay because you changed your mind) if you do cancel in the cooling-off period.

- If you sign up to a website for a month's free trial and you have to submit your credit card details, ensure that you read the terms and conditions thoroughly. If you do not understand them, ask for help. If you don't want to pay after the free trial period, you need to cancel your subscription and erase your credit card details on that website or close your account.

7.8 Standing up for yourself and saying no

It's your money, so you should choose what you do with it. If you find it hard to say no to deals or special offers, remember that there are likely to be more deals and special offers soon. If you miss this one and plan for what you will do next time, you will not be missing much. You might actually end up better off financially because you may decide you do not need the product anyway.

7.9 Loans

'Student Loans are a MAJOR commitment that I truly didn't understand. I thought that I would complete school and they would find me a good job (like they said) and I'd make good money and pay it back and that would be that. HA! Not even close! I had a psychotic break from the stress of trying to keep up with my schooling (in addition to the demands of daily life) and had to drop out of school. There I was, owing all this money with no way to pay on it. I've ALWAYS struggled financially and have NEVER been able to work up to my potential. Nevertheless, it is now almost 20 years later and this debt is STILL hanging over my head! Student loans are different and can't just be written off as a bad debt (like credit cards). I had no idea the burden I was taking on at the time. I believed that I would go to school, get a good job, do good, etc., etc. There was no contingency plan. Nobody even made me aware that it COULD go any other way!'

Audra, research participant

Any loan is a commitment until you have paid it off.

⊘ To **pay off a loan** means to pay back the money that you borrowed and any added interest, administration fees or other charges.

A college or university loan is a very large amount of money to borrow. If you have a particular career path you want to pursue (e.g. if you plan to be a lawyer or doctor) and you feel confident that you will be able to pay off the loan, then it is a suitable path to take.

If the loan is for a house or car and your current job is stable, then a loan might be a viable option, but make sure you think about how you will pay for it.

⊘ A **stable job** is a job you are unlikely to lose.

You should also be aware of interest.

⊘ **Interest** is a percentage that is added to your loan per month or year. This is one way that banks and companies make money. The interest also has interest added to it and this is known as cumulative interest.

Ask the bank or company offering you the loan exactly how much you will have to pay back and over what period of time, including interest and cumulative interest. If you feel unsure, talk to an independent financial advisor.

7.10 Credit cards

Many non-autistic people find it difficult to use credit cards without getting into a great deal of debt. Credit cards can be very useful for making particular purchases such as holidays or home electronics because some credit card providers include additional insurance when you buy things with your card.

However, credit cards are like a loan and you have to pay the money back to the credit card company. Depending on how long it takes you to do this, you may also have to pay interest and others fees. There are two ways of doing this:

- Pay the amount in full at the end of the month (or when you receive the credit card statement).

- Pay back the money in instalments, which may incur interest and cumulative interest. If you choose this option, it is important to clarify exactly how much you have to pay back each month and for how long. Do this by contacting the credit card company.

A **credit limit** is how much money the credit card company is prepared to allow you to spend per month. It does not mean you have to spend that amount of money or that the money is yours.

Before spending any money on a credit card, always plan out how you will pay that money back.

One way of reminding yourself to do this is to stick a post-it note on your computer monitor, to remind you to calculate how you will pay the money back to the credit card company if you make a purchase.

Top 10 things to remember from Chapter 7

1. Many people struggle with managing money. This does not mean you are inferior to people who are good at managing money. We all have different strengths and weaknesses.

2. There are many different methods of budgeting, including computer programs, apps for smartphones, abacuses and hand-drawn charts and graphs. If one type of budgeting system does not work for you, try another.

3. It is important to spend some money on things that make you happy and improve your quality of life. However, it is also important to minimize debt where possible. This is why budgeting is important, because it can tell you how much money you can spend on the things you want without getting into debt.

4. Some companies or banks may try to convince you to sign an agreement for a financial product (e.g. a credit card). Do not give in to this pressure. Make sure you give yourself enough time to think about your decision.

5. Some things can usually only be bought using a loan – for example, to buy a house you need a mortgage, which is a type of loan, or you may need a loan to buy a car or a student loan to get a university degree. Make sure you plan how you will pay the loan off and what (if any) problems there might be and how you could overcome them.

6. Some websites offer a one-month free trial of a product or service. However, they usually ask you to submit your credit card details. These deals often work on the basis that businesses think you will forget you signed up and then you will pay for the service after your month's free trial because you forget to cancel your subscription. Write on your calendar/journal when you need to cancel the subscription.

7. Ask about cooling-off periods when buying a financial product. This is a period of time in which you can change your mind.

8. It can be easy to think you have understood the commitment and the terms and conditions of paying a loan, but talk the situation through with someone you trust to ensure you really have understood everything and planned effectively.

9. Some people have someone else to look after their money. Make sure that you monitor this situation. You should still be involved in making decisions, and nobody should take your money away from you without your say-so.

10. If you want to buy something, think about what the consequences might be and ask yourself, 'Does my budget allow for this?'

Resources

Websites

Money Saving Expert
www.moneysavingexpert.com
This website contains information on how to save money and offers explanations about some financial common financial issues that people have.

Managing Money
www.managingmoney.org.uk
An online course on how to manage money. There is also a workbook version of the website, which is available to purchase from www.nas.org.uk.

BudgetTracker from the Money Advice Service
https://secure.budgettracker.com/login.php?sp=nouser
A website that you can use to help work out your budget.

My Money
www.mymoney.gov
A US website to help you manage your money.

Money Smart
www.moneysmart.gov.au
An Australian website to help you manage your money.

8

WORK

In this chapter

8.1 Introduction

Work is often an essential part of adult life, because it means you can earn money to buy the things you need and want. The income from a job is also less likely to be static than the income from benefits, and there is potential to earn more money. This increases your likelihood of staying safe. For example, it reduces the likelihood that you will struggle to pay off debts. In turn, this makes it more likely you'll be able to keep your home and possessions, because you won't have to sell your home or your possessions to pay off the debt. Jobs can also increase self-esteem and self-worth, which can have benefits for your mental health. This is turn helps to reduce the likelihood of suicide due to depression. It also means you have more control of your life, when compared with state benefits such as social security, ESA (employment support allowance in the UK) or a pension, since a government can choose to reduce the amount you receive. Jobs sometimes also come with other benefits.

⊘ A **benefit**, in the context of a job, means things you receive because of your job, such as a company car or healthcare.

A job that meets your needs can also allow you more choices in where you live, what you do in your free time and the quality of the food you eat. But there are some issues to be aware of that will help you keep your job and the benefits that come with it.

Olga Bogdashina has written some excellent books about sensory issues, which include strategies. Rudy Simone and Sarah Hendrickx have written books about employment for people on the autistic spectrum. Ashley Stanford has written one of my favourite ASD-related books, *Business for Aspies*. (See the resources section at the end of the chapter for details of these books.)

It may be possible for you to borrow these books from your local library if you are unable to buy them.

Please remember, though, that the aim of this book is to address safety issues; it is not about how to get a job.

8.2 People at work

'Get a boss or colleague to mentor you. I had the help of my boss who I filtered everything through. Helped so much. Was the only job I kept for 10+ years.'

Jennifer, research participant

If you are lucky to have a boss who takes the time to get to know you and wants to accommodate you, this is great. Jennifer talks above about how her supportive boss enabled her to keep her job for more than ten years.

One way of building this relationship with your boss would be to ask if they would like to have a chat with you to get to know you. Small talk (chitchat) can be very difficult for people on the autistic spectrum, but this particular conversation is really worth having.

Explain to your boss what you find difficult and what would help. Come prepared with a list of things that help you; otherwise, you might sound as if you are moaning (complaining). If you don't have all the strategies you need, that's OK. A boss will just be glad you've shown some initiative and that you're positive. In this conversation, listen out for your boss telling you any small positive details about their life, such as supporting a football team or having kids. Later on, you can ask, 'How's your team doing in the league this year?' or 'How are your kids doing?' On a first meeting with your boss, it's not usually advisable to ask them if they like football or have kids, but be listening out for people telling you these small details, as they can be conversation starters during social times of the day. They also help to make you appear friendly.

However, be aware that there are some bosses who don't care about their employees, particularly in industries that have a high staff turnover.

⊘ A **high staff turnover** means that staff leave or get fired a lot.

In these situations, Georgie's advice may be very useful:

'I have one or two people who I trust at work. They have a similar work ethic and are more socially skilled. I run things by them if I can to get advice on any troubling matters.'

Georgie, research participant

Look and listen for people who you could get on (get along) with at work – people who have similar interests or people who have similar work attitudes, but who are socially skilled (if you feel this is where you have difficulties). Ask them for advice.

⊘ **Getting on/getting along with someone** means that you both like each other and can spend time together or speak to each other without being annoyed by each other. It doesn't necessarily mean that you are friends with them.

Conversation strategies

Rather than just going up to someone and saying, 'I heard you talking about soccer' (or another topic that interests them), I recommend that you look for a time when they are not busy and when they are alone – for example, when they're making tea or waiting for the photocopier – and ask them about what you think they might like – 'Hey, do you like football?' or 'Do you have kids?' Even though you know the answer, because you weren't part of the conversation you overheard it's politer to ask. Maybe they have a photo or ornament of an animal on their desk. So you could say, 'Oh, I was walking by your desk and saw you had a lizard. That's really cool – do you have a real one?' Make sure that you don't just ask questions but also say something about you (e.g. 'I have a lizard'). After a couple of questions, if you are only getting one- or two-sentence responses and they are not asking you questions, try talking about another topic. If, again, you only get one- or two-sentence responses and no questions back, then either they are busy or they may not want to talk to you.

Running things past someone means to ask someone's opinion of something, or to ask someone to clarify something. For example, if someone said something and you were a bit confused, you could say, 'Run that past me again,' or if you wanted to ask a friend about something you were confused about, you could say, 'Hey, Mary, can I run this past you? Last week...' If you need a visual representation of this, think of it like a tape player. The tape is running when someone is speaking; to run something past you again means to rewind the tape and hear what the person said again. Unlike a tape, of course, the person can elaborate on what was said and explain anything you might not have understood.

8.2.1 Others' expectations of you

'Do your best, you can't do anything more.'

Angharad Siân, research participant

> Do your best does not mean work so hard that you get burnt out or have a nervous/mental breakdown.

Many people on the autistic spectrum find it hard to know what other people expect of them. Obviously, you can ask your manager/boss what they expect of you, but in this section I wanted to convey some other information that might be helpful.

I found it hard to understand the expectations of others. You need to define boundaries to keep yourself safe from being burnt out and safe from exploitation.

To be **burnt out** means to be unable to work, due to stress.

Below is a guide to questions you might ask yourself when setting your boundaries for work situations. When you have decided what your boundaries are, I recommend that you write them down in a notebook which you store on your desk, or write them in an email to yourself, or store them on your mobile/cell phone's memory (if you work in an office with a 'clear desk' policy – i.e. no personal effects allowed on your desk).

Is there a particular way instructions can be provided to you that works best? For example:

- verbal instructions

- written instructions

- not being asked to do something when you haven't finished the task you are currently working on.

Also, think about if there are ever any exceptions. For example, if you are very stressed, then you might only be able to respond to people via email.

What do you need in your sensory environment and what don't you need?

- Having a telephone that rings on your desk may be too stressful or unpredictable.

- Your contract may specify particular working hours. Are you prepared to work beyond these hours and not receive pay for the extra time you worked?

- Are you prepared to work extra hours if you get paid the same rate of pay as your usual hours?

- How many extra hours are you prepared to work per week? Bear in mind that time away from work (in the evenings and at weekends/days off) is important for your mental wellbeing and stability.

Again, there may be exceptions to the above. For example, if you were working for a company that made and set up stage equipment, there may be particular times in the year during which you work longer hours. This is part of the job. If this does not work for you, consider a change of job. If you choose to do extra work, consider your motivation. This might include the following:

- There may be a particular boss that you like, and perhaps you are willing to do a few extra hours a week because you want to be nice to them. Make sure that you decide for yourself how much extra you are prepared to do. (Note: If you are romantically attracted to a boss, doing extra hours is unlikely to make them want to date you.)

- You may feel that doing the extra work such as a college course will be beneficial as it may allow you to get a better-paid or higher-level job.

- You may choose to do the extra because you do not want to cause an argument or just want a particular task done. Be firm with yourself about how many extra hours you will work before it has a negative impact on your personal life. Perhaps set yourself a working week limit – for example, you will only work 45 hours a week.

It can be very difficult to balance pleasing a boss and being taken advantage of, but decide what your limit is. Make sure you consider your wellbeing. If you became unwell, the company you work for would lose an employee and would be paying you sick pay, and they would lose the quality of your work. This would be bad for them as well as you. If you look after yourself, this will enable you to stay well and the company will benefit from your productivity.

You can review your job description, which is the job you are agreed to do. But a job description is only a guide (sometimes you may be asked to do things that are similar to what is described in the job description and this is OK). If you are being asked to do activities that are not in the job description, and you are finding this happens often and that it is difficult for you, tell your manager.

8.2.2 Social expectations at work

There may be particular work events, such as away-days or team-building days, that you are expected to attend. These days have a different structure to a normal working day and may involve playing team games such as paintballing. This can be very confusing for someone on the autistic spectrum, so it's important to explain to your boss the things you might need to know and that perhaps having someone as a buddy (i.e. a work colleague assigned to help you to participate in the day) might be useful. Many people on the autistic spectrum experience social anxiety, and this high level of anxiety can make the day intolerable. It is important that your boss understands this, that you are not being difficult or uncooperative but that some things might cause you great distress. In this situation, assigning you a specific job – perhaps one that is out of the way of lots of people – might be helpful. For example, you could be the person who is stopwatch timer (if the activity requires one) or the photographer, so you can still be part of the team but you have a defined job role.

There may be other events such as dances or dinners that require you to take a 'date'. People who are single do take people who they are not necessarily romantically attached to, but you may not want to do this. Remember that not all non-autistic people enjoy the kinds of events described in this section. Perhaps you could ask your boss if there is anyone else going who also does not really enjoy the event; perhaps you would like to sit with that person.

Sometimes it's nice to know you are not the only person not having fun.

It's OK to say, 'I don't want to go to this event because I will find it too overwhelming.' These events are designed to help people bond and have a good time, but they can be scary and overwhelming for people on the autistic spectrum.

8.2.3 Ways of coping with demands of others

Once you know what your boundaries are, you now need to know what you will do if someone attempts to push (make you change) your boundaries. Below are some ways that you might achieve this:

- Tell the person who is asking you to do the extra work that you need time to decide if you can do this. You might say, for example, 'I need to check my schedule, to work out if I will have time to do this.' If you use a schedule or calendar, it might help to block out some time that you spend away from work. Having this clearly marked in your calendar may help you to feel more confident when saying you do not have time to do something.

- If you find confrontation hard, reply by email. (You can do this even if you have time in your diary, but feel your wellbeing would be affected if you did this extra work, or if you feel the person is just using you.)

- If you are unsure what to do, ask another colleague or supervisor for advice.

- If someone is trying to make you feel bad for saying no, explain the consequences to you of doing this extra work. For example: 'I can appreciate that you want me to do this extra work, but if I work longer than my contracted hours, this will affect my health and I will struggle to come to work at all.'

- You could also discuss this with your boss in a less confrontational way. For example, you could say that you are finding it hard to know what the most important piece of work to be done is, and ask them to help you go through your schedule. This may help your boss realize how much work you have been asked to do. Your boss may also be able to advocate for you and ask others not to put pressure on you.

- If you are a member of a union, ask the advice of the union rep in your workplace.

A **union rep** is a representative of the union.

- Go to a member of the HR (human resources) department and ask for advice.

- If you would benefit from moral support, go to meetings with a colleague you trust when asking for help.

- In meetings, agree action points (things you and the other person will do), write them down and email the person you had the meeting with to ask them to confirm that the action points you have written down are accurate.

8.3 Added complications higher up the career ladder

'Remember that maybe intellectually you can perform well in a job, but as the job gets higher up the ladder, skills other than intellectual skills are required as well. Mainly social skills. I was never good with those and in the end I could not cope with all the networking and such I had to do to perform well in my job. Stick to a level at which you can be proud and feel fulfilled but yet does not require you to chitchat with colleagues and bosses at social events too often. If you cannot do that, you won't be able to understand office politics, nor will you be able to get involved. And at a certain level, this is a required skill. You will only get unhappy or eventually burn out.'

Fushin, research participant

Networking is when people meet normally within a work context and share ideas and information, which they hope will result in benefits for a business.

An example of networking

When I was working at a computer shop, I met someone who was a technician in a school; he gave me his business card and offered me work experience, which boosted my confidence. Giving out business cards is an example of networking.

Networking can be very difficult for someone on the autistic spectrum. This can be for many reasons, including sensory issues and because there is so much information to interpret and respond to.

A work colleague or a supportive manager may be able to help you. I have a lot of experience with networking and have found two useful strategies:

1. I am an associative thinker. This means, unlike most non-autistic people, I link my thoughts and sentences together via association, rather than context. For example, if I were in Battersea (in London) at a networking breakfast, I might be talking about pigs with a food distributor and then switch the topic of conversation to my special interest (which normally has the strongest association) of Pink Floyd because in 1977 they released an album called *Animals*. The front cover featured a pig flying over Battersea Power Station in London.

   Someone thinking in a contextual way might talk about something in context – for example, about the venue or possible business deals.

   Knowing that non-autistic people generally think in context is useful in trying to decide what I should say next.

2. My special interest in autism, which is the area I work in, is my biggest strength. When I meet someone new, I try to find out if they have any links, interest or experience in autism.

8.4 Meltdowns and explaining autistic behaviour

A meltdown is not the same as a tantrum. One definition of a meltdown could be an inability to cope with the world around you and an inability to process information or choose what to do next. Meltdowns can result in a person yelling or swearing.

Always try to find the cause of the meltdown. Why did it happen?

If this is something you experience, it is important to be very aware of the signs that a meltdown might happen. Using a book such as *The Incredible 5-Point Scale* by Kari Dunn Buron (see resources section at the end of this chapter) may be useful in helping you to define which behaviours you exhibit before you reach an uncontainable state and what you can do (or what others can do to help you) to avoid becoming inconsolable. Meltdowns are not your fault; please don't feel embarrassed by them. Be assertive in learning ways to avoid them as much as possible, as they can make you vulnerable. During the meltdown you will be less aware of what is happening around you and this could mean someone could steal your things, for example. Don't use meltdowns as an excuse not to do things before you have explored all possible strategies to prevent having a meltdown.

8.5 Workplace bullying

Bullying is when someone deliberately does something to cause you harm or upset. The type of harm they intend to cause you could vary greatly. For example:

- Physical harm could be cuts and bruises.

- Emotional effects could be crying, feeling upset, feeling angry or bad about yourself, being pressurized into doing something you do not want to do. This can result in a breakdown (when you feel you can no longer cope with life).

Unfortunately, bullying is something that many people on the autistic spectrum and non-autistic people encounter in many different situations.

My experience of bullying

People take great comfort in knowing that I have been bullied. I guess this is because it means they are not alone; they see I'm relatively successful and think, 'Well, if Robyn can do it, I can do it!' I have been bullied throughout my life. When I was in college, aged about 17, other people on my course called me names, blew up condoms so they could spit in them and throw them at me, deliberately did things to annoy me, said they had voted me off the course and generally made me feel unwanted. I tried yelling at them, which made it worse, and telling tutors, which didn't help because they thought that it was me who was causing the bullying. I would say things to the bullies that only seemed to make them want to bully me more. For example, in the UK we use pounds. One student kept talking in dollars – 'I bought my new car for $1000' and so on. I would shout at him, 'WE DO NOT USE DOLLARS IN THE UK!' This made him want to speak in dollars even more, because he liked the fact that I shouted at him. It meant he had made me angry, which meant I shouted loudly and he thought this was funny.

Then I had a support assistant follow me around to classes. This made things better and I was left alone, since he knew what to say to the students who weren't nice. Then a year later I was walking back to college and saw two of my former bullies. They said, 'Hello, Robyn, you shit,' so I went to the head of security, whom I had met since I now lived in college, and I asked him to watch the CCTV back. Although he couldn't see them on the film, he knew I was trustworthy. One student happened to be employed at the college, so the head of security went to see the boss of the person who had bullied me and told him what had happened. The head of security got the two students together and asked them who they had seen the previous day on the way out of college. At first they said no one, but then they turned to each other and said, 'Oh shit, Robyn.' They were told if they ever bullied me again they would both lose their jobs.

Although this was satisfying, I had spent the previous six or seven years being bullied, while the bullies got away with it. What changed was that I just happened to know the head of security and just happened to be standing near a CCTV camera.

You must also understand there is a difference between bullying and teasing. Sometimes people might tease another person (see Chapter 1 for more information on teasing).

8.5.1 Red flags/signs that you're being bullied at work

- If someone is doing something repeatedly that is causing you harm or distress (this could be subtle like knocking a pot of pens over your desk or spilling tea or coffee on your work), then this is probably not an accident, even if they claim it is.

- If you feel that your deadlines are unmanageable, this may not be bullying. Your manager might just not have anticipated how long it will take you to get tasks done (this is not a personal failing on your part necessarily). Ask your manager for help. If they are willing to help and support you, then this is probably not bullying. If they say they are busy, they should be able to tell you how to overcome the problem. If this happens often, ask to make an appointment with your manager to discuss it.

- If you are being asked to do someone else's job (e.g. if you were being asked to clean the walls, when there is a cleaner employed to do this), unless there is a good reason why you are being asked to do this, then this could be bullying.

- If someone else is getting you to do their work so that they don't have to do anything, this could also be bullying.

- If someone is making unpleasant or rude remarks about you (e.g. 'Look at her – isn't she ugly?'), this may be bullying. Even if you feel that what they are saying is true, if it is unpleasant, ask yourself, 'Does their remark help me do my job?' Does what they are saying having anything to do with the person saying it? For example, if one of your colleagues in an office said that your dress sense was rubbish, is it up to them and are they your boss? If the answer the above is no, then you might be being bullied. Does the person laugh or smile after they have made negative comments? If the answer is yes, this is also a sign you are being bullied. If someone has negative comments to make, they should use tact and their criticism should be constructive.

8.5.2 What to do if you are being bullied

Speak to or email your manager, supervisor, a trusted colleague, friend or union representative. Explain the signs that make you think you are being bullied. Make a timeline of exactly what happened when and how it made you feel and ask them what you should do.

If you feel uncomfortable saying you are being bullied (some people may feel they are accusing someone unnecessarily), then you can tell them what happened and how you felt about it, and ask what you should do. But don't do this in an accusing way.

A really common mistake people make is to think people are staring or looking at them. Yes, sometimes others might stare or look at you, but make sure you check to see if that person ever looks or stares at anyone else. I would be inclined to ignore staring. So what? Let them stare! But if you feel you cannot do this, ask a friend for help.

8.6 Other people's business

People on the autistic spectrum are sometimes described as lacking empathy. Many people on the autistic spectrum actually don't lack empathy skills, in my experience, especially for others on the autistic spectrum. This isn't because people on the autistic spectrum do not care for non-autistic people, but because the non-autistic world seems so different to the autistic way of thinking that it is hard to relate to. But that does not mean it is impossible, or that non-autistic people all have amazing empathy skills, because they don't.

If you have had experiences of being bullied or harassed or being unhappy at work, and you see that another colleague appears to be having similar difficulties, it could be tempting to try to help them by confronting the person you think is bullying them.

It is probably best not to intervene; people have to deal with their own problems. If someone comes and solves their problems on their behalf, this does not allow them to learn new skills for themselves.

Also, it could have very bad consequences for you, such as getting physically hurt.

The way a non-autistic woman might deal with this situation, as long as the life of the person being bullied was not in danger (in which case call 999 or your country's emergency number), would be to:

- Ask the person to lunch and discuss the situation with them. For example, say, 'I saw Harry giving you a hard time last week. Is everything OK?'

To **ask someone to lunch** means to ask them if they would like to eat lunch with you.

- Talk to colleagues you know and who also know the person you think is being bullied about what the best thing to do might be.

- Raise a concern (speak to the manager and say you're worried about the person you think is being bullied).

- Make an effort to smile at the person you think is being bullied and say good morning when you get to work or when they get to work.

- Go to the desk of the person you think is being bullied and tell them where you sit (even if they know that). Say that if they ever want or need to talk, you would be happy to help them out. (You would be less likely to do this with a male colleague because they might think you were flirting.)

8.7 Sex work

Sex work is governed by the laws of the country in which it is taking place. In some parts of the world it is completely illegal; in some places it is OK if the woman is working alone (i.e. without a pimp); in other places it is OK as long as it is done in a brothel. It is important to familiarize yourself with the relevant local laws and regulations (especially if you travel to a different country or state).

Some women on the autistic spectrum have become sex workers. Some women do this because it makes them feel that they belong somewhere, because it earns money and perhaps because they feel no emotional connection to the acts (types of sex) they are performing on men or women or the acts performed on them. Some women may feel this is the only work they can do or are worthy of.

However, being a sex worker puts you at great risk. These risks include:

- *Physical violence from others.* There is a risk that a client could cause you physical harm. Because you are in a bedroom or hotel room or car, you may have fewer escape routes available to you. If you are naked, this may limit where you can go and also means that you do not have your mobile/cell phone or other belongings with you.

- *Emotional effects.* You may not feel any emotions at the time or feel that you are completely able to separate yourself from the situation and not feel anything. Be aware that after work, when you have time to process what has happened during the day, you could find the experience upsetting and it may affect relationships outside of work.

- *Control from others.* A pimp is someone who controls one or more women in the following ways:

  - who they have sex with at work

  - when they work

  - how much money they charge

  - how much money they can keep.

  Because it is hard for women on the autistic spectrum to understand another's intentions, it could be that you end up being controlled by a pimp who is acting as though he is your friend when really he just wants to make money from you. It is important to consider when someone is 'appearing' to be your friend. One warning sign is if the person pretending to be your friend has more control over you in any way (e.g. money or what you do) than you have over yourself.

- *Infections and diseases* can be passed on by any kind of sex, including oral, anal and vaginal. Always use protection (condom or femidom).

- *Rape and sexual assault.* Your clients may be intoxicated with drugs or alcohol. All sex work has some risk involved, especially for women on the autistic spectrum, due to difficulties predicting other people's intentions and reading social cues. There are 'safer' but not risk-free ways of working within the sex industry, and contacting the organizations included in the resources section in Chapter 2 may be a way to find out how you can do this work safely in your country and state.

8.8 Is freelancing or self-employment an option for me?

This isn't strictly a safety topic, but I really wanted to include it because there are so many people out of work and I think sometimes self-employment isn't explored. You can become self-employed from a young age using your skills.

To freelance is to sell a service you provide to a company on a contract for a limited time (e.g. a six-month project). Normally, freelancers work for many different companies at once, but they can choose when they start and finish work each day and they can also choose how much of their day is spent on each project. Freelancers often work from home. Usually, they don't work as part of a team, or they may work as part of a virtual team and communicate with others via email and Skype.

To be self-employed is to set up a company and sell products and/or services to companies or individuals. You choose when you start and finish work each day, where you work and what work you do.

'I started freelancing many years ago after getting depressed and frustrated about all the jobs I could easily have managed, but didn't get because I didn't fit in socially. I hate job interviews, because I never come across like what I really am. Now all my contacts with my clients are through email and the occasional phone call, which makes my life a lot easier and also a lot more fun! Most clients are very happy with my work and when they are not, it is their right to criticize me about my work, but it's not about me personally, so I can just take it in and move on. I have a lot more self-esteem now than I had when working below my level (because those jobs I did get) and getting nowhere with job applications. Of course, it also helps that I can fill my day as I see it fit instead of doing time from nine to five each day. I work until my work is done, then I'm free, whether I have worked two hours that day or 12. I don't mind. I love the fact that I don't know how much work I will have in a month or in a year. I would hate to know that I have to work each day from nine to five for another 35 years from now. ;) I also get to work where I can get the most done. I have a special room in my own house and I can even take breaks when I want and how often I want. And pet my pet animals for a break or do some household chores.'

Carol, research participant

To run a business or work freelance takes a lot of skill. But it is possible to be successful.

- Consider what your special interest/obsession is. Could this be what you do as a freelancer or self-employed person? If not, what skills does it give you?

- Research online how other people with similar business have acquired clients.

- Get a web presence – for example, a free blog at blogger. com or wordpress.com.

A **web presence** means that what you do (business-wise) can be found on the internet.

- Make sure you write down all the money you spend and use a bookkeeping program or spreadsheet.

- Get a very good accountant (use recommendations from others).

- If your special interest doesn't fit into a work activity easily, then perhaps the skills that you use to engage with that interest do. For example, if you enjoy painting warhammer figures, maybe you could make jewellery or paint ornaments?

It is very important that you are aware of both the advantages and the disadvantages of being freelance/self-employed.

You may find it useful to mark each advantage and disadvantage out of 10, 10 being very important and 1 being least important. Add up the total of the advantages and compare it with the total of the disadvantages. If the disadvantages have a greater score, then self-employment or freelancing is probably not a good option for you.

8.8.1 Advantages and disadvantages of being self-employed

ADVANTAGES

- You work from home so you are in control of your sensory environment.

- You choose your working hours to suit you.

- You choose when you have a break.

- You choose when you eat and drink.

- You choose to take time off when you feel like it.

- You choose how you communicate with other people (e.g. via email or phone or face to face). This can vary from day to day.

- You choose which companies (and bosses) you accept work from and which you don't.

- You can avoid office politics since you don't work in an office with other people.

- If you do extra training and gain particular qualifications, this can make you more valuable. For example, a chartered psychologist who is also an educational psychologist can do a wider variety of work. If you pay for your own training courses, then you directly benefit from the extra money this enables you to earn, rather than an employer benefiting financially.

- You can develop your business in different directions. For example, you might start as a hairdresser but then decide that you will also train as a beautician.

- You have less stress from being expected to do your job and perform socially.

Disadvantages

- You have to find your own clients.

- There is no security. If a job goes wrong, you may well lose money.

- You have to buy your own medical insurance (in the USA or other countries that don't have free healthcare).

- You have to set up your own pension.

- You have to set up insurances (such as public liability).

- You have to arrange to pay taxes (in the UK you can do this either via a self-assessment tax form or through an accountant who will do everything that needs to be done for you for a fee).

- If you have a difficult client, you have to deal with them to get paid or end the working relationship.

- You are solely responsible for every aspect of your business, such as paying the internet bill and adhering to relevant laws.

- If you are unwell and unable to work, you will not get paid.

Top 10 things to remember from Chapter 8

1. Work can have some benefits for safety such as greater financial stability and positive effects on your mental health.

2. It is important to manage your expectations of others and to check you understand what is expected of you.

3. Moving up the career ladder can result in new problems such as the need to network; however, you may be able to learn skills to overcome this.

4. Meltdowns happen for some people on the autistic spectrum. It is important to discover your trigger for the meltdown and have a plan of what to do if this happens.

5. People, including non-autistic people, sometimes get bullied at work. Being bullied is not OK and you shouldn't have to put up with it.

6. Some people do not like others giving them advice they have not asked for.

7. If you are considering working as any kind of sex worker (I do not condone this; it can be very dangerous and damaging to a person), ensure you understand the law in the area of the country you are working.

8. Some people on the autistic spectrum have become successful by starting their own business or freelancing.

9. Running something past a trusted colleague or friend at work can be a helpful way of checking that you are doing the right thing or have understood something completely.

10. Many people on the autistic spectrum feel they have understood something such as an instruction but actually have not completely understood what was being asked of them or why. Always check that you fully understand.

Resources

Books

Bogdashina, O. (2003) *Sensory Perceptual Issues in Autism and Asperger's Syndrome: Different Sensory Experiences – Different Perceptual Worlds.* London: Jessica Kingsley Publishers. ISBN: 1843101661

This book explains the many different types of sensory issues people on the spectrum experience. It also contains a sensory profile tool, which may be a useful starting point for assessing your sensory issues, particularly if you are unable to see an occupational therapist.

Buron, K.D. and Curtis, M. (2003) *The Incredible 5-Point Scale: Assisting Students with Autism Spectrum Disorders in Understanding Social Interactions and Controlling Their Emotional Responses.* Shawnee Mission, KS: Autism Asperger Publishing Co. ISBN: 1931282528

Don't be put off that this is a children's book – it is a fantastic resource with many useful strategies in it, which are simple to implement. There is also a version for adolescents.

Buron, K.D., Brown, J.T., Curtis, M. and King, L. (2012) *Social Behavior and Self-Management: 5-Point Scales for Adolescents and Adults.* Shawnee Mission, KS: Autism Asperger Publishing Co. ISBN: 1934575918

This is the adolescent version of the 5-Point Scale, so the activities are more sophisticated than the ones in version above.

Hendrickx, S. (2008) *Love, Sex and Long-Term Relationships: What People with Asperger Syndrome Really Really Want.* London: Jessica Kingsley Publishers. ISBN: 1843106051

Sarah Hendrickx is a professional who works with people on the spectrum. Her partner has Asperger's syndrome. In this book she explores issues around sex and relationships for people with Asperger's syndrome.

Simone, R. (2010) *Aspergirls: Empowering Females with Asperger Syndrome.* London: Jessica Kingsley Publishers. ISBN: 1849058261

This book is divided into chapters which focus on particular areas of life that affect females, such as relationships and work. Rudy uses quotes she has gathered from women on the spectrum to explain the issues they face.

Stanford, A. (2011) *Business for Aspies: 42 Best Practices for Using Asperger Syndrome Traits at Work Successfully.* London: Jessica Kingsley Publishers. ISBN: 1849058458

Ashley Stanford is married to a man with Asperger's syndrome, and she knows a great deal about autism and difficulties that are not necessarily unique to autism but many people on the spectrum have in common, such as executive functioning. This book is useful for many situations other than just work, and would be applicable whether you work in business or not.

9

MOODS, EMOTIONS, FEELINGS AND MENTAL HEALTH

'If you're gonna be safe you've got be strong psychologically.'

Dr Tony Attwood

In this chapter

9.1 Introduction

My personal and professional experience has taught me that many people on the autistic spectrum often experience one or more of the following at some point in their life:

- clinical depression

- feelings of worthlessness

- feelings that nothing will change

- feeling suicidal

- anxiety

- anxiety disorders such as generalized anxiety disorder (GAD) and post-traumatic stress disorder (PTSD)

- extreme levels of stress

- loneliness

- being unable to leave the house

- obsessive compulsive disorder (OCD)

- eating disorders such as anorexia nervosa and bulimia

- low self-esteem

- social anxiety

- lack of confidence

- self-harm

- problems with sleep

- difficulties with self-identity including gender and sexuality.

Being on the autistic spectrum can create challenges that non-autistic people do not have. People on the autistic spectrum have a great deal to offer the world, but sometimes, as a person on the autistic spectrum, you have to navigate through things that are very difficult emotionally.

🔍 **Navigate**, in this context, means to learn how to get through the difficult time, situation or emotion you are having.

9.2 Stephen Fry's weather analogy

Some people on the autistic spectrum find analogies helpful. I would like to share with you a quote from the actor and author Stephen Fry. Although he is not on the autistic spectrum, I feel this is very worthwhile. I have found it insightful and useful for understanding myself. Stephen Fry has bipolar disorder (sometimes called manic depression). This means that he has periods of time of being very depressed and periods of time when he is manic.

> To me mood is the equivalent of weather. Weather is real. That's the important thing to remember about weather. It is absolutely real. When it rains it rains. It is wet. You get wet. There is no question about it. It's also true about weather that you can't control it. You can't say if I wish hard enough it won't rain and it's equally true that if the weather is bad one day it will get better and what I had to learn was to treat my moods like the weather. On the one hand denying that they were there and saying I can't... I'm not really depressed. Why should I be depressed? I've got enough money. I've got a job. People like me. There is no [reason] to be depressed. That's as stupid as saying there is no reason to have asthma or there is no reason to have the measles. You know you've got it. It's there. It's not about reason. You don't get depressed because bad things happen to you. That's getting pissed off and annoyed. That's reasonable. Someone hits you in the face you go 'Ow!' ...but depression is something that happens like weather to you inside you and it's not about... It could be triggered by something unfortunate. (Stephen Fry, transcript of a video *An Uppy-Downy, Mood-Swingy Kind of Guy*; Big Think 2010)

What Stephen is expressing is that bipolar (and other mental illnesses and conditions) happens to people and is not in their control. Just as the weather changes, mood changes. Mental illness can happen to anyone. Stephen Fry has two houses, a car, a good job, friends, money, but he still suffers from bipolar, which includes bouts of depression.

There are things you can do to help to manage your emotions and mental health.

9.3 Strategies for emotions and emotional competency

Throughout a day you are likely to experience lots of different emotions. Sometimes it is very helpful to be able to name these emotions and to understand what they feel like and how they alter the way you think. It's also helpful to understand why they happen. This skill is part of being emotionally competent.

Often people on the autistic spectrum find it hard to differentiate between subtle changes in emotions. You could describe emotions in different shades, as you would colours. There are many different shades of blue (cyan, navy, royal, etc.) and each one is still blue, but it is subtly different to the shade that preceded it and the one that follows it.

Some people on the autistic spectrum say they know when they are extremely sad or extremely happy but are not aware of emotions between these two extremes.

You can use scales with a word to label the strength of the emotion from 1 to 10 and the thoughts that go with it (e.g. irritated: 'I wish she would be quiet for a bit').

It can be helpful to learn to identify emotions, because then you can respond to them and this may help your wellbeing. For example, if you knew the difference between being hungry and being anxious (hunger is not an emotion but could be confused with anxiety because both might give you stomach ache), then you either eat or do something to feel less anxious. If you can understand and label your own emotions, you can begin to understand them and other people's emotions better.

9.3.1 Starting to think about emotions

To help you to learn about emotions, you might just want to think about emotions in the simplest way possible. For example, happy and sad. Happy and sad are two opposites (extremes). Some people would describe happy as a positive emotion and sad as a negative emotion, because being happy is normally in response to good things happening and being sad is normally when something bad has happened.

Write two lists, one of things that make you happy and one of things that make you sad.

Things that make me happy

Things that make me sad

Some people find a numerical scale a good tool, such as *The Incredible 5-Point Scale* (see resources) to use with emotions. Table 9.1 is a scale of happy and sad.

Table 9.1 Scales of happy and sad

Sad					Happy				
1	2	3	4	5	6	7	8	9	10

You could try writing some experiences in order of most happy (under 10) and most sad (under 1). You might find using your special interest helpful; Table 9.2 is an example of this.

Having each number associated with an experience may help you work out how you are feeling if you compare how you are feeling now to the experiences you have written on the table. Paula's special interest is the London Underground. Her favourite line is the Victoria Line.

Table 9.2 Scales of happy and sad – using a special interest

Sad					Happy				
1	2	3	4	5	6	7	8	9	10
Fire alert and evacuation	Snow, meaning no trains	Cancelled train	A train being delayed	Using the tfl.gov website to plan a journey	Looking at the underground map	Seeing old underground trains in a museum	Taking the Victoria Line from Brixton to Stockwell	Taking the Victoria Line from Brixton to Kings Cross St Pancras	Taking a Victoria Line train from Brixton to Walthamstow Central

The next step on from this would be to name, label or describe in one word each number on the table. For example, if 1 is you when you are most sad, you might say you would be feeling 'distraught'.

You might label number 10 (the most happy you have ever felt) as 'euphoric'. This will help you to understand that emotions have opposites and different intensities. Sometimes people describe mood by comparing it to temperature. For example, Dr Tony Attwood's CAT Kit uses this method to help people understand emotions (see the resources section). Another method could be to use *The Incredible 5-Point Scale* (again, see the resources section at the end of this chapter). It's also important, once you understand that emotions have different intensities, to find out what each intensity looks and feels like to you.

This example, slightly adapted, comes from *The Incredible 5-Point Scale*:

Emotion: Distraught.

Looks like/behaviour: When I cry uncontrollably for five minutes or longer.

Feels like: I feel the world has ended and cannot do anything except sit and cry. Crying intensity, to me, means my eyes sting and get red and sore.

Think about what your behaviour looks like and what it feels like or, if this is difficult, scenarios/situations when you have felt these emotions:

- happy
- sad
- angry
- anxious.

9.3.2 Complexities of emotions

When we start to talk about emotions such as anxiety, this creates questions such as 'What is the difference between being worried and being anxious?' It is then important to add more definitions and more emotions to distinguish between them and decide if they are either a completely different emotion or just a different intensity of the same emotion.

The Emotion Annotation and Representation Language (EARL) is a suggested format from the Human-Machine Interaction Network on Emotion (HUMAINE) (see the resources section at the end of this chapter). It lists 48 emotions (see below). Look at the list of emotions and write down examples of when you have felt these emotions. (This will take you some time, and you may want to ask others for their opinions/memories of when you may have experienced these emotions.) Speaking with a non-autistic person may be particularly useful if you find this task difficult. The list is very comprehensive and you could choose to think about only some of the items in the list. If you find it hard to choose, perhaps pick ten at random, by running your finger over the list and stopping every three seconds; the emotion your finger is on is the one that you choose.

- Negative and forceful

  - Anger

  - Annoyance

  - Contempt

  - Disgust

  - Irritation

- Negative and not in control

  - Anxiety

  - Embarrassment

  - Fear

  - Helplessness

  - Powerlessness

  - Worry

- Negative thoughts
  - Doubt
  - Envy
  - Frustration
  - Guilt
  - Shame
- Negative and passive
  - Boredom
  - Despair
  - Disappointment
  - Hurt
  - Sadness
- Agitation
  - Shock
  - Stress
  - Tension
- Positive and lively
  - Amusement
  - Delight
  - Elation
  - Excitement
  - Happiness
  - Joy
  - Pleasure

- Caring
    - Affection
    - Empathy
    - Friendliness
    - Love
- Positive thoughts
    - Courage
    - Hope
    - Pride
    - Satisfaction
    - Trust
- Quiet and positive
    - Calm
    - Content
    - Relaxed
    - Relieved
    - Serene
- Reactive
    - Interest
    - Politeness
    - Surprised

(Humaine 2013)

'I think the most important thing about moods is to remember that they WILL change even if it doesn't feel that way, and they do drastically alter the perception of reality. There is an old saying, "Never make decisions when you are sad or promises when you are happy." Of course "never" is a word that causes difficulty for most of us on the [autistic] spectrum, but what it means is, you should be very careful in considering how your mood may affect your choices and lead you to do the wrong thing.'

H, research participant

9.4 Gluten and casein

Many people on the autistic spectrum benefit from a gluten-free and casein-free (GF/CF) diet (i.e. they eat no gluten or casein). People have said that they are less anxious and digest food better when on a GF/CF diet.

Gluten is found in all kinds of different products such as wheat, rye and other grains. Also, products such as sausages sometimes contain it, so read food packaging carefully.

You might consider trying a GF/CF diet, particularly if you live near or have access to a large supermarket, or you can buy food online. Many food manufacturers now make gluten-free products. There are many books now available, which provide information and recipes on this topic (see the resources section at the end of this chapter).

Be aware that a GF/CF diet does not work for everyone. You might also want to consider going to a nutritionist or dietician to be tested for allergies. Also, if you have difficulties with your bowels – for example, regular diarrhoea (e.g. once a week) or constipation – then talk to your family doctor.

9.5 Routines

'Anxiety is something I'm working on. I've tried a lot to fix it but in the end the strongest thing will always be support and routine. Take me out of my routine and I fall over sideways like a dinosaur in a mass extinction. I can't give much advice on this one yet because it's a work in progress, but don't let others force you to change.'

Stella, research participant

Many people on the autistic spectrum rely on routine to make them feel safe. One reason may be because they are predictable.

It's very important, however, to be aware that sometimes routines need to change. For example, if your lunchtime routine is to go to Subway, and one day Subway is closed, then you need to go somewhere else to buy your lunch, because you still need to eat. You may also need to reassure yourself that it is OK to have to change routine sometimes.

9.5.1 A way of visualizing routines

Single train track

Life could be compared to a series of train tracks which incorporate your routines, and you are a train going along the train track.

Single train track

If a change happens (e.g. at work), it may be helpful to imagine that a large brick wall has suddenly landed in front of you; because you are on a single track you can go no further. Perhaps this results in you having a meltdown.

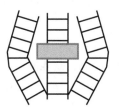

Multiple train tracks

To overcome the large wall on your train track, you need to find a way of creating multiple options/choices/directions, so you can take a diversion until you have got past the wall and can continue on with your normal routine.

Figure 9.3 An example of visualizing a routine using train tracks

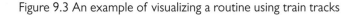

Although your routine may be very important in terms of your wellbeing, you also need to learn as much as possible to be able to cope with some change, without the change adversely affecting your life.

9.6 Strategies that may help you to be flexible when routines change

- Choose a good way to display your routine. This means a way that you will feel confident using and one that meets your needs. Below are some suggestions:

  - A photo routine (a series of photos tacked on to a board in the order that they will happen).

  - As above but with symbols.

  - Write out a schedule with time slots:

  - 9.00–9.30 read emails

  - 9.30–10.45 attend team meeting

  - Electronic schedule/calendar.

  - 'To do' list (a list of things you need to do in the order you will do them).

  - Write a 'to do' list and colour-code items on the list in order of priority or number the items in the order in which you will do them.

- Choose transition activities. Some people find it very important to do short activities such as walking to the photocopier and back to their desk (while at work), listening to a piece of music or doing some stretching exercises, petting an animal or hoovering between different tasks or activities. This is a way to help them cope with the change of activity. Also, if something changes, these are activities that can be used to make you feel more secure because they are familiar.

- If something does change, it may reduce the amount of time you will have to get a particular day's tasks completed. Review your routine/schedule and ask yourself what you can alter to incorporate the change. Perhaps there are low-priority tasks that you can take off another day's schedule and put on tomorrow's schedule.

- If you feel you cannot cope with a change, do something that calms you. Have this planned beforehand. If you work in an office with cubicles, pin an instruction sheet on your cubicle wall. At home, you could put this information on a whiteboard, chalkboard or the refrigerator.

- If something changes at work, it may not impact on your personal life (outside work), and it may only be a change for today. Perhaps tomorrow will be back to normal.

- If a change is permanent (i.e. for ever), remember that things in your life have changed to get to your current daily routine/schedule. For example, your school schedule was probably different to your schedule now, and you got through that change. You are likely to be able to get through this change, because you have dealt with routine change at least once in your life before.

- Ask your boss/manager, supervisor, co-workers or friends for help.

- Ask yourself: 'Is my schedule and the information being provided to me supporting my learning style?' For more information on learning styles, you could read Dr Wendy Lawson's book *The Passionate Mind* (see the resources section at the end of this chapter), which also contains a learning styles quiz (there are also many of these quizzes online). Sometimes just having the information displayed in a better format for you can reduce the difficulty in change. For example, if you got a letter from the council to say that your recycling would be collected on a different day of the week, you could call the council and ask them to tell you what the letter said. Being able to hear the information, rather than just seeing it, may make it easier for you to process the information.

- Plan ahead. If you are moving office, for example, visit the new office several times before you move. Take photos and compare where you work now (what's good and what's bad) with the new office (what's good and what's bad). You could display this digitally in a PowerPoint presentation, make a small book or write a short document. This strategy could work for other new things, such as moving house.

- If someone you like is leaving work, or they are leaving your life, having feelings about this is natural. It is important to find a way to express those feelings, such as through poetry or art. Some people find that a less direct way of releasing emotions is useful (e.g. a sport such as swimming or jogging).

9.7 Depression

Depression, just like any other emotion, has extremes. Depression can be a feeling of unhappiness – as if nothing is going right – that lasts for a few days. But if you have had this feeling for two weeks or longer, there is a possibility that you may have an illness called clinical depression. Clinical depression is treatable, and people usually recover.

'I have also been depressed for a long time (starting from when I was about 15 years old). I am not depressed any more since I stopped using the contraception pill (which depletes my energy) and since I try to hold on to the question: "What if there is just a one per cent chance that something I really really want in life will come true? Is that worth battling on for a little while more?" Because it usually is, and the depression usually subsides after a while. Also, always seek help, share with others about your depression. Everyone feels depressed at times and it's even harder dealing with it on your own. If you have no one, try sending an email to the Samaritans. Contact with them is free and they are all over the world and will respond to your email quite fast.'

Carol, research participant

Depression can develop for lots of reasons. If you find yourself feeling depressed, it is important to investigate the physical and psychological causes. Usually, this will involve seeing a doctor. Above, Carol talks about how the contraceptive pill affected her, although it's important to know that not everyone will react to the pill in the way Carol describes. If you find you do react negatively to the pill, discuss this with your family doctor, as there are alternative contraceptive methods.

Focusing your thoughts means to concentrate on one thought.

You could focus your thoughts on the positive things that have happened that day.

Many people on the autistic spectrum feel that they have never been able to meet any of their goals or aspirations and feel that they never will. But you need to keep trying. If you do not keep trying, then you will never know for sure that you would have always failed. You need to look for things you can change (even if they are small) that may improve your quality of life.

Carol also talks about the Samaritans (a UK charity – see the resources section for contact details).

9.7.1 Ways of thinking about depression

Quite often, when someone feels depressed they go to their family doctor who asks them questions about how they have been feeling in the last two weeks. This can be very difficult for someone on the autistic spectrum to think about and the questions could seem confusing. Two weeks may be too long a time, or you may just not be sure if you have felt the way the doctor is asking.

A useful tool to read might be the Hamilton Depression Scale (see the resources section at the end of this chapter). The questions are concise and it may help you to formulate sentences (or write down) about the way you are feeling.

My experience of depression

I have had depression. I found that although psychiatry can be very beneficial for many people, it can be very disempowering.

I was in a bookstore one day and came across a bright orange book called *Mood Mapping* by Dr Liz Miller (see the resources section for details). The book outlines a series of activities in a structured format. I followed the instructions and felt more in control.

I took melatonin for short periods and found that sleeping properly improved my mood.

My family doctor also gave me some very helpful advice. He said that if I wanted to come off antidepressants, I would need to replace them with something such as going to the gym.

I was quite scared of the gym at first, as I am a small woman and felt a little intimidated. My local mental health trust had a small gym. At the gym I met Ty. Ty is a gym instructor who taught me how to use the equipment. Over a few weeks I decided I really liked the gym. I joined a local private gym. I was given a gym routine and used to go five times a week for roughly an hour each time. I found this helpful. As I reduced the dose of antidepressants I took, I increased the amount of time at the gym.

I also used mood mapping as described in Dr Liz Miller's book and put it into a behavioural plan. Each day I aimed to have three mood maps (you draw four a day) that had to be in the middle, and if my mood dropped (meaning it become too negative), I had to deal with it to make it go back up (i.e. to make me happier). If I managed this, I could have an After Eight mint (they are my favourite). If I could do this for a whole week, I could go to the cinema.

I had to be disciplined with myself but I got through it. I lost weight and found greater self-confidence, as well as successfully coming off my medication and finding an interest in going to the gym, which provides me with additional social contact that has been very beneficial.

Note: It is important to make sure you follow a health professional's guidance when coming off medication.

9.8 Trying to prevent being overwhelmed by emotions

'Learning to see things objectively has helped a lot with mood, that and proper self-care (wearing sunglasses, ear plugs and watching my diet). Paying attention to my emotional wellbeing and making sure pent-up feelings are released and processed (through writing, art and music). Mainly, whenever something doesn't go well, or seems wrong, I try very hard to see it two ways at once: there is good in every situation, and bad in every situation. When I feel myself focusing on the negative, I try very hard to flip to the other side of the coin, so to speak, and find what went right or well or what good can come of something I wasn't anticipating.'

Aspergirrl, research participant

9.9 An emotions analogy

Sometimes people think that people on the autistic spectrum emotionally overact (e.g. get more upset or more angry than is necessary). However, I think that many people on the autistic spectrum need strategies to help them to process emotions effectively, as this is not always an innate skill.

The following analogy tries to describe this:

One way of considering emotions could be to imagine that everyone has a jar in their head. When something happens, an emotional token falls into the jar. For example, if you saw a piece of your favourite cake, a happy token would fall into your jar. Tokens are passed around the brain via a hose pipe, so there is a constant flow of emotions.

But people on the autistic spectrum do not have a hose pipe. So their emotional tokens build up and up and up, and there is NO flow of emotions.

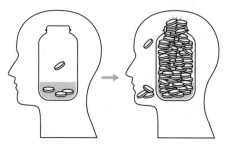

Eventually, the jar overflows and the person has a meltdown and/or is overwhelmed by emotions.

To overcome this problem, a person needs to release their emotions slowly.

9.9.1 Releasing emotions

Below is a list of ways you may be able to release emotions:

- *Music.* You can interact with music in several different ways:

    □ Listen to music.

    □ Listen and walk/exercise to music.

    □ Play music on an instrument.

    □ If you cannot play an instrument, drum the beat of music with a hand drum.

    □ Write music.

□ Write rhymes and rap over them or use samples (there are computer programs that can be used to create these).

□ Sing your favourite or familiar song to music or *a capella* (without music).

□ You may find that listening to music with headphones, earbud-type headphones or through speakers gives you different experiences. You may also find that a particular volume is your threshold (i.e. you cannot bear to listen to music louder than this). If you are hyposensitive to sound, you may need the music at a particular volume to get any emotional effect.

• *Art.* There are many ways of interacting with art and many kinds of art materials.

□ Look at art in a book, in a gallery or on the internet.

□ Draw what you see around you.

□ Draw your special interest/obsession.

□ Draw what has happened to you today, this week or in the past, or what you hope will happen to you in the future.

□ Use storyboarding to chronicle what has happened that has upset you.

   If you do not like to draw, consider using charcoal, different kinds of paint (e.g. acrylic, watercolour or oil), clay (different kinds), collage, needlework/knitting.

   Also consider what you use to access these materials (e.g. paintbrushes or your fingers) and what kinds of paper you use – what weights and textures do you like best?

• *Sports.* You may find that running, jogging, swimming, going to the gym or any other kind of sport is very helpful. Although this might not seem to deal directly with emotions, it can be beneficial for some people (including me). For example, when I am anxious, I have a lot of energy going into the anxiety, so by exercising I am using that energy in a positive way.

- Take a break, go for a walk or imagine you are somewhere else.

- In a place far from other people, scream, yell, shout or stamp your feet!

- *Write*. For example:

  ▫ Keep a journal.

  ▫ Write stories either based on your life, the lives of others or imagined scenarios.

  ▫ Write poetry.

- *Worry box*. Keep a small box such as a shoe box by your bed. At the end of each day, write in a small notebook (you could also keep this by your bed) things that worry you or that are preventing you from going to sleep. Tear out the paper you have written on and post it or put it into the worry box. Some people place worry dolls (a small doll you make) in the box and tell the doll what they are worried about and close the lid, so the worries are stored there until the morning. In the morning, you can open the box and deal with your worries, rather than lying awake worrying, having poor-quality sleep and then finding it harder to deal with your worries in the morning because you are tired.

- *Mood mapping*. I like Dr Liz Miller's method. It is a systematic way of charting emotions. (Again, see the resources section at the end of the chapter.)

- *Stim*. Self-stimulating, often known as stimming, is a repetitive movement such as flapping, rocking, twirling or swaying, which is calming to many people on the autistic spectrum. Sometimes people who do not know about autism try to stop people stimming, but there is nothing wrong with it as long as it does not hurt you or anyone else, or stop you or anyone else from doing anything.

These activities do not always have to focus on what has upset you or what has happened that day – you need to process positive emotions too.

9.10 Suicide

To commit suicide means to kill yourself. People may feel suicidal for many different reasons.

If you feel suicidal, it may seem as if the feeling won't go away, but these emotions can go away. When I interviewed Dr Tony Attwood for research for this book, he talked about a 'depression attack' – acute periods of depression – and feeling suicidal as 'wanting to end life because it would end the pain'. Normally, this is when something has gone wrong. I have seen this kind of behaviour in many people on the autistic spectrum. Dr Attwood recommends writing a plan. You need to contact someone or, if someone is with you, tell them how you feel, and they should stay with you. Dr Attwood says it is important for someone to be with you and shadow you (i.e. they must be able to see you). It is likely that you will want to be alone, but it's important that the person who is with you stays in the same room; they could sit on the opposite side of the room, but they must be able to see you

The person with you needs to say, 'The feeling will go, don't know when, but it will go.' When you feel this way, the person with you should not ask you about what's wrong or tell you not to kill yourself; they should keep calm. When you are sufficiently calm, they could talk to you about your special interest. Dr Attwood says to use your special interest like a thought blocker – to stop you thinking about the problem that made you feel suicidal. When you are calm, then you can deal with the problem that made you feel like this.

Here are some other things you could do:

- If you find talking helps, talk to someone who will listen to you but who doesn't know you. See the resources section at the end of this chapter for organizations that may be able to help.

• If it is very late at night, try to sleep. You may feel differently in the morning, even if you are convinced you won't. If nothing else, the sleep will give you more energy to cope and seek help. If you live near a friend, consider asking them if you could you stay with them overnight. As Dr Attwood says, having someone with you is important.

• Go to the A&E or ER department at your local hospital and ask for help.

9.11 Anxiety

Anxiety is a normal human emotion which everybody experiences at some point in their life. It can be hard to know if you have an anxiety disorder as opposed to just anxiety. If anxiety is stopping you from doing everyday activities or is reducing your quality of life, then it is important to discuss this with your family doctor.

There are many different experiences of anxiety. For some people, anxiety is intense worrying (worrying that stops them from doing everyday activities); for others, anxiety is when they have sweaty palms, increased heart rate or stomach pain. People get anxious about all kinds of things including changes to routine, throwing things away or the uncertainty of life.

Below are some of the common types of anxiety disorders (this is not an exhaustive list). You can use the NHS Choices website (see the resources section) to search for more information on all of these conditions.

9.11.1 Generalized anxiety disorder (GAD)

This is when you worry all the time. It can affect your sleep, concentration and ability to think. Normally, the anxiety is not about one specific thing or event. The anxiety could be about different things and these could change throughout a day or week.

9.11.2 Post-traumatic stress disorder (PTSD)

This is when something traumatic happens in your life (e.g. being bullied or abused) and this then causes anxiety after the event.

9.11.3 Obsessive compulsive disorder (OCD)

This is when you have an obsession such as contamination and a compulsion such as washing your hands. The compulsion is something you feel you have to do, and you feel that if you do not do your compulsion, then something bad will happen. It is important to know that OCD obsessions do not just have to be about contamination or making everything symmetrical; some people who have OCD have ruminations, which are intrusive thoughts.

9.11.4 Social anxiety/phobia

Social phobia is defined as 'a fear of negative evaluation from others – the fear of being judged and criticized. It is a fear of social situations that involve interaction with other people' (Anxiety UK 2013).

'I suffered from social anxiety so much that I stayed indoors for about two years, only going outside with my boyfriend. He took almost everything out of my hands, so in a way made it possible for me to escape the outside world. One day I got fed up with this and decided that I would change it. I set up a weblog (for motivation during the project) and wrote on it my daily or weekly attempts at leaving the house. All my thoughts and experiences I wrote down as well as poems and advice I found online. After about 1.5 years I was able to set up a strategy that worked for me and now it's about 2.5 years after this "project" and I usually have no trouble at all leaving the house by myself. This has made me a lot more independent and also took some strain off my boyfriend and our relationship.'

Carol, research participant

Carol explains the system she used to help her overcome her social anxiety:

- She set up a weblog (sometimes called a blog).

- She wrote on it about her attempts to leave the house and other information she found on the topic.

- She also wrote poems.

- She designed a strategy using the information she had learned.

- She used the strategy and overcame her anxiety.

Blogs can be a fantastic way to communicate either anonymously or as yourself with other people. See www.blogger.com or www. wordpress.com for more information and to set up a free blog.

9.12 The worry cycle

'Forgive yourself for moods, explain to friends about your moods, explain how you worry about little stuff. If you get stuck in the worry cycle, ask someone to clarify your thoughts.'

Jacinta, research participant

A **worry cycle** is when you worry about something repeatedly and can't stop worrying. This often occurs when there are 'unknowns'. These are things that you do not know the outcome of – for example, if you will ever get married.

Sometimes when you worry about something for a long period of time, the worry can seem to increase. It can become overwhelming and cause a meltdown. This repetitive worrying is known as a cycle because it goes round and round.

It is important to tell your friends about your moods. Explain what being on the autistic spectrum means for you (e.g. that you get very anxious and can't stop worrying). Forgive yourself. Do not feel guilty that this is the way you experience the world – you did not choose it, and you just have to work with what you've got.

9.13 Worry and anxiety strategies

Here is a list of ways you might be able to break a cycle of worrying:

- Talk to a friend. Explain what is worrying you and ask them to help you figure out if what you are worried about is likely to happen. Sometimes talking about worries can be calming.

- Come up with a plan B/contingency plan for if your worry does happen. The planning process and knowing what you will do if it happens might help you reduce your anxiety. If you begin to worry, you can think about what you will do if what you are worrying about happens.

- Ask yourself: 'If this worry happens, will the world continue or will the world end?' It is highly unlikely that the world will end due to your worry.

- If you are worried about the world ending, think carefully. Do you mean you think a large meteor will hit the earth? If that happens, we will all probably die immediately. You will not know the world is over and feel no pain, so it is not worth worrying about. Do you mean that there will be terrible storms? If so, then we have overcome this in the past. Do you mean global warming will heat up the earth too much? We have many new technologies now that are helping us to use energy better. Think logically about what would happen.

- Write down your worries.

- Probably the biggest, most important and hardest skill to learn is that sometimes you have to accept that things have gone wrong. Some things cannot be rectified without a lot of emotional pain, and this may not be worth it. Especially if you can't know for sure if a problem is solvable, you may just have to make the best of what you've got.

9.14 Overcoming anxiety and increasing self-esteem

Many people on the autistic spectrum experience high levels of anxiety and low self-esteem. These two things are often linked. For example, if you were anxious about going into a shop and asking for something, and therefore did not go into shops, this would increase your anxiety because you would feel you could not do it. It would also lower your self-esteem because you might start to think and feel that you are inadequate or a bad person as a result of the things you find difficult, when everyone else appears to find it all so easy.

Low self-esteem is very dangerous because it means you are more likely to not take care of yourself and keep yourself safe because you do not feel worth it. Below are some strategies that can be used to help you.

9.14.1 Small steps strategy

- You need to establish why your self-esteem is so low. Write down the answers to the two questions below. (Gunilla Gerland does something similar with drawing a staircase – see the resources section.)

  - Is it that you feel you can't do something (e.g. job) or can't be something (girlfriend, good friend, etc.)?

  - What problems have you encountered to make you feel like this?

- Next, write down a long-term goal (e.g. to get a job to feel good about myself).

- Next, write down things you could do to overcome the difficulties you have encountered reaching your goal in the past. Are there ways you can think of to overcome them?

- Write down some small goals. An example of a small goal could be to ask on an online forum how other people overcome a particular problem (e.g. difficulty with eye contact). Try to think of one thing you could do to work towards overcoming each difficulty.

- Make these goals achievable – something you feel you can do but something productive towards your long-term goal.

- Once you succeed at this small step once, do it again ten times if you can (you don't have to do it ten times in one day). Some small goals may not need repeating (e.g. if a small goal was to ask online how people overcame making eye contact, you only need to ask that once).

- If you fail to do one of the goals, why was this? And what can you do to prevent this happening again? Can you split your goal down into even smaller steps? If you don't know the answer, then is there someone you can ask for help in understanding the situation? Sometimes it is helpful just to talk about it with someone else. As you talk about it, you are thinking and this allows your brain to process the information again. This may help you to think about what went wrong and what you can do next time.

Also consider asking online for help. You do not need to give people lots of detail on your problem. For example, just ask: 'I am finding it hard to apply for jobs as it makes me so anxious. Has anyone else experienced this and overcome it?' (See Chapter 6 for more information on online safety.)

9.15 Accepting there are things you can't do right now (but that can change)

If there are things you can't do, then it's important to understand that this does not make you a bad person. Not everyone in the world can do the same things – for example, not everyone has a maths PhD and not everyone can cook. You need to focus on things you can do and enjoy doing and not dwell on (continue thinking about) the things you can't do.

'[I have] been told that I should not be such a coward. "Just do this or that", but these things are not easy for me at all. Makes me feel stupid and less worthy.'

Carol, research participant

9.16 Strategies from Dr Tony Attwood

Dr Tony Attwood suggests these strategies:

- Tony encourages clients to identify abilities and qualities. For example, an ability might be to be very good at maths and a quality might be to be patient. If you find this hard, then ask your friends, family and work colleagues what is good about you.

- Tony also uses people's special interests. If you are interested in animals and have a favourite kind of animal such as dogs, you could list the qualities of dogs: dogs do not have bad days, they are always pleased to see you, they like to have fun, they are not complicated to communicate with. Do you share any of these same characteristics?

- In Tony's clinic, ring binders are used for different things. One strategy is to ask people who know you what qualities you have. Or perhaps you already know some of your qualities – for example, being trustworthy, kind or clever. It might be difficult to evaluate your own qualities and perhaps you might even feel you do not have any, so make sure you ask people you know as well as making your own evaluations. Add a blank page into the ring binder for each quality and write the name of the quality on the page. Then when you feel (or others feel) you have demonstrated that quality, you (or they) can write it on the page. You could also include photographs, pictures or screenshots/printouts from a computer demonstrating particular qualities.

- Another strategy Dr Attwood uses is to ask his clients to create a collage of images that represent a person's life and qualities. Some clients have made CDs with different tracks that describe them. For example, if you felt you were a calm person, you might have a piece of music that represents calm to you. This can be a good way to start looking at the qualities you have.

- Some people also find it helpful to think about qualities they would like to have. If you admire a celebrity or book/ film character, what abilities and qualities do they have? And do you ever demonstrate these qualities? Each of these characters can have their own page in your ring binder and again you or other people can write down when you demonstrate a particular quality.

9.17 Obsessions

Many people on the autistic spectrum become obsessed with a particular topic; this could be a person you know or a historical figure, or even a whole subject area such as animals. This might mean:

- You want to talk about the subject to everyone you meet.

- You don't want to talk about anything else.

- You feel distracted by your obsession when you are trying to do other things.

- You can become very successful at your chosen subject.

- You can memorize lots of facts and useful information.

- Because of the amount of thinking you do on the topic, you may find you develop new ideas nobody else has thought of.

- You may be very good at problem solving within your particular topic.

Clearly, there are some huge positives. For example, Temple Grandin is very famous – and on the autistic spectrum. Her special interest/ obsession might be described as animals. She has created a career for herself working with animals.

However, sometimes obsessions can be problematic – for example, when an obsession is about another person who does not feel the same way as the person who is obsessed with them, or is uncomfortable with the idea that someone is obsessed with them. Or if your obsession/special interest was the Victoria Line on the London Underground and there was a strike, this would mean that there would be no trains that day. Life does not end in these circumstances, but for someone on the autistic spectrum it can be very difficult to cope with. Sometimes obsessions/interests are used as escapism, so this means you use them to get away from other things such as bullying or teasing. This is OK, but we all still have to function in the world to become independent. If you are independent, you have more choices in life.

It is important that professionals working with people on the autistic spectrum don't get obsessions/special interests and OCD (obsessive compulsive disorder) mixed up. If this happens to you, it might help to explain that, in literature written about autism, obsessions/special interests are sometimes described as circumscribed interests.

9.17.1 Strategies if obsessions are a problem

- If the obsession is with a living person who does not want you to be obsessed with them, sometimes writing one or two paragraphs to explain the situation to yourself can be helpful. It means that you are processing the information and then putting it on a piece of paper. For example, Jane is obsessed with Claire, but Claire is not interested in spending time with Jane. Jane is also interested in science. So she might write:

  Jane is obsessed with Claire, which means she wants to talk to and spend time with Claire, but Claire does not want to spend time with Jane. This is OK because each person has their own feelings, which can be different from another person's. It is important to respect other people's feelings, because otherwise Jane could get into trouble as it is disrespectful. Jane would be unhappy if people were disrespectful to her, so she must be respectful to others to earn their respect. If Jane starts thinking about Claire or begins to start a conversation with her, Jane will start to recite the periodic table or listen to music on her iPod.

- I have written the above in the third person, but you can write in the first person, using 'I' instead of your name. Note that I have incorporated Jane's interest into her strategy.

- Prepare what you will think about as an alternative to your obsession. Choose something very specific. Some people find lists helpful (e.g. the periodic table or pi).

- Explain to the person you are obsessed with that you are on the autistic spectrum and/or that you find it hard not to talk to them. Agree on what they will do in response. Having the same response will help you not to talk to the person because you will be able to predict what is happening and redirect yourself to another activity. Note that the response you may agree is that the person will ignore you.

- The person you are obsessed with may not wish even to engage in a conversation with you. If this is true of your situation, stop trying completely. You will have to write your own strategy.

- If the person is willing to spend some time with you, then perhaps you could agree when these times are or other limits such as how many questions you can ask them.

- If you really find nothing works, perhaps draw an association map (see Chapter 10). Find one of the things you associate with that person that you could be interested in without contacting or thinking about that person and arrange some activities or borrow some books from the library to find out more about this topic.

9.18 A strategy for dealing with emotions

I have found the instructions below useful for people who have difficulties with emotions. This strategy can be used with any emotion, although the example is for anxiety. This strategy was inspired by *Social Behavior and Self-Management: 5-Point Scales for Adolescents and Adults* by Kari Dunn Buron (Buron *et al.* 2012), and adapted by Robyn Steward.

Many people on the autistic spectrum find it hard to know how they are feeling or see the escalation of an emotion such as anxiety. People exhibit emotions through behaviour. Anxiety can be very debilitating, so having strategies for anxiety can be helpful. The scale below is designed to help you and other people around you know when you're anxious and what you or they can do about it.

The instructions include questions to help you fill out the scale. Ask people who know you for help in recognizing the things you do (the behaviours you exhibit) when you're anxious or the things that help.

Anxiety escalation scale

Question 1: What behaviours do you exhibit when you're anxious? Examples:

- drumming fingers
- withdrawing
- not speaking
- flapping
- pulling T-shirt over part of your face or burying your head in your T-shirt/jumper
- putting thumb or fingers in mouth
- groaning
- pacing
- procrastinating about what is making you anxious
- vocal sounds
- vomiting
- unable to concentrate
- increased heart rate
- not being able to sleep
- sweating.

Question 2: What is your behaviour when you are calm? Examples might be:

- able to concentrate for 30 minutes
- focus on task you are doing.

Question 3: Put your behaviours in order of escalation (i.e. least anxious to most anxious behaviours). Put them into five groups (group 5 being the most anxious) on the 'Anxiety escalation scale'. It's OK if you can't split them into five groups, but have a go anyway). For group 1 (calm), write your answers from question 2 above.

Level of anxiety	Anxious behaviours
5	
4	
3	
2	
1	

Question 4: Think about the things that help you for each level of anxiety. This may be hard to do, and you might need to ask for help and try things out. Below are some examples. Place them in the 'Things that help to reduce anxiety' column with their corresponding number. For example, if you have rated a behaviour as 5, then write things that help that behaviour in the 5 box. For example:

Level of anxiety	Things that help to reduce anxiety
5	flapping, talking about IT
4	chewing finger, time alone for five minutes
3	listening to music
2	
1	

Examples of things that might help:
- Listening to music (specify artists or tracks). You may need to test out which pieces of music help you calm down. If you are not sure, monitoring your pulse can be a useful tool (i.e. when your pulse is slower, you are calmer).
- Watching a YouTube video, looking at photos of familiar things, going for a walk, taking five minutes out of a situation alone, wearing ear plugs.
- Writing down what makes you anxious, writing down possible outcomes of situations you are anxious about, writing down options for the situations you are anxious about.

- Having a specific time in the day in which to think about your anxieties, so you can tell yourself that you are not going to worry about what makes you anxious now, but you will think about it at the specified time.

Things that help to reduce anxiety

1. Name the levels of anxiety. For example, you could call level 5 'most anxious', or you could describe/label it as 'out of control'.
2. Use the 'Anxiety escalation scale' to fill out the behaviours for each number.
3. Use the 'Things that help to reduce anxiety' table to fill out the things other people (and you) can do to help.
4. Collate your answers into the 5-point scale sheet below.

Level of anxiety	Behaviour	Things that help to reduce anxiety
5		
4		
3		
2		
1		

I hope this helps. If it seems confusing at first, ask for help.

Top 10 things to remember from Chapter 9

1. If you find analogies helpful, Stephen Fry (a British actor who has bipolar disorder) describes mood like your own personal weather. Just as you cannot control whether it is raining or not, you cannot control whether you are depressed. You didn't choose it to happen.

2. There are many different types of mental health issues that affect people on the autistic spectrum.

3. There are things you can do to improve your mental health.

4. Emotions can be hard for people on the autistic spectrum to understand. However, it is possible to learn and gain control of them.

5. Gluten and casein and bowel difficulties (such as irritable bowel syndrome) can affect mood.

6. Sometimes routines need to change. This can be difficult for people on the autistic spectrum. However, there are strategies, such as making a visual timetable, that can help you cope with the change.

7. It is important to release emotions. You can do this in many different ways – for example, through art, music or exercise.

8. Sometimes making small steps towards a goal can really help. Breaking down a task into small steps in itself can be empowering.

9. Sometimes people on the autistic spectrum have very low self-esteem. It is important to find a way to see the things you are good at and feel good about yourself.

10. Many people on the autistic spectrum can be obsessed with a topic or a person. Sometimes a person may not want you to be obsessed with them. It is important to be aware of how others may perceive your behaviour.

Resources

Books

Attwood, T., Callesen, K. and Moller-Nielsen, A. (2009) *CAT-Kit: The New Cognitive Affective Training Program for Improving Communication.* Arlington, TX: Future Horizons. ISBN: 1932565736
The CAT-Kit was developed by Dr Tony Attwood and colleagues and offers a range of resources for helping people on the autistic spectrum to understand and deal effectively with emotions.

Buron, K.D. and Curtis, M. (2003) *The Incredible 5-Point Scale: Assisting Students with Autism Spectrum Disorders in Understanding Social Interactions and Controlling Their Emotional Responses.* Shawnee Mission, KS: Autism Asperger Publishing Co. ISBN: 1931282528

Don't be put off that this is a children's book – it is a fantastic resource with many useful strategies in it, which are simple to implement. There is also a version for adolescents.

Buron, K.D., Brown, J.T., Curtis, M. and King, L. (2012) *Social Behavior and Self-Management: 5-Point Scales for Adolescents and Adults.* Shawnee Mission, KS: Autism Asperger Publishing Co. ISBN: 1934575918

This is the adolescent version of the 5-Point Scale, so the activities are more sophisticated than the ones in version above.

Gerland, G. (2013) *Secrets to Success for Professionals in the Autism Field: An Insider's Guide to Understanding the Autism Spectrum, the Environment and Your Role.* London: Jessica Kingsley Publishers. ISBN: 1849053707

Gunilla is on the autistic spectrum herself, and has many years' experience of working with people on the autistic spectrum. In this book she shares some of the techniques she uses, and explains how many people on the autistic spectrum think and why.

Jackson, L. (2001) *A User Guide to the GF/CF Diet for Autism, Asperger Syndrome and AD/HD.* London: Jessica Kingsley Publishers. ISBN: 1843100553

Luke is on the autistic spectrum. In this book he talks about how to work with a gluten-free casein-free diet.

Lawson, W. (2010) *The Passionate Mind: How People with Autism Learn.* London: Jessica Kingsley Publishers. ISBN: 1849051216

Wendy is on the autistic spectrum. In this book she explores the difference in the way people on the autistic spectrum learn and how they might be supported.

Miller, L. (2008) *Mood Mapping: Plot Your Way to Emotional Health and Happiness.* Emmaus, PN: Rodale. ISBN: 1905744773

Liz Miller has worked in various heath positions. She has bipolar and wrote this book about mood mapping, which offers 30 days of activities as well as other information. You will need quite a lot of emotional competency to begin with before using this book. If you are not sure whether you're ready for this I would suggest trying *The Incredible 5-Point Scale* (see details above) first.

Websites

Hamilton Depression Scale

http://healthnet.umassmed.edu/mhealth/HAMD.pdf

This is not supposed to be used as a way to diagnose yourself with depression, but it may be a helpful tool to use to chart your emotions over a two-week period before seeking medical help from your family doctor. If you feel your life is in danger you must contact a doctor immediately.

Emotion Annotation and Representation Language (EARL)
http://emotion-research.net/projects/humaine/aboutHUMAINE/start-here
EARL is a tool to help you think about different kinds of emotions.

NHS Choices
www.nhs.uk
The NHS Choices website provides information on health-related matters, for example contraception. There is a A–Z list of medical conditions, and also a search box where you can type in key words to find out more information about particular health-related topics.

Organizations

Samaritans
www.samaritans.org
Many people find it helpful to talk to someone they don't know when they are upset or emotionally distressed. The Samaritans provide 'listeners' – people who are trained to offer anyone contacting them someone to listen to them, and will keep the information confidential.

National Suicide Prevention Network (US)
www.suicidepreventionlifeline.org
A US organization which offers support if you are in emotional distress or feeling suicidal.

Lifeline (Australia)
www.lifeline.org.au
Lifeline offers multiple ways of contacting someone if you are experiencing suicidal feelings or are in emotional crisis.

10

USEFUL SKILLS AND STRATEGIES FOR MULTIPLE SITUATIONS

In this chapter

This chapter contains strategies that I think will be useful in multiple situations.

10.1 Contacting people strategy

I have made many references to this throughout the book.

Many people on the autistic spectrum have difficulties knowing how often to contact people. These could be friends, romantic partners, estate agents, your manager or anyone else you may have contact with.

There are social rules people adhere to that are not generally discussed or written down (known as unwritten rules). Some people understand these rules intuitively or by copying other people, or from conversations with others which do not specifically state the rule but help to clarify it. Here is a strategy you could use.

The table below is meant only as a guide. You could make your own chart/table and ask how often it is OK to contact people. How often you should contact someone depends on the context, person and mode of contact (phone, email, etc.). If you contact someone too much, they might think you're obsessive, annoying or bothersome.

Table 10.1 Contacting people

Person	Method of contact	Frequency
Mum	Phone	Once a day. RULE: not before 8am or after 10pm.
Sister: Tara	Text	As often as she replies to me. RULE: wait till she replies to a message I sent. Typos generally do not matter. I must only send one additional message if I make a mistake.
Friend: Mark	Facebook message	OK to message more than he replies, but to check with him that this is OK. RULE: do not talk about sex a lot, as he does not like me in a sexual way and this may stop him speaking to me.

10.1.1 If you need more concrete rules

Some non-autistic people do not communicate with other people often. Do not be offended by this; this is just the way some people communicate.

Over a period of time, you may find that these rules do not apply to particular friendships. It is impossible for me to identify which friendships rules don't apply to you; the above is intended only as a guideline.

- With friends, managers, supervisors, romantic partners and family members, agree how often you can contact them.

- If you message, text or email someone, wait for a week for them to reply. You may have to contact them sooner if your message or request is urgent. Sometimes people just forget to reply to messages. If you see them face to face, you could ask them, 'Did you get my message?'

- In business and work situations, you could add a line of text to the end of your message that asks for a reply by a particular time – for example, 'Please could you let me have your answer by 4pm tomorrow. If I do not hear from you, I will call you.' Or you could write, 'I will give you a call next week.' Remember that the person you are emailing may have other things that need to be done by a particular time.

- If you have sex with someone, this does not mean they are a close friend. A close friendship is something that is built up/created over time.

- After sending someone a message, if you feel that you have made a non-critical mistake (i.e. the person will still be able to understand you), it is normally best not to send another message but to wait for a response. If you are unsure of how critical the information you left out or misspelt is, grade it out of 10, 10 being critical, 1 being insignificant. If it's not 9 or 10, then wait for a response before sending another message.

- At work it is acceptable to send several emails. For example, you might send one email about one subject and another about a separate subject, if you are collaborating with that person. But clarify how frequently it is OK to email them and then set yourself a limit – for example, if you have sent someone three emails, do not send another until they have replied to one of your emails.

- When using instant messaging or Facebook, if the person does not ask open-ended questions (e.g. 'How are you?'), they may be busy so may not be able to chat with you now.

- If you are unsure if a person wants to talk to you on instant message or on the phone, you can ask them, 'Is now a good time to talk?' or 'Do you have time to talk?'

- Equally, if you do not want to talk to someone, you can say, 'I'm really sorry but I don't have time to talk to you right now' or 'I am in the middle of doing something.'

It's important to understand that these rules may need to be adapted for your personal circumstances. If you have a friend who texts or messages you a lot, you could reply with the same level of frequency.

If someone is contacting you too much, you can ask them not to contact you so often.

If you find waiting for a reply hard, try to distract yourself with other things or thoughts. You could make a list of things to do if you were waiting for someone to contact you.

10.1.2 What to do if it is hard waiting for someone to reply

It's very common to find waiting for a reply frustrating and anxiety-provoking. Some messages obviously don't require a reply, in which case you probably won't get one. For example, if someone texts you and asks, 'Are we still on for meeting at 1pm for lunch?' and you reply yes, then you probably won't get a reply to your message. But other messages and calls do require a reply, and bugging someone (i.e. repeatedly texting, calling or messaging them) will annoy the other person and may jeopardize your friendship.

So here are five things you could do while you're waiting:

1. Prepare a thought, such as a philosophical question or the lines from a play, to think about when you start wondering if the person has replied or why they haven't replied. Every time you start thinking about the person, think about your thought. Using your special interest here might be helpful too.

2. Write a 'to do' list of stuff you can be getting on with. Perhaps you'll become so engrossed with what you are doing that you'll forget you are waiting and it will be a nice surprise when you get a reply.

3. You might be anxious as to whether the person is OK or not or what reason they might have for not replying. Until you have information to suggest that they are not OK, it is best to assume they are and carry on with your life; otherwise, you might well be worrying for no good reason. This is easier said than done, however, so you need to think through this issue. Think about it logically. Do you have any evidence this person isn't OK? What other reasons could there be for them not replying? What can you do to relax?

4. These situations can be very stressful for people on the autistic spectrum, so have a list of relaxing activities. Sometimes it can be hard to choose an activity, so number your list, and then when you are anxious and need to relax, choose a number at random and do whichever activity is that number on the list.

5. Don't assume the person hasn't replied because they don't like you! It's more likely that they are just busy.

10.2 Acting

Many non-autistic women get out of bad situations by acting or pretending.

Being able to act or pretend can be very hard for people on the autistic spectrum. However, it is possible. There are professional actors who are on the autistic spectrum, but you do not need to be a professional actor to use acting techniques in social situations.

Many non-autistic people pretend their mobile/cell phone is ringing. You could also try this in a situation you wanted to get out of – for example, if you felt uncomfortable with another person and wanted to get away from them.

It would be advisable to practise this with a good friend or in front of the mirror before you need this skill in a real situation, because it needs to look convincing. Remember that the person you're trying to get away from will not know that your cell/mobile phone was not really ringing and that you are not really speaking to someone.

This scenario is designed for when you do not know someone well and might find yourself alone with them in a club/bar, at their home or another place (except your own home).

- Consider how you phone might ring. For example, do you normally have it on a vibrate setting? This is a good setting to have your cell phone on because that way nobody will know that it did not really ring.

- How do you answer the phone? Do you press a button or swipe the screen? Make sure you hold the phone away from the person you are trying to get away from, so they do not see what is on the screen.

- How do you usually answer the phone? What does your voice sound like? And what do you say (e.g. hi or hello)? If you use this strategy, it might be helpful to decide on someone you will pretend is ringing you. The person needs to be someone you trust and someone who is unlikely to be with you when you use this strategy (e.g. your mother, father or cousin). Choosing a cousin could be a good solution because that way you can call them by their first name as opposed to Mom or Dad, which may look suspicious or cause your friends to tease you.

- How many seconds do you need to wait before speaking after saying hello? To make it sound as though you are talking to someone (because you are acting as if they had called you), they would be speaking to you, and you would be listening while they spoke and therefore not speaking. You could write a script which you could imagine reading through in your head so the timing is correct. For example, you answer the phone with 'Hi!' and then in your script the other person says, 'Hello, how are you?' This takes about five seconds – read the sentence out loud and time it with a stopwatch if you need to.

- It is now perfectly acceptable to walk away from the person you are trying to get away from. You could say something like 'I can't hear you well – there is very little signal. I will just move somewhere where the signal is better.' When you do this, make sure it sounds the sort of thing you would say – for example, some people would not use the word 'signal' and might say 'reception' instead – and that your voice tone sounds calm (a friend may be able to help you do this).

- Leave the building where the person you want to get away from is.

- You can now stop pretending as if you are speaking to someone on the phone and go somewhere else. Go to a public place where you could call someone to pick you up or ask for help if you need it. A public place is good because if the person was following you, they are less likely to attack or hurt you when there are other people around because those other people could call the police.

If you want to use this method, make sure you practise so that it is convincing.

10.3 Giving too much information and knowing what information to give

This is a skill that everyone has to learn to be able to communicate effectively. It can be a very hard skill to learn. This is how I learnt it. When I put my hand up to ask a question at school, a teacher chose me but told me to give a short answer. At the time this was frustrating and annoying, but it taught me how to answer concisely. Below is a game that you can play by yourself or with others which may help you to develop this skill.

You will need:
- a time-keeping device or timer of some kind (e.g. a stopwatch or sand timer – you could also use a wrist watch or computer clock)
- paper and a pen
- pair of scissors
- small box, container, a hat or a bag (optional).

Instructions
1. On the piece of paper write down your favourite topics/interests/things you enjoy talking or thinking about. Leave enough space around each topic so there is room to cut it out.
2. Cut out the topics so that each one is on a separate piece of paper.
3. Place the topics in a bag, hat or box or lay them out on the table with the blank side of the paper facing you.
4. Pick a topic from the bag/hat/box/table.
5. Set your time-keeping device for five minutes (if you find this too easy, you can reduce the amount of time).
6. Write down the important points of the topic. (Another way to make this game harder is to write down the important points of an event that has happened or the important points from a TV programme.)
7. Prioritize the points you have written down.
8. Stop writing when the timer ends.

You can then repeat steps 3–8. When you have reduced the time to 60 seconds, you could try doing this task verbally rather than writing it down. You could record this on a dictaphone or your computer or into another device that records sound. Or play the game with a friend.

The objective of this is to practise rather than win. Prioritizing may be difficult at first, so ask yourself, if someone else read what you had written, could a particular point be left out and the reader still be able to understand the topic?

10.4 Difficulty explaining events in order

A lot of people on the autistic spectrum find it hard to explain an event in chronological order. Many of my clients have explained situations to me, and rather than start at the beginning of what they are trying to tell me, they have started at the point when the most important thing happened.

If you need to explain a series of events, it may help to write them down in a list and either number the items in the order they happened or cut them out and place them on a table in chronological order.

You could then draw them on a timeline. If you find this difficult talk about each point with someone else and work out what goes where on the timeline together.

10.5 Prioritizing – self-advocacy tree

If you find it hard to make a decision or choice when there are a great number of variables (things) that affect that choice, it may help to prioritize them.

You can either draw or make a self-advocacy tree. Figure 10.1 is an example.

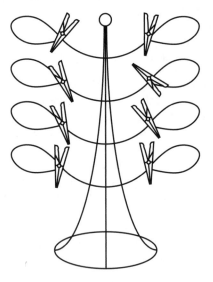

Figure 10.1 Self-advocacy tree

Instructions

This example uses school because for most people it will be familiar, but you can use this strategy with any situation.

- Draw eight leaf shapes on a piece of card or paper, and then cut them out.
- Write on the leaf shapes eight aspects or variables of school that you feel are important to enable you to learn – for example, food, IT, teachers, being understood by others, having friends, sensory environment, break time when needed, choice of subjects.
- Using a mug tree and some pegs, place the leaves (variables) on the tree in order of importance. The most important goes at the top and the least important at the bottom of the tree.

This example deliberately uses a subject that you have experience of, but you could use this tree to make a decision about something else. For example, if you are choosing which university to go to, list the things that are important to you and then ask yourself which university most provides for these needs.

Clearly some decisions are more complicated and can be very anxiety-provoking. However, thinking about the problem or decision in a visual way might be useful to some readers. Other uses could include deciding which work task you do first or how long you spend on them – the higher the priority, the more time you spend on the task.

10.6 Association vs. contextual thinking

Lots of people on the autistic spectrum think by association rather than context. There is nothing wrong with thinking in this way, but be aware that the majority of non-autistic people think in context which can be useful when thinking about social situations.

10.6.1 What is a context?

A context is made up of variables that affect your perception of a situation. For example, when you were at school, if you had a friend come to your house, and your parents and their parents allowed swearing or bad language, then that is OK. But when you see your friend at school, it is not OK to use that language because home and school are two different social contexts and they have different rules.

At home, your parents make the rules. At school, teachers make the rules. The teachers must take into account all the children's needs, whereas in your home your parents consider only their needs, your needs and the needs of any other members of your family.

This is why it can be hard to understand situations and people's behaviours. As in the example above, without knowing that home and school are different contexts, you may not understand why it is OK to swear at home but not OK to swear at school, since you are with some of the same people.

Quite often I see clients who have clearly not understood the idea that there are different contexts and each context has different rules. When analysing a situation, it is important to consider the context. *Autism as Context Blindness* by Peter Vermeulen is a useful book on this subject (see the resources section at the end of this chapter).

Context is also an issue that needs consideration when having conversations with people. When you are speaking to someone, they expect that any subject you begin to talk about will be related by context to the previous subject you were talking about. However, many people on the autistic spectrum think associatively, so to communicate clearly with non-autistic people who do not know what you are thinking, you need to say why you are going from one topic to another (i.e. how you made the association).

For example, if you were talking about the film *Spider-Man* and then changed the topic to the M&Ms store – because there is an M&Ms store on the same street as the AMC cinema on Broadway in New York, which is where you saw the film – the person you are speaking to may be confused. To make this change understandable to the listener, who won't know what you're thinking unless you tell them, you would need to say something like 'I saw *Spider-Man* at the AMC cinema on Broadway and on the same street is an M&Ms store, which I visited on the way to the cinema.'

One way to help you understand your own thinking is to draw a map of your thoughts. If you feel people have not understood the connections you have made in a conversation between different ideas and concepts, or if people have told you this has been difficult for them, can you draw your thought process? For example: 'I thought about Broadway in New York and then I thought about the time I went to the M&Ms store.' You could also draw it as a flow diagram, like the one used in Chapter 5. Do this with a non-autistic friend and discuss what they think about the conversation. This might help you both understand each other better.

10.6.1 How can I make my thinking make sense to other people?

It may help to draw a mind map. This is like a spider diagram of how your thoughts connect with one another, so other people can see how your thoughts connect.

See *Autism as Context Blindness* for more information (in the resources section at the end of this chapter).

10.7 Social conversations

Part of being socially successful is being able to converse (not necessarily with speech) with people. First of all, ensure that you know what (if any) sensory issues you have and how you can best accommodate them (e.g. ear plugs or coloured lenses).

Below is a strategy for finding something to talk about:

- In preparation for a social gathering, think of five topics of conversation you could have with someone. Base these on the news (radio, newspapers), or (if in work) specific industry-related events or news, or (if not at work) a shared interest (you might have to ask the person). Family and holidays are also good options. Include in your list some questions you could ask associated to each topic. The topics you choose must be positive.

- When you talk to someone is a social situation, start with 'Hello, how are you? What do you do (i.e. what is your job)?' (unless you know what job they do because you have met them before).

- When they tell you what they do, consider if you can relate to this in any way. Have you ever studied this topic? Or have you ever worked in the industry? The person should ask you what you do. You can choose to continue talking about work. This is particularly relevant if you are at an event that is related to your work. Remember that conversations should be 50 per cent sharing information and 50 per cent receiving information from the other person.

- Next, use one of your topics. If the person does not talk for more than two sentences or ask you a question, move on to the next topic.

- If you have tried three topics, and the person has not said more than two sentences or asked questions about each topic, then go and talk to someone else.

- If you need to get out of a conversation, say that you need the restroom/toilet or that you are going to get a drink, or smile, make eye contact (or look at the bridge of the person's nose) and say, 'It was nice speaking to you, I better go back to my desk now.' If you are on public transportation, you can just say, 'It was nice speaking to you.'

- If you are trying to start a conversation with someone and you are unsure whether they want to talk to you, if you are sitting or standing next to them, use a statement such as 'It's lovely weather today' or 'It's busy here'. If they respond, then this is a cue to begin a conversation

- If someone asks you for your phone number in a situation that is not work-related, and you don't want to tell them but want to be polite, you could say, 'No, I'm sorry, I don't know my number.'

10.8 Dealing with anxiety

10.8.1 Creating an anxiety book

If you are going to a situation that makes you anxious, you might find it helpful to plan out what you would do if whatever is causing the anxiety actually happens.

You can either buy a book for this (an address book would be suitable) or a notepad, or use your your mobile/cell phone. For example, if someone was travelling on a bus route they had never been on, they might list the following things as possible anxieties:

- a bus not coming

- not knowing where the bus stop is

- not knowing when it is my stop

- not having change to pay the driver

- not knowing where to sit

- someone talking to me

- someone on the bus who smells or the bus itself smelling

- forgetting my belongings

- getting mugged

- getting bullied or teased.

They could place these anxieties under B (for bus) in the address book and then include a small action plan of what to do if any of these things happen. For example:

B

Bus not coming:

1. Save into my mobile/cell phone the telephone number of the bus company.

2. Call the bus company or use mobile internet to see if I can obtain information.

3. If this is not possible, I can wait for 15 minutes. If this means I will be late to my destination and someone is meeting me there, I should call or text them to let them know I will be late.

10.9 Abuse

If you feel your life is in danger, leave immediately, call the police and ask for help.

Beware of being isolated. If someone tries to destroy your relationships with your friends and family this is a sign of abuse.

10.9.1 Definitions of abuse

Emotional abuse/verbal abuse includes non-physical behaviors such as threats, insults, constant monitoring or 'checking in', excessive texting, humiliation, intimidation or isolation.

Stalking means being repeatedly watched, followed or harassed.

Financial abuse is when someone uses money or access to accounts to exert power and control over a partner.

Physical abuse refers to any intentional use of physical force with the intent to cause fear or injury (e.g. hitting, shoving, biting, strangling, kicking or using a weapon).

Sexual abuse refers to any action that impacts a person's ability to control their sexual activity or the circumstances in which sexual activity occurs, including restricting access to birth control or condoms, or ignoring someone's refusal to engage in sexual activities by repeatedly using emotional, verbal or physical pressure.

(loveisrespect.org 2013)

10.9.2 Keeping an abuse diary

If you feel that you are being abused in any way or if you think there is a chance you might be, then keeping a diary of when this happens can be a good way to help you find out whether or not you are being abused. Many people who are being abused at the time do not consider what is happening to them to be abuse. But if someone is making you unhappy regularly and you have told them how you feel but it keeps happening, use the following technique to help you make sense of what is happening to you.

Keep a diary of when abuse happens, what happens just before (e.g. you are at a party, or your partner has come home drunk) and what happens afterwards. Do this for a month or two, and then look at what you have written. Are there any patterns? If you can't see any patterns or the abuse is less frequent than this, try keeping the diary for a longer period of time. Ask a friend to look at what you have written and ask them if they can see any patterns. Abuse normally comes in patterns, so if you can see a pattern (e.g. my boyfriend is violent towards me every Tuesday or when he is drunk), then talk to the person who is abusing you about this (if they are willing to discuss it) and decide upon what you could both do to avoid these situations. Continue to keep a diary to see if things improve, but if things don't improve or if the abuser blames you for their behaviour, do not put up with being made to feel unhappy. Leave the relationship and stop contact with the abuser.

10.10 Black-and-white thinking

Sometimes people on the autistic spectrum are described as thinking in black and white. This does not mean seeing the world without colour. It means thinking a person is either all good or all bad, when actually people make some good decisions and some bad decisions. The reason people make what appear to be bad decisions may be because they are dealing with a life-or-death situation or because they made a mistake. People are not machines. But this does not make it OK for people to abuse you. Many people have friends who have attributes that they find annoying, but this does not mean they do not like their friend; they just find that one attribute annoying. It is important, if something goes wrong in any relationship or situation, that you do not catastrophize it and decide this means everything in the future will go wrong or that you must leave the relationship or not be friends with the person. (An exception to this would be if the other person had been abusive.) You need to think rationally. Sometimes this is hard for people on the autistic spectrum. Strategies such as the non-autistic (NA) council (see Chapter 1) and talking to people who know you can help you to see the world not just in black and white, but you need to accept that other people may have different opinions and views to you. Do not just dismiss someone's idea because that is not how you naturally think. Being on the autistic spectrum has some wonderful attributes, such as being able to focus on tasks, but it also has its downside – the negatives. But being non-autistic has its positives and negatives too.

10.11 Growing self-esteem

When I talked to Dr Tony Attwood about how people have to grow self-esteem, I came up with the idea that you can conceptualize self-esteem as a plant or flower to grow it. As Dr Attwood says, people need praise, and he suggests that you let people around you know that you need to be praised when you have done something well. Receiving praise is like watering your self-esteem plant/flower. This will mean your plant/flower will grow and you will be more likely to stand up for yourself.

Tell the people who care about you, such as your family, friends, co-workers and boss, that you need praise. You could say, 'I find it hard to know when I'm doing well. Please tell me when I do well.'

Last words

Nobody chooses to be autistic. But if you are on the autistic spectrum, it is important to accept that being on the autistic spectrum is part of who you are. Find out what your strengths are (the things you are good at) and try to find ways of using those strengths and overcoming your weaknesses. Remember, you are not alone.

Top 10 things to remember from Chapter 10

1. It is important not to contact someone too much. They may feel that you are harassing them, even if this was not your intention.

2. It can be hard waiting for a reply to a message. Strategies that may help include concentrating on a specific thought or task.

3. Many non-autistic people and people on the autistic spectrum use acting skills to help them get out of risky social situations.

4. Many people on the autistic spectrum explain things out of chronological order and this can make it hard for others to make sense of what the person is saying. Using a timeline may help you explain things in a way other people can understand.

5. The non-autistic world is built around different contexts (e.g. there are different rules at school and at home). It can be hard to understand contexts but it is essential that you do so.

6. Some people on the autistic spectrum think by association. This means that they think of things in groups rather than in chronological order or context. In conversation this can seem strange to other people and you need to explain how you link one topic to another.

7. If you feel you are being abused, keep a diary of when abuse happens. Show this diary to the police or someone you trust (but not the person abusing you) and ask for help.

8. Many people on the autistic spectrum can be described as black-and-white thinkers, meaning that they find it hard to see the grey area of a situation. For example, if someone broke the law to save someone's life, even though this is technically wrong, many people dependent on the law that was broken would feel this was acceptable as it saved someone's life. As someone on the autistic spectrum wanting to interact within the non-autistic world, it is important for you to work on flexibility of thought, such as understanding grey areas and respecting other people's perspectives. This will help you understand other people.

9. You need to grow self-esteem. Just as you would water a plant, you need to be 'watered' with praise for things you do well. You need people to tell you when you do a good job and, when something goes wrong, someone to help you generalize skills so that you don't make the same mistake again.

10. The biggest difficulty I see facing many people on the autistic spectrum is their difficulty seeing the positives in a situation. You have to make the best of any situation.

Resources

Book

Vermeulen, P. (2012) *Autism as Context Blindness.* Overland Park, KS: Autism Asperger Publishing Co. ISBN: 1937473007

The world we live in consists of many contexts, and many people on the autistic spectrum find it hard to differentiate between contexts and adapt their behaviour accordingly. This book explores what context means, how it affects us and what this means in the world of autism.

Final Thoughts

Writing a book has been one of the hardest things I have ever done. I started writing this book thinking I was thick. I really couldn't understand why anyone would want to hear what I had to say. This is the person who got kicked out of school with no GCSEs.

I realized that I'm not thick but that I am slower to learn new concepts (like apostrophes) or things I don't have a lot of available information to associate the new information to. Yet I also have a lot of knowledge in my head about autism and I understand things many professionals don't, because not only have I lived it but I've also worked with people on the autistic spectrum and I see how autism affects people in different ways.

As a woman on the autistic spectrum, I am excited to be part of gender-specific writing for people on the autistic spectrum, as there are only a handful of books written for women on the autistic spectrum, even fewer when you count those written *by* women on the autistic spectrum.

I wouldn't consider myself a good writer – I like to speak more than write – but I really hope you have learnt at least one useful thing from this book.

It's a Sunday afternoon in the UK, the sky is blue and I'm off down the pub to eat a roast dinner.

Appendix A

Record Sheets for Reporting Abuse

If you think you may be being abused and feel you can't tell anyone, tick one or more of the boxes on this chart and leave it where someone you trust (not the abuser) will find it; they may be able to help you. This doesn't technically break the 'don't tell anyone rule' because you have just ticked a box.

Someone has done this to me or I have seen it happen to someone else

Physical			
Hit		Pushed	
Punched		Threatened with a knife or other sharp object	
Kicked		Threatened with a gun	
Spat at		Threatened with a syringe/needle	
Smashed face into glass/glass thrown in face		Cut/stabbed	
Burnt		Had objects stuffed down throat	
Objects thrown at me/them		Clothes torn	

Verbal		
Called names e.g. retard		People have said sexually inappropriate things or asked inappropriate questions
Yelled/shouted at		People I did not know have shouted at me down the street
Been gossiped about		
Sexual		
Had sex but did not want to		Been touched in my private parts (e.g. breasts, thighs)
Had sex but did not want to and told the other person that I did not want to		Been sent messages with sexual content I did not want
Been asked to touch someone's private parts (e.g. penis, vagina)		

Appendix B

Erogenous Zones Diagram

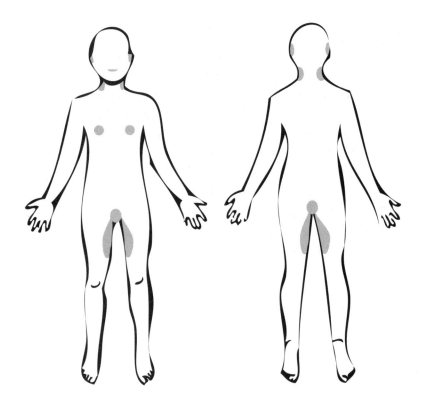

References

Anxiety UK (2013) 'Social Phobia/Social Anxiety Disorder.' Available at www.nhs. uk/ipgmedia/national/Anxiety%20UK/Assets/SocialPhobia.pdf, accessed on 22 July 2013.

Baron-Cohen, S., Leslie, A.M. and Frith, U. (1985) 'Does the autistic child have a "theory of mind"?' *Cognition 21*, 1, 37–46.

Big Think (2010) 'An Uppy-Downy, Mood-Swingy Kind of Guy.' Available at http:// bigthink.com/videos/an-uppy-downy-mood-swingy-kind-of-guy, accessed on 22 July 2013.

Bogdashina, O. (2003) *Sensory Perceptual Issues in Autism and Asperger's Syndrome: Different Sensory Experiences – Different Perceptual Worlds.* London: Jessica Kingsley Publishers.

Buron, K.D. and Curtis, M. (2003) *The Incredible 5-Point Scale: Assisting Students with Autism Spectrum Disorders in Understanding Social Interactions and Controlling Their Emotional Responses.* Shawnee Mission, KS: Austism Asperger Publishing Co.

Buron, K.D., Brown, J.T., Curtis, M. and King, L. (2012) *Social Behavior and Self-Management: 5-Point Scales for Adolescents and Adults.* Shawnee Mission, KS: Austism Asperger Publishing Co.

Gerland, G. (2013) *Secrets to Success for Professionals in the Autism Field: An Insider's Guide to Understanding the Autism Spectrum, the Environment and Your Role.* London: Jessica Kingsley Publishers.

Humaine (2013) 'HUMAINE Emotion Annotation and Representation Language (EARL): Proposal.' Available at http://emotion-research.net/projects/humaine/ earl/proposal, accessed on 22 July 2013.

Krantz, P.J. and McClannahan, L.E. (1993) 'Teaching children with autism to initiate to peers: Effects of a script-facing procedure.' *Journal of Applied Behavior Analysis 26*, 1, 121–132.

Laugeson, E. and Frankel, F. (2012) *Social Skills for Teenagers with Developmental and Autism Spectrum Disorders: The PEERS Treatment Manual.* New York, NY: Routledge.

loveisrespect.org (2013) 'Types of Abuse.' Available at www.loveisrespect.org/pdf/ Types_Of_Abuse.pdf, accessed on 22 July 2013.

Metropolitan Police (2013) 'Definitions.' Available at http://content.met.police.uk/ Article/Definitions/1400008450549/1400008450549, accessed on 22 July 2013.

NHS Choices (2013) 'Signs and symptoms of pregnancy.' Available at www.nhs. uk/conditions/pregnancy-and-baby/pages/signs-and-symptoms-pregnancy. aspx#close, accessed on 22 July 2013.

US Department of Justice (2013) 'Sexual Assault.' Available at www.ovw.usdoj.gov/ sexassault.htm, accessed on 22 July 2013.

Index